T0302143

Transformational Innovation in the Creative and Cultural Industries

Interest in the management of creative and cultural organizations has grown at pace with the size of this sector. This textbook uniquely focuses on how innovation in these industries transforms practice. Uncovering the strategic role of innovation for organizations in the creative and cultural sector, the book provides readers with practical guidance to help traverse seismic disruptions brought about by global health and economic crises. The authors examine how innovation in business models, products, services and technology has disrupted the competitive landscapes of the arts world. Innovations are characterized as deriving from other industries as well as via exogenous shocks that privilege some companies over others. Case studies bring to life how innovation is used strategically in different ways around varying competitive forces.

Enhanced by conceptual tools and replete with industry examples, this textbook is an ideal resource for students and reflective practitioners to understand how innovation can be a productive tool for transforming their own creative and cultural industry practice and performance during a period of rapid technological change and unprecedented societal challenge.

Dr Alison Rieple is Emeritus Professor of Strategic Management at the University of Westminster in London, UK.

Dr Robert DeFillippi is Emeritus Professor of Strategy and International Business at Suffolk University in Boston, USA.

Dr David Schreiber is Chair of Creative & Entertainment Industry Studies and Associate Professor in the Mike Curb College of Entertainment and Music Business, Belmont University, USA.

Discovering the Creative Industries
Series Editor: Ruth Rentschler

The creative and cultural industries account for a significant share of the global economy. Gaining and maintaining employment and work in this sector is a challenge and chances of success are enhanced by ongoing professional development.

This series provides a range of relatively short, student-centred books which blend industry and educational expertise with cultural sector practice. Books in the series provide applied introductions to the core elements of the creative industries. In sum, the series provides essential reading for those studying to enter the creative industries as well as those seeking to enhance their career via executive education.

Consumer Behaviour and the Arts
A Marketing Perspective
François Colbert and Alain d'Astous

Business Issues in the Arts
Edited by Anthony Rhine and Jay Pension

Arts and Cultural Leadership
Creating Sustainable Arts Organizations
Kenneth Foster

Fundraising for the Creative and Cultural Industries
Leading Effective Fundraising Strategies
Michelle Wright, Ben Walmsley and Emilee Simmons

Managing the Arts and Culture
Cultivating a Practice
Edited by Constance DeVereaux

Managing Organizations in the Creative Economy, Second Edition
Organizational Behaviour for the Cultural Sector
Paul Saintilan and David Schreiber

Transformational Innovation in the Creative and Cultural Industries
Alison Rieple, Robert DeFillippi and David Schreiber

For more information about this series, please visit: www.routledge.com/Discovering-the-Creative-Industries/book-series/DCI

Transformational Innovation in the Creative and Cultural Industries

**Alison Rieple, Robert DeFillippi
and David Schreiber**

LONDON AND NEW YORK

Cover design: peepo / Getty Images

First published 2023
by Routledge
4 Park Square, Milton Park, Abingdon, Oxon OX14 4RN

and by Routledge
605 Third Avenue, New York, NY 10158

Routledge is an imprint of the Taylor & Francis Group, an informa business

British Library Cataloguing-in-Publication Data
A catalogue record for this book is available from the British
Library

ISBN: 978-1-032-07534-1 (hbk)
ISBN: 978-1-032-07153-4 (pbk)
ISBN: 978-1-003-20754-2 (ebk)

DOI: 10.4324/9781003207542

Typeset in Calvert
by Deanta Global Publishing Services, Chennai, India

Contents

List of Figures
and Table

FIGURES

TABLE

Preface

In preparing this book, we have attempted to balance the subtleties of innovation as an academic disciplinary perspective with the practicalities of how innovation and transformation unfold in real life, with a focus on the creative and cultural industry sector. Hence, our book provides reviews of key innovation concepts (e.g. crowdsourcing, digitization, product, process, business model and technological innovation) and related management concepts (e.g. intellectual property protections, collaboration, supply chain management) that provide the necessary background knowledge for understanding the forms of innovations impacting creative and cultural industries. We also outline the drivers in each industry cluster influencing how such innovations impact industry practice and transformation.

Our second focus is on providing the reader with a rich array of real-world examples of innovation in practice. We have identified over 20 innovation exemplars, which are mini cases that detail specific industry practices reflective of transformational innovation. These exemplars include North American, European and Asian examples and cover the full range of industries associated with each of the three CCI clusters: Cluster One: Digitizable media (advertising, film, photography, publishing, recorded music and video games); Cluster Two: Physical products (fashion goods, furniture and furnishings); and Cluster Three: Ephemeral experience providers (art galleries, festivals, live music, museums and performing arts).

Additionally, our book includes four major case studies of significant innovation transformations across our three CCI clusters. Digitizable Media focuses on Tencent, a Chinese multinational that dominates the full spectrum of Cluster One industries. The physical products cluster features two major end-of-chapter case studies. One is fast fashion and the competition between major players in this sector. The second case focuses on IKEA, a Swedish business that has grown into the world's largest furniture manufacturer. Cluster Three (experiential experiences) provides our concluding major case focused on Cirque du Soleil (CdS) (French for Circus of the Sun), a Canadian performing arts company whose principal business is to provide live shows that are a hybrid of circus, acrobatics, theater and dance. Each of these cases provides a complex example of how the various transformational drivers specific to each CCI cluster are interwoven and invite innovative responses by the focal organization and its various ecosystem partners.

This book has been a collaboration of complementary perspectives and sensibilities forged into a unifying perspective on our subject. Two of our authors (Alison Rieple and Robert DeFillippi) are innovation and strategy scholars with deep expertise in examining how innovation transforms cultural and creative industry practices, while David Schneider brings deep scholarly and practitioner expertise in digital entertainment and the organizational and leadership challenges facing its practitioners.

Acknowledgments

We are grateful to Jonathan Mayes, Head of Strategic Partnerships and Impact, Clore Leadership Programme, and former lead on policy and investment strategy for orchestras in Arts Council England and Director of Residencies and Regional Programme with the Philharmonia Orchestra for his insights into the role of innovation ecosystems in classical music performance and recording.

We thank Yesim Tonga Uriarte, Assistant Professor at IMT School for Advanced Studies Lucca, for her private correspondence with Bob DeFillippi regarding trends in festival organizing and innovation. Her counsel as a collaborator in previous research with Bob DeFillippi on festivals and innovation is deeply appreciated in the service of our discussion of festivals in our current book.

We thank Jason Allen for his insights into the role of AI in the creative arts.

We would also like to thank our families and long-suffering spouses (Gordon, Kate and Jane) for their unstinting support during this book's journey to completion.

About the authors

Alison Rieple

Dr Alison Rieple is Emeritus Professor of Strategic Management at the University of Westminster in London, UK. A degree in music was followed by an early career in the Probation Service. After leaving probation she undertook an MBA and PhD at Cranfield School of Management. Since then, her teaching and research have focused on strategic management, entrepreneurship and innovation, notably in the creative and cultural industries such as music and fashion. She is the co-author of two strategic management textbooks, was co-editor (with Bob DeFillippi) of a book published in 2016 on the role of design in disruptive innovation and has written numerous book chapters. She has authored more than 100 scholarly articles. Alison has been a book and article reviewer for numerous publishers and journals and has served on the Editorial Board of *Management Decision*, the *Design Management Journal* and the *International Journal of Entrepreneurship and Management*.

Alison was Director of Research at Westminster University's Harrow Business School and was founder and director of the IDEaS (Innovation, Design Entrepreneurship and Strategy) Research Centre. She has supervised more than 25 PhD students. She has served on the academic board of the Design Management Institute, in Boston, Mass., and the Design Management International Conferences. She has also worked internationally as a business development and consultant for both public sector and commercial organizations, and now undertakes pro-bono consultancy for the Cranfield Trust, a charity which provides free management consultancy advice to other charities. When not working Alison enjoys playing bridge and singing in one of London's large symphony choruses.

Robert DeFillippi

Robert DeFillippi is Emeritus Professor of Strategy and International Business at the Sawyer Business School, Suffolk University, Boston, USA. Dr. DeFillippi is an international scholar in innovation, and he has held visiting scholar and/ or visiting professor appointments at Imperial College and Cass Business School, London; the Center for Research in Innovation Management at the University of Sussex, Brighton, UK; Polytechnico di Milano and Bocconi University, Milan; Queensland University of Technology, Brisbane, Australia; and University of Kyoto, Japan. He also has been a Fulbright consulting scholar at IMT in Lucca, Italy, and Freie Universitat, Berlin, Germany. Dr. DeFillippi holds an MA, MPhil and PhD from Yale University in Organisation Studies. He is a founder and emeritus director of the Center for Innovative Collaboration Leadership (CICL), Sawyer Business School, Suffolk University. He previously served on the Editorial Board of the *Journal of Media Business Studies* and was Consulting Editor and Associate Editor of the *International Journal of Management Reviews*.

His previous scholarship has included theoretical and empirical research contributions to the study of co-creation, industry clusters, project-based careers, temporary organizing and innovation in creative and cultural industries, including advertising, design, festivals, film production, music, publishing, stock photography and video games. He was co-editor of the book series Business Innovation and Disruption in Creative and Cultural Industries with Patrik Wikstrom for Edward Elgar Press. This four-volume book series was dedicated to understanding the disruptive forces that are reshaping creative industry boundaries and challenging conventional business models and business practices worldwide. He is the author of over 40 scholarly and applied journal publications and book chapters and ten scholarly books.

His academic administrative career has included chairing the Strategy and International Business and the Management departments and serving as Academic Director, Innovation and Design Management concentration in the Executive MBA at Suffolk University. His post-retirement activities include serving as board member and director of volunteers for the Sarasota Institute of LifeTime Learning (url: sillsarasota.org), a premier public lecture series on foreign policy and international affairs in Sarasota, FL.

David Schreiber

Dr. David Schreiber is Associate Professor and Chair of the Creative & Entertainment Industries program at Belmont University in Nashville, TN. Dr. Schreiber is an international scholar of the creative industries and has held a visiting scholar appointment at Queen's University in Belfast, Northern Ireland. He has written textbooks on organizational behavior in the creative economy and has published on topics related to symbolic capital and its role in decision-making in the music industry and the use of sub-cultural capital in artist branding. Furthermore, David is a member of the Academy of Management (AOM), European Group of Organization Studies (EGOS), the Music and Entertainment Industry Educators Association (MEIEA) and International Music Business Research Association; served as Associate Editor; and served on the board of MEIEA for nearly a decade.

David received a Bachelor of Arts from the University of Wisconsin Stevens Point, but after working in the music industry for eight years, he realized his true passion was to be found in teaching. He returned to the University of Miami for a Master of Music, and subsequently a Doctor of Philosophy from the University of Westminster in London, England.

Prior to accepting his current position at Belmont University, Dr. Schreiber taught at Greenville College, Minnesota State Mankato and Albright College. He has worked in multiple areas of the music industry, including Regional Manager at Schmitt Music, Marketing and Business Development Manager for Shiny Penny Productions, in the licensing and royalty department of Miami Records, as Business Development Manager at Pivot Entertainment and managed artist Dean Fields.

Introduction to Trans- formational Innovation in the Creative and Cultural Industries

Alison Rieple, Robert DeFillippi and David Schreiber

Chapter 1

Introduction

This book focuses on the way that innovation within the Creative and Cultural Industries (CCIs) transformed the industries in which they were applied. Several strands of theory have explicitly related innovation to industry evolution and transformation (Malerba, 2006). One of the earliest and perhaps most prominent of these perspectives was Joseph Schumpeter's in his 1942 treatise *Capitalism, Socialisms and Democracy*. Schumpeter said that some

DOI: 10.4324/9781003207542-1

forms of innovation contribute to *gales of creative destruction* – the "process of industrial mutation that incessantly revolutionizes the economic structure from within, incessantly destroying the old one, incessantly creating a new one" (Schumpeter, 1942: 82–3). In this way innovation disrupts the prevailing industrial order and provides opportunities for the emergence of new players by making obsolete the prior dominant design and basis of value creation (Abernathy and Utterback, 1978). The dominant design, which might be centered on a technology, product or set of key industry features, controls the way that firms compete in an industry and thus the type of organizations that succeed and prevail. Once a dominant design is established the focus shifts from transformational to incremental innovations that alter the technological sophistication, quality and scope of an industry's offerings without altering the structure of relations between established actors. It is these *transformational* innovations that we are interested in in this book. We want to show how they emerged, their sources, what made them successful and who were the major actors in the process.

We group the CCIs into three major clusters (Figure 1.1):

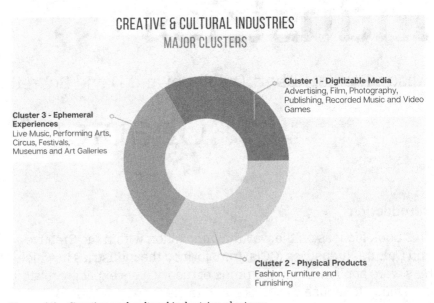

Figure 1.1   Creative and cultural industries clusters.

1. *Digitizable Media*, including advertising, film, photography, publishing, recorded music and video games

Transformational Innovation

2. *Physical Products*, including fashion, furniture and
    furnishings
3. *Ephemeral Experience Providers*, including live music,
    performing arts, festivals, museums and art galleries

The industries in each cluster may be different from some of
their fellow cluster members, but they share core strategic
challenges and critical drivers that make them comparable and
which innovation needs to address. Thus, although there may
be some overlaps, the innovations in each cluster tend to be
specific to the cluster. We will discuss these in more detail in
later chapters.

But before we move on to the definition of and characterization
of the CCIs in Chapter 2, and why we have grouped them in
this way, we first explain what innovation is, and why it is so
important in the CCIs. The first thing to say is that innovation
is not creativity, or invention, with which it is often confused,
although both creativity and invention may be part of the
innovation development process. Here we define invention as
the first occurrence of a new idea, creativity as the expression
of an original idea and innovation as the implementation of a
significantly new idea in a specific context.

In some industries it is almost impossible to separate
invention from innovation. In biotechnology, for example,
the development of, say, a new gene modification technique
happens through practical, applied, creativity in the laboratory.
In some other industries, such as fashion, creativity and
innovation are often used synonymously, although they are
not necessarily the same thing. One fashion firm that we
know, Swarovski, is an Austrian company that makes glass
and crystal products. It makes an internal distinction between
the two concepts in its own products (source: personal
communication). Although both are basically based on glass,
the sparkly ones used in fashion as decorative elements are
not especially innovative or sophisticated in their attributes
and are labeled creative products whereas the other types are
innovative in the way that they were developed and used. For
example, colored zirconia required changes to be made to the
company's production processes, and consequential changes to
the highly technical processes in other industries in which they

are used. We, too, make a distinction between creativity and innovation.

There are many ways of defining and characterizing innovation. A small new idea that is applied to improving an existing product or service is known as an *incremental* innovation and is very common. It is easy to implement and is less likely to encounter the sort of resistance that a major innovation would engender. At the other extreme are *radical* innovations. These are new ideas that are very different from what has gone before, and that may come up against serious opposition as people don't understand or like what they see. As Machiavelli said: "For he who innovates will have for his enemies all those who are well off under the existing order of things, and only lukewarm supporters in those who might be better off under the new" (Machiavelli, 1532).

The third category is those innovations that *transform* the ways that the whole industry operates. Most of the transformational innovations that we discuss in this book are radical, although not all radical innovations are transformational. What makes them transformational is if they disrupt the activities and operations of the whole industry and its customers, suppliers and partners. Not all radical innovations succeed: only 40% in one study were judged to be successful (Kadareja, 2013). (Although it has to be said that defining innovation success is a minefield, something that is beyond the scope of this book to discuss. See Edison et al. (2014) and More (2011) for reviews.)

A similar concept to transformational innovation is that of *disruptive innovation*. In its commonplace definition (that the innovation disrupts existing arrangements), this would be an alternative to our concept of transformational innovation. However, it has come to have a specialist, narrower, meaning as put forward by Christensen and colleagues[1] (Wessel and Christensen, 2012; Christensen et al., 2015; 2016; Christensen, 1997) and therefore is not a term that we will use in this book.

Table 1.1 shows some examples of the different types of innovations in the CCIs, which we will discuss further in the following chapters.

Table 1.1 Examples of different types of innovations in the CCIs

		Incremental Innovation	Radical Innovation	Transformational Innovation
Chapter 3 Digitizable media	**Publishing**	New physical formats (paperbacks, tabloid newspapers)	Word processing software Audiobooks	Digital publishing platforms Subscription models for digital content access P2P file sharing
	Music	Long Play (LP) or "full-length" album format	Audio compression and MP3 technology	Video streaming
	Motion pictures	Cinemascope widescreen format for movie projection	CGI (Computer-generated imagery)	
Chapter 4 Physical products	**Fashion**	Improved fabrics	Computer-aided fashion designing	Online retailing Just in time manufacturing
	Furniture and furnishings	Improved materials and manufacturing techniques	Flat-pack self-assembly furniture	Self-service retailing
Chapter 5 Ephemeral experience providers	**Performing arts**	Use of enhanced sound technologies and LED lighting to improve audience experience	3D Holographic concerts and wearable technologies that provide a more interactive experience	Digitization and live streaming
	Art galleries/ museums	Online gallery and museum enhancements, including digitized museum tours	Virtual museums, virtual reality and augmented reality displays	AR/VR/XR

WHERE ARE INNOVATIONS TO BE FOUND?

Innovations can be found across a huge range of activities and contexts. There are four categories of innovation that we are especially interested in: product/service, technology, process/ systems, and business model. In many cases, as we shall see, there are many areas of overlap between these. Companies can innovate at the product level but also simultaneously innovate at the process and business model levels. In fact, a product innovation may also need innovation in processes/systems and business model if it is to be successful.

Product/Service

Product/service innovation involves the invention, development and making of a physical object or a way of providing a service that is significantly different from those that have gone before. Examples of product innovations are:

- streaming video/audio
- online retailing
- 3D printers
- digital cameras

Examples of service innovation are:

- multichannel retailing
- video/clothes rentals
- subscription services for performing arts
- online payment systems

You might think that some of these innovations are a mixture of service and physical product (online retailing, for example), and we would agree with you. It's sometimes very hard to separate out the different elements, especially for products that involve digitization. It is also sometimes difficult to decide whether these are incremental or radical. It is possible to trace incremental developments in retailing that finally emerged as radical innovations in the form of online retailing, or e-tailing.

Using our definition, many of the new products that are commonplace in the CCIs are not *significantly* different from their predecessors. A pop artist might release a new single every month or an album every few months. Unless the new release does something significantly different in terms of, say, how it is recorded or written, or is significantly novel in the inherent aspects of the music's composition, it's simply a new creative work but not in our definition an innovative one. Similarly in fashion, designers bring out new items of clothing every few weeks. As with recorded music, unless this involves a new way of constructing or designing the garment, or brings in new materials, it would be considered creativity but not innovation.

Technology

Product innovation is often, if not always, dependent on another category of innovation, technology. Technological innovations are sometimes invented in universities, or maybe within a company, but the uses to which they are put are more widespread than can be commercialized by the originator. An example of this would be 3D printing/additive manufacturing (Vanderploeg et al., 2017), which was created by a Californian inventor called Chuck Hull in the early 1980s, but which has since moved far away from his lab to be found in industries as different as architecture (where it has transformed the design process); fashion (where it is allowing personalization and customization of fashion items); and art and performance (where it is being used to design art installations, modern sculptures, characters and prop design).

Technological innovations can alter the industry's success factors, culture and routines (its "recipes") and, if transformational, result in advances so significant that "no increase in scale, efficiency, or design can make older technologies competitive with the new technology" (Tushman and Anderson, 1986: 441). Examples are the MP3 or sound compression technologies that led to the transformation of the recorded music industry from a physical product to digital streaming. This allowed for transformational changes to the industry's business model, away from a physical manufacturing and distribution model to one that was eventually built around online payments for digitally-delivered products.

Processes and Systems

Some product and technological innovations also change the way that the organization needs to operate, and process and system innovations need to be brought in in parallel if the innovation is to succeed. 3D printers need to be linked to software that can be downloaded and shared, not only over the Internet but also via internal systems such as corporate intranets.

Some companies have also introduced new systems and processes that fundamentally change the way that the organization operates, for example, by changing the activities and procedures needed to develop, produce and deliver its products and services (its value chain). If these innovations are significantly more effective than competitors', those competitors will need to also change their processes/systems if they are not to go out of business. Figure 1.2 shows how innovation has affected the book publishing industry.

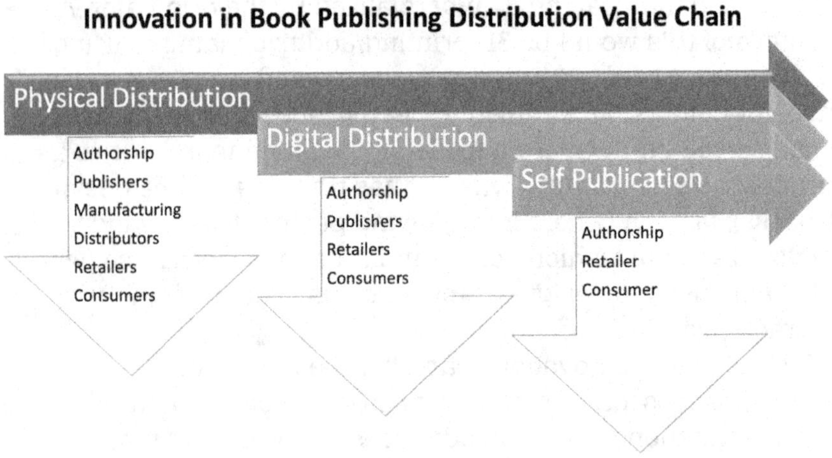

Innovation in Book Publishing Distribution Value Chain

Figure 1.2   Innovation in the book publishing distribution value chain.

In this way the rules of competition in the industry are transformed. Examples include Amazon.com, which was the first major Internet bookseller (set up in 1995), and a pioneer of the online ordering and postal delivery of books, and subsequently online delivery more generally. Along with the, then radically new, concept of selling books over the Internet, the value chain that it set up in order to fulfill its orders was also highly innovative. Another more recent example is the development of Blockchain and digital currencies such as Bitcoin and Ethereum, which are transforming the ways that electronic transactions are made.

Business Models

Although process and system innovations can be transformative internally within the company by increasing the efficiency and effectiveness of the value chain, systemic innovations if extensive and radical enough can form a new business model. In this the whole way of doing business is transformed. It is arguable that this is what Amazon did when it created its online marketplace and what digital currencies are doing now. Transformation usually involves significant disruption to suppliers, distributors, consumers and even competitors. Many business model innovations involve partnerships with competitors or other collaborators, and many have come about because of the availability of digital technologies such as the Internet and Electronic Data Interchange (EDI). Some of the most transformational recent business model innovations have involved the removal of intermediaries, such as retailers, to be replaced by direct interaction between the consumer and the provider. Sometimes this has cannibalized the company's own retail outlets; examples in the fashion industry include companies such as H&M and Zara, who are increasingly selling their own goods online rather than in their shops. In the music and film industries online downloading and streaming of songs and videos long ago virtually killed off record and video retailers.

HOW INNOVATION IS DEVELOPED

Certain features, within and outside the organization, appear to be beneficial to the innovation development process. One factor is being located within an innovation-supporting environment (Gong and Hassick, 2017). Fashion has long been known to concentrate in clusters, in Paris, New York or Milan for example. The US and Indian film industries in Hollywood and "Bollywood" and the music industry in Nashville are highly clustered geographically. California's Silicon Valley offers a whole range of supportive elements for software developers, a culture of risk-taking and enthusiasm for new ideas; government-supported venture capital and R&D funding; information sharing and cooperation between competing firms, research institutions and universities; sophisticated local customers; and plenty of resources to bring an innovation to fruition, including chip designers, specialist software writers and patent lawyers.

Many innovations are developed internally. In a large company there should be no reason why the necessary resources cannot be found by the organization itself, except – and it is a big "except" – that large organizations are often committed to existing products and may be organizationally resistant to anything that would require them to alter existing ways of working. Managing this type of change is challenging. Some large companies solve this so-called innovator's dilemma (Christensen, 1997) by setting up separate divisions that attempt to mimic the entrepreneurial spirit of start-ups. The problem then is to make sure that the new venture is not marginalized by the rest of the company. Sony's divisions include Game and Network Services, Music, Pictures, Electronics Products and Solutions, Imaging and Sensing Solutions and innovation-focused divisions such as Sony Computer Science Labs, which work in "chaotic creativity to find new solutions for Japan's future" (Nikkei.com, 2021). Ensuring that innovative new ideas are allowed to flourish is achieved by having senior directors from the Group Board also sit on the Boards of the various subsidiaries. By participating in this way they can force through innovation-based challenges to established ways of doing things.

Because of these sorts of problems, innovations are often brought about by new firms with an entrepreneurial mindset and no existing infrastructure to be dismantled. Their problem, instead, is to obtain the resources they need from outside the organization. This is where venture capitalists and a supportive environment come in. The types of complex innovation found especially in culture- or technology-based industries require knowledge and inputs from a wider variety of people and technologies than can be found within a single organization. For example, despite its size, Sony's Blu-ray DVD and the Cell processor which is a key component of the Playstation 3 (PS3) video game console were developed with partners that included IBM and Toshiba. As Sony said "Amid advances in digitalization and networking, external partnerships – such as with other companies, education and research institutes at universities, and non-profit organizations – are increasingly important for two purposes: bringing together the wide range of motivations that drive users and creators to develop new businesses and/or engage in research and development, and expanding the scope of the creation of new products and businesses to increase customer value" (Sony Annual Report, 2020: 35).

Disney, too, has successfully managed alliances with animation companies such as Pixar to produce innovative animation-based feature films. Disney ultimately acquired Pixar, and this feature of incorporating alliance partners and/or spinning them off as independent companies is another common consequence of collaborative innovation. This provides incentives for potential partners who may end up with a considerable capital gain if the new company is acquired by their larger partner or floated as an independent company on a stock market (Reuer and Tong, 2010; Vandaie and Zaheer, 2014). For example, Kiva Systems was a start-up that developed an innovative robotic system to pick, pack and move orders within a warehouse, replacing the employees that previously would have done the job. In March 2012 its partner Amazon.com bought the company for $775 million, making Kiva's founders very wealthy.

A recent development in the innovation process is open innovation. This is where a firm seeks out external communities to provide it with what it needs. Open innovation came out of the open-source software model, where products such as the Linux operating system were developed using a wide net of participants, many of whom had no formal affiliation to the organization and could be located in any part of the world. The development of innovative tangible products using similar principles is harder, yet many CCI industries are doing it. Companies with crowdsourcing-type open innovation models set up contact points with the "outside world". These may be other organizations, or may be individuals sought through websites that advertise innovation challenges such as NineSigma, Big Idea Group and Innocentive. In crowdsourcing, an organization posts (typically online) an innovation challenge and invites outside parties to volunteer solutions for review. The winner can in some cases reap considerable rewards. CCIs such as advertising, video production, filmmaking and photography, have used this model.

THE PERILS OF INNOVATION

Many writers seem to assume that innovation is inherently a good thing and something that all firms should aspire to.

However, it is by no means automatic that innovation will lead to success, or indeed, that it should be a competitive priority for all companies. Most studies suggest that a high percentage of innovations fail commercially, and a high proportion of the resources devoted to new product development go to unsuccessful projects. Some estimates put new product failures as high as 90% (e.g. Fisher, 2014). However, this figure is hugely debatable as it is almost impossible to agree on what failure means. Much of the learning that takes place during the innovation development process will be transferred to another product, probably a direct successor to the original one. Should that count as a failure or simply a stage on the way to ultimate success?

However, as a general point these sorts of statistics imply that to be successful, innovators have to develop capabilities in the innovation development process (which we discuss more in Chapter 2), and they should expect to fail repeatedly. But if they are successful, their performance is likely to be superior to their peers, especially if they transform the rules of competition in their industries.

The risks of innovation fall into four major categories:

1. the costs of development and time-scales needed for success
2. the unpredictability of take-up
3. the imitation of the product may be imitated before enough returns have been generated by the original innovator
4. the need to focus on existing products and organizational routines

The Costs of Development and Time-Scales Needed for Success

The time-scales before an innovation is likely to become a commercial success can be long and costs very high. Although a recent study suggested that innovative companies on average generate 3.6% higher annual total shareholder returns than their peers (Harnoss and Baeza, 2019), many companies find it hard to achieve a positive return on their investment in innovation. Some studies have suggested that it takes eight years on average before an innovation reaches profitability, but within this average are very different patterns, depending on the novelty or complexity of the innovation: the greater the complexity and novelty, the longer the time-scales can be (Gross et al., 2018). Surprisingly little research has examined this, no doubt because of the definitional and measurement difficulties involved (see for example McKinsey and Co's, 2018 review).

An example of slow commercialization is the development of colorization in filmmaking. Four different versions of Technicolor systems were developed between 1916 and 1938, each an incremental improvement on the previous version. However, the costs of colorized filmmaking slowed the introduction of this feature in commercial film production during the 1930s and 1940s. Color filmmaking only thrived after 1947 when the competitive threat from television made adopting it imperative. In 1947, only 12% of American films were made in color. By 1954, that number rose to over 50% and had largely displaced black and white film by the 1960s (Cook, 2004).

By contrast, the introduction of sound in filmmaking was quite rapid. In late 1927 Warner Brothers studio released *The Jazz Singer*, which was mostly silent but contained what is generally regarded as the first synchronized dialogue (and singing) in a feature film. By the end of 1929, Hollywood was almost all "talkie", with several competing sound systems (soon to be standardized). Sound strengthened the market position of major studios in numerous countries: the higher expense associated with the talkie film overwhelmed smaller competitors, while the novelty of sound lured vastly larger audiences for those producers that remained.

Unpredictability of Take-up

Building market awareness and demand for a new product, even a fundamentally good one, takes time. Apart from the need to tell potential buyers about the product, there is always a problem in overcoming consumers', or collaborators', resistance to something new (Huang et al., 2021; Mani and Chouk, 2018; Trenerry et al., 2021). Gaining buy-in to a significantly new idea often requires customers, suppliers, other collaborators and even competitors, to change their behavior, and in the case of another company alter their own value chains and production processes. Not surprisingly many firms will wait to see whether the innovation is likely to be successful before they commit their own resources to accommodate it. Some types of products, such as recorded music, fashion or trend-driven electronics, also have a different sort of bandwagon effect, where consumers will only buy a product if they see someone else buying it.

Another problem is that products which are developed for one country do not necessarily succeed elsewhere. The length of time that new products take to reach "take-off" varies widely within countries. In Europe, Scandinavian countries have the shortest time – four years, nearly half that of Mediterranean countries (Tellis et al., 2003). National culture partly explains these differences, although economic factors are also important – take-off is faster in wealthier countries and more open economies. As the developers of an innovative product are often under great pressure to kill it off if it does not succeed quickly, introducing it in a country that is more likely to show early sales can help to convince critics, both inside the company and outside, of its potential. An early success can also generate profits, which the innovator can use to improve the product and promote it more aggressively.

The Product May Be Imitated Before Enough Returns Have Been Generated

Innovations, once launched and visible, may quickly spawn imitations that may be superior, or have access to a better distribution network, and so eat into the originator's sales and profits. Patents, design rights and recently NFTs are ways of protecting the intellectual property of some innovations. However, there is only a limited amount of protection afforded by such legal mechanisms. Patents are available to all and can be imitated, products deconstructed and *reverse engineered*, designs are visible and copyright legislation and redress to the courts is not always effective, especially in some international contexts.

For these reasons some of the most successful innovators adopt strategies such as technology and market diffusion S-Curves in which they attempt to pre-empt imitators by developing the next generation of product before competitors have had a chance to imitate the last one properly (Brown, 1992). Essentially these innovators commit to a trajectory of continuous innovation and improvement that retain and build on advantages enjoyed during the initial offering (Foster, 1986). These advantages in turn may evolve from initial functionality, reliability or simplicity of use to lower cost of purchase or replacement (Christensen, 1997). Such trends have been observed in numerous digitally based innovations employed in filmmaking, television and music.

Need to Focus on Existing Products and Organizational Routines

Innovation is often very disruptive to an organization's own existing operations, and this is a risk that many are not prepared or able to take or are allowed to by their shareholders. One well-known example is that of Kodak which had difficulty in embracing the new digital photography process because of the risk of destroying their own successful film-based business (Tidd and Bessant, 2020). Christensen (1997) refers to the choices that businesses must make between catering to their customers' current needs or adopting innovative products and technologies which will answer their future needs as the innovator's *dilemma*.

The implication is that not all companies are, or should be, primarily focused on innovation, or radical innovation at least. Some are very good at *exploitation*, successfully getting returns from existing products and services rather than *exploration* – the seeking-out of novel opportunities. This can sometimes last for decades. Because dedicated processes and systems are needed in order to exploit existing products, changes to these in order to accommodate new products are likely to be expensive. Routines have to be adjusted to take in the needs of the new product, plant and machinery may have to be retooled, and distribution and supplier contracts renegotiated. Exploiting firms may encounter difficulties if they recruit highly innovative types, who will be regarded with some suspicion as they attempt to change the status quo. Even firms that are strong at exploration are often better at some aspects of the innovation process than others.

The need to focus on one type of operation is one of the reasons why highly innovative industries such as music, video games and fashion are characterized by many partnerships between firms, especially between larger companies and smaller organizations that focus on a specialized aspect of the innovation process. The different stages of innovation, from invention to full commercialization, often require both types of organization at different times. Given the difficulties each type of organization has in developing the other's competences (and so-called ambidextrous organizations that are equally good at both are rare), firms often turn to outside partners to fill the gap. The major music companies employ many, and wide-ranging A&R (artist and repertoire) teams seek out new artists and small independent record companies that they can sign to the label. The label then puts all its marketing and sales might behind the new signing, exploiting the "product" while the independent label or individual musician can concentrate on exploring, discovering and creating new music (Gander et al., 2007; Gander and Rieple, 2004).

To summarize, innovation can be risky and expensive, and not all organizations are able to do it well. However, for those that are able to, the gains are potentially huge, especially if their innovation is one that transforms the industry and how it operates. It is these transformational innovations that we focus on in this book.

DEFINING THE CREATIVE AND CULTURAL INDUSTRIES

The industries that we focus on in this book, the *CCIs*, sometimes described as the *creative economy*, are a heterogeneous group that has been defined in myriad ways by many different people. All CCIs involve the use of creativity to a great extent in the development and provision of their products and services (it is of course arguable that all organizations use creativity in their product/service development and provision: we don't engage in that debate in this book, simply acknowledge that it exists). A new term "Creative and Digital Industries" recognizes the importance of digital content and online services within the creative economy (CIF, 2021). A subset of the CCIs focus additionally on cultural aspects, defined by UNESCO as "industries that combine the creation, production and commercialisation of contents which are intangible and cultural in nature; these contents are typically protected by copyright and they can take the form of a good or a service". Many, although not all, CCIs also create wealth through the generation and exploitation of intellectual property (DCMS, 2020a; Caves, 2000; Throsby, 2001).

Many authors have provided their own definitions. Paris (2010) suggests that the CCIs encompass all activities characterized by a creative process, with three common characteristics:

- The creative act exists independently of market demand.
- The value of a good has a social dimension (for example, going to a concert with friends, wearing clothes to identify yourself as part of a "tribe" of like-minded individuals).
- Prescription (i.e., cultural commentators) plays an essential role and contributes significantly to the success of the works.

His definition encompasses some very different industries such as fashion, advertising, gastronomy and design. Busson and Evrard (2013) are more exclusive and list seven CCI sectors: heritage, performing arts, the book industry, the music industry, video games, film and television. Pellegrin-Boucher and Roy's (2019) wider-ranging list includes architecture, cinema, photography, the art market, plastic arts, design, fashion (textiles, clothing, accessories, perfumes, cosmetics, luxury), heritage (museums, monuments), advertising, performing arts (shows, theatres, festivals, concerts), radio, TV, music, video games, gastronomy, living arts (decoration, furniture, tableware) and publishing (books, press).

In addition to authors, bodies such as the UK government's Department for Digital, Culture, Media and Sport (DCMS, 2019) and the US' Creative Economy Coalition (arts.gov, 2021) provide definitions because they are interested in providing research and support to industries which are important contributors to the national economy and the country's well-being. They include (DCMS, 2019; arts.gov, 2021):

- advertising and marketing
- architecture
- crafts
- design: product, graphic, fashion
- film, TV, video, animation, VFX/SFX, radio and photography
- IT, video games, software and computer services

- publishing (the US's term is Internet broadcasting and publishing)
- museums, galleries, libraries and heritage
- music, performing and visual arts
- music production, distribution and sales

We return to looking at the critical challenges or success factors operating within these industries in the next chapter. But first, we look at their social and economic importance.

THE ECONOMIC CONTRIBUTION OF THE CCIS

The UK and US governments believe that the CCIs are important contributors to the social and economic well-being of their countries (OECD, 2020). This is also true of other countries such as France, Japan, China and Brazil (Park, 2022; OECD, 2020). In Europe, the CCIs are responsible for 4% of the EU's GDP and over seven million jobs, mainly in small businesses (Eurostat, 2021). They represent a source of wealth and job creation, particularly since they are relocatable only with difficulty; they require rare talents and knowledge that is difficult to substitute, rooted in specific know-how and heritage (Pellegrin-Boucher and Roy 2019). As an economic comparison, in France CCIs represent slightly more than twice the size of the accommodation and catering sectors (Pellegrin-Boucher and Roy 2019). In the UK almost one in eight businesses are in the creative economy, more than the automotive, aerospace, life sciences and oil and gas industries combined. They contribute £101.5bn gross value added (GVA) to the UK economy, account for almost 12% of UK services exports and employ over two million people. These are sectors that have seen high levels of growth in recent years (DCMS, 2019; Goldman Sachs, 2020; Statista, 2022). Similar figures are to be found in other countries including in less developed parts of the world.

As an indication, Figures 1.3 and 1.4 show the scale of the worldwide economic contribution of a few of the major CCIs that we discuss in the remainder of this book.

These data provide a clear indication of the importance of the CCIs. In turn these industries depend heavily on innovation for their economic success.

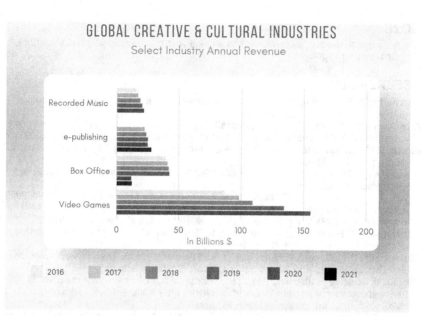

Figure 1.3 Global creative and cultural industries, select annual revenues $bn. *Source:* Recorded Music (International Federation of the Phonographic Industry) IFPI.org. *Source:* e-publishing, Digital Media Report 2021 – Video Games: Statista Digital Market Outlook. *Source:* Film. Global box office revenues. *Source:* Statista, 2022. *Source:* Video Games, Digital Media Report 2021 – Video Games: Statista Digital Market Outlook

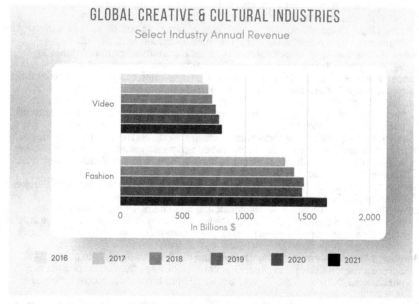

Figure 1.4 Global creative and entertainment industries, select annual revenues $bn. *Source:* Video, Digital Media Report 2021 – Video: Statista Digital Market Outlook. *Source:* Fashion, Size of the apparel market worldwide from 2011 to 2020 ($ bn): *Source:* Statista.com

NOTE

1   It is beyond the scope of this book to engage with this debate, which is sometimes virulent and ongoing!

REFERENCES

Abernathy, W. J. and Utterback, J. (1978). Patterns of industrial innovation. *Technology Review*, 80 (7): 40–47 (June–July).

Arts.gov. (2021). US' creative economy coalition. Available from: (https://www.arts.gov/sites/default/files/Research-Art-Works-Milwaukee.pdf). Accessed August 15, 2021.

Brown, R. (1992). Managing the "S" curves of innovation. *Journal of Business & Industrial Marketing*, 7 (3): 41–52.

Busson, A., and Evrard, Y. (2013). *Les Industries Culturelles et Créatives: Économie et Stratégie*. Vuibert.

Caves, R. E. (2000). *Creative Industries: Contracts Between Art and Commerce (No. 20)*. Harvard University Press.

Christensen, C. (1997). *The Innovator's Dilemma*. Harvard Business School Press.

Christensen, C., Raynor, M., and McDonald, R. (2015). What is disruptive innovation?. *Harvard Business Review*, December: 44–53.

Christensen, C, McDonald, R., Altman, E. J., and Palmer, J. (2016). *Disruptive Innovation: Intellectual History and Future Paths*. Harvard Business School.

CIF (2021). Creative industries infographic. Available from: https://www.creativeind ustriesfederation.com/sites/default/files/2019-12/UK%20Creative%20Industries %20Infographic.pdf. Accessed June 18, 2021.

DCMS (2019). Creative Industries Economic Estimates – Business Demographics, January. Available from: https://www.gov.uk/government/organisations/department-for-digital -culture-media-sport. Accessed March 3, 2022.

DCMS (2020a). Sectors Economic Estimates, GVA, December. Available from: https://www .gov.uk/government/publications/dcms-sectors-economic-estimates-methodology/ dcms-sector-economic-estimates-methodology. Accessed February 8, 2021.

Edison, H., Ali, N. B., and Torkar, R. (2014). Towards innovation measurement in the software industry. *Journal of Systems and Software*, 86 (5): 1390–407.

Eurostat (2021). Culture Statistics. Available from: https://ec.europa.eu/eurostat/statistics -explained/index.php?title=Culture_statistics. Accessed April 29, 2022.

Fisher, A. (2014). Why most innovations are great big failures. *Fortune*, October 7.

Foster, R. N. (1986). *Innovation: The Attacker's Advantage*. Summit Books.

Gander, J., and Rieple, A. (2004). How relevant is transaction cost economics to inter-firm relationships in the music industry? *Journal of Cultural Economics*, 28(1), 57–79.

Gander, J., Haberberg, A., and Rieple, A. (2007). A paradox of alliance management: Resource contamination in the recorded music industry. *Journal of Organisational Behaviour*, 28(5), 607–624.

Goldman Sachs (2020). *State of the Music Industry*. Available from: https://www.toptal .com/finance/market-research-analysts/state-of-music-industry#:~:text=In%20May %202020%2C%20Goldman%20Sachs,billion%2C%20made%20in%20October%202016. Accessed July 14, 2022.

Gong, J. and Hassink, R. (2017). Exploring the clustering of creative industries. *European Planning Studies*, 25(4): 583–600.

Gross, R., Hanna, R., Gambhir, A., Heptonstall, P. and Speirs, J. (2018). How long does innovation and commercialisation in the energy sectors take? Historical case studies of the timescale from invention to widespread commercialisation in energy supply and end use technology. *Energy Policy*, 123: 682–699.

Harnoss, J. D., and Baeza, R. (2019). *Overcoming the Four Big Barriers to Innovation Success*. Boston Consulting Group. Available from: https://www.bcg.com/en-nor/ publications/2019/overcoming-four-big-barriers-to-innovation-success. Accessed May 29, 2021.

Huang, D., Jin, X., and Coghlan, A. (2021). Advances in consumer innovation resistance research: A review and research agenda. *Technological Forecasting and Social Change*, 166: 120594.

Kadareja, A. (2013). Risks of incremental, differential, radical, and breakthrough innovation projects. *Innovation Management*. Available from: https://innovationm anagement.se/2013/07/29/risks-of-incremental-differential-radical-and-breakthrough -innovation-projects/. Accessed December 12, 2021.

Machiavelli, N. (1532). *The Prince: Second Edition, 2010*. University of Chicago Press.

Malerba, F., (2006). Innovation and the evolution of industries, *Journal of Evolutionary Economics*, Springer, 16(1): 3–23.

Mani, Z. and Chouk, I. (2018). Consumer resistance to innovation in services: Challenges and barriers in the internet of things era. *Journal of Product Innovation Management*, 35 (5): 780–807.

McKinsey and Co. (2018). How to take the measure of innovation. Available from: https://www.mckinsey.com/business-functions/strategy-and-corporate-finance/our-insights /how-to-take-the-measure-of-innovation. Accessed March 2, 2022.

More, R. (2011). What is success in innovation? *Ivey Business Journal*. Available from: https://iveybusinessjournal.com/publication/what-is-success-in-innovation/. Accessed July 14, 2021.

Nikkei.com (2021). Inside Sony's mysterious lab. Available from: https://asia.nikkei.com /Business/Companies/Inside-Sony-s-mysterious-lab-30-researchers-pursue-unique -projects. Accessed March 2, 2022.

OECD (2020). Culture shock: Covid-19 and the cultural and creative sectors. Available from: https://www.oecd.org/coronavirus/policy-responses/culture-shock-covid-19 -and-the-cultural-and-creative-sectors-08da9e0e/. Accessed April 18, 2022.

Paris, T. (2010). *Manager la Créativité*. Pearson Education.

Park, S. D. (2022). Policy Discourse Among the Chinese Public on Initiatives for Cultural and Creative Industries: Text Mining Analysis. *SAGE Open*, 12 (1): 21582440221079927.

Pellegrin-Boucher, E. and Roy, P., eds. (2019). *Innovation in the Cultural and Creative Industries*. Wiley.

Reuer, J. J., and Tong, T. W. (2010). Discovering valuable growth opportunities: An analysis of equity alliances with IPO firms. *Organization Science*, 21 (1): 202–215.

Schumpeter, J. A. (1942). *Capitalism, Socialism and Democracy*. Harper and Brothers.

Sony (2020). Annual report. Available from: chrome-extension:// efaidnbmnnnibpcajpcglclefindmkaj/https://www.sony.com/en/SonyInfo/IR/library/ corporatereport/CorporateReport2020_E.pdf. Accessed November 14, 2021.

Statista Search Department. (2022). Video Games, Market Data Analysis & Forecasts. *Statista*. Available from: file:///Users/davidschreiber/Downloads/study_id39310_vi deo-games%20(1).pdf. Accessed July 30, 2022.

Tellis, G. J., Stremersch, S., and Yin, E. (2003). The international takeoff of new products: the role of economics, culture, and country innovativeness. *Marketing Science*, 22(2): 188–208.

Throsby, D. (2001). *Economics and Culture*. Cambridge University Press.

Tidd, J., and Bessant, J. R. (2020). *Managing Innovation: Integrating Technological, Market and Organizational Change*. John Wiley & Sons.

Trenerry, B., Chng, S., Wang, Y., Suhaila, Z. S., Lim, S. S., Lu, H. Y., and Oh, P. H. (2021). Preparing workplaces for digital transformation: An integrative review and framework of multi-level factors. *Frontiers in Psychology*, 12: 822.

Tushman, M. L. and Anderson, P. (1986). Technological discontinuities and organizational environments. *Administrative Science Quarterly*, 31 (3): 439–465.

Vandaie, R., and Zaheer, A. (2015). Alliance partners and firm capability: Evidence from the motion picture industry. *Organization Science*, 26 (1): 22–36.

Vanderploeg, A., Lee, S. E., and Mamp, M. (2017). The application of 3D printing technology in the fashion industry. *International Journal of Fashion Design, Technology and Education*, 10 (2): 170–179.

Wessel, M. and Christensen, C. M. (2012). Surviving disruption. *Harvard Business Review*, 90 (12): 56–64.

Critical Challenges and Success Factors in the CCIs

Defining Three Clusters of CCI Industries

Alison Rieple, Robert DeFillippi and David Schreiber

Chapter 2

Introduction

In this chapter we describe some of the generic critical
challenges and success factors in the Creative and Cultural
Industries. We then go on to define our three industry clusters,
based around the features that distinguish them from the other
CCI industry types.

FIVE CRITICAL FEATURES OF THE CREATIVE AND CULTURAL INDUSTRIES

Before we move on to explaining our categorizing of the CCIs
into three clusters, we first cover some of the generic features of
the CCIs that distinguish them from other industries and which
provide critical challenges for anyone seeking to innovate.

DOI: 10.4324/9781003207542-2

Such challenges, sometimes known as critical success factors (Dziurski, 2016), are essential considerations for innovators; unless an innovation addresses these core concerns in some way, it is unlikely to be successful, and even less likely to be transformative.

CRITICAL FEATURE 1: CREATIVITY IN THE PRODUCT/SERVICE

Perhaps the most important feature of the CCI is that they all involve the use of creativity to a great extent in the development and provision of their products and services. Almost all CCI offerings are new, not necessarily innovatively new (as discussed previously), but novel in that each one is intentionally different from others (Bouquillon et al., 2021). This distinguishes them from industries such as: a) brick-making or pharmaceuticals, for example, where the aim is to make identical copies of the same brick or drug over and over again at the lowest possible cost: financial services, where the aim is to provide customers (whether individuals or other companies, the so-called business to business, B2B, services) with the solutions they need with little customization or c) agriculture, where the aim is to utilize land productively to produce food. For many in the CCIs success comes from achieving recognition for their novelty or difference (Wohl, 2022).

Central to this process is the creative individual, designer or artist (in its widest sense), typically intrinsically motivated and rewarded by factors other than purely economic ones (Cnossen et al., 2019; Paris and Mahmoud-Jouini, 2019). As has been suggested (Paris, 2010; Pellegrin-Boucher and Roy, 2019), the creative act can be independent of any market demand. For creativity-focused individuals, as well as the organizations that they work in, rewards may come in the form of symbolic capital rather than economic capital. Strategies may be aimed at generating reputational resources, perhaps in the shape of an award or nomination, or more informally the respect of fellow industry practitioners. Bourdieu even suggested that in some cases symbolic capital can be created by demonstrating a *disinterest* in economic reward (Bourdieu, 1996). It is certainly a truism that "creatives" are supposedly antipathetic to the "suits", the "them and us" division between those who are artists engaged in aesthetic production and those motivated by practical outcomes and financial incentives. Such stereotypes may have a grain of truth in them, but ultimately all those working in the creative industries have to be cognizant of both the need to make money and the lure of fame and celebrity.

The problem is how. Novelty is difficult for consumers to process unless it has some degree of familiarity. Schatz (1981) described the *curious bind* as the need to match or relate to existing, familiar, goods while also generating excitement by introducing aspects that are new and different. Achieving this balance of distinctiveness and "sameness" is tricky: if it is too similar, then the product risks being judged as derivative, if too new, then cultural intermediaries and consumers may not have the conceptual frameworks needed to evaluate it.

CRITICAL FEATURE 2: ECONOMIC PECULIARITIES

Because of the inherent novelty in the CCI product/service, economic success is not always predictable (Loots and van Witteloostuijn, 2018). This situation is made acute by the large numbers of possible new artists and works allowed by low barriers to entry. As we discuss in the next section, some success is due to a bandwagon effect in which a product or service "catches the wind". But bandwagons are unpredictable, and in some cases high production costs and weaker sales than anticipated have resulted in large losses: *Heaven's Gate*, a film directed by the award-winning director of *Deer Hunter* nearly destroyed the film studio United Artists (Welkos, 2004; BBC, 2015). Even more unusual (when compared to other product types) is that the success of a product is not always proportional to its quality (Rosen, 1981; Frank and Cook, 2010).

Some of the CCIs are classic examples of a *winner takes all* type of industry: the few major successes finance the majority of products, which are commercial failures (Karpik, 2007). In music, film, TV, fashion and architecture a few extremely successful large firms dominate, leaving a very small percentage of market share to be allocated among a large number of small companies. Similar dynamics apply to the individual artist; the amount earned by the top actors, architects, fashion designers, musicians or artists is many times that earned by their less fortunate colleagues. In some of the CCIs, competition based around standards creates the winner-takes-all situation because of "increasing returns to adoption". This is where the incentive for customers to adopt a standard increases with the number of users who have already adopted it, because of the greater availability of complementary and compatible goods and services. These include shows for TV and film networks and programs for computers (Tidd and Bessant, 2020).

CRITICAL FEATURE 3: CULTURE AND THE ROLE OF PRESCRIPTION

Uncertainty is thus an important problem for many of the CCIs. The symbolic qualities of cultural products also mean that there is, in the words of Richard Caves (2000), an *infinite variety* problem: there is a never-ending list of meanings, qualities and messages that might be used to signify the product. The symbolic and aesthetic dimensions may be more or less strong in different sectors but are always present.

In fact, one of the causes of the uneven sales of creative/cultural products is the role of prescription by cultural intermediaries who help to interpret the cultural product. Prescription matters because creative and cultural goods have a social dimension. This includes listening to the same music as your friends, going to the cinema in a group or wearing clothes that are recommended by trusted influencers and that identify yourself as part of a "tribe" of like-minded individuals.

Editorial institutions and actors such as critics, reviewers and celebrities with a public following have the function of selecting works and promoting them to the wider public (Caves, 2000). This can take the form of awards and charts that rank books, songs, films, clothes and games, as well as social media sites such as YouTube, Instagram and Facebook (Morning Consult, 2021). These can help to sway sales enormously, but the process and outcome are often unpredictable. Prescriptions can be circulated through real and virtual networks to produce the bandwagon effect. In this way organizations in the CCIs are engaged in what Appadurai (1988) described as a *tournament economy*.

CRITICAL FEATURE 4: INTELLECTUAL PROPERTY

Intellectual Property (IP) laws play an important role in providing the foundation for ownership and the business models that drive the CCIs. They are designed so that owners can be recognized for their work and also achieve financial benefits from it. IP laws aim to strike a balance between providing financial incentives for the originator and the interests of the public by creating an environment where creativity and innovation can thrive.

Almost all CCI products and services result in some form of intellectual property (Handke, 2018). There are a number of different means of protecting IP, according to the type of CCI output and national location, although they are not always effective at preventing someone from imitating or copying the originator's work. What they do offer, however, is a means of protection or recourse when others try to profit from those creations or use them in ways that harm or tarnish the reputation of the originator.

Different countries recognize different forms of intellectual property, and there are subtle differences between countries or economic territories (NI business info, 2022). Some categories of protection are provided automatically, and others have to be applied for. The main categories include:

- patents, which protect product inventions and new processes, including service methodologies
- trademarks and service-marks, which protect logos, words and other branding elements
- registered design rights, which protect the visual design of a product
- copyright, which protects art, writing, music, film and computer programs
- trade secrets

PATENTS

A patent is an exclusive protective right granted for an invention of a new product or process (Caplanova, 2020). In order to seek a patent registration (and it has to be applied for) the invention must be "new, functional, useful and original" (Caplanova, 2020). Once patent protection is granted the owner can sue others if they use the patented item without permission. In exchange for this right, the patent owner makes technical information about the invention publicly available in a published patent document (WIPO, 2022). It is for this reason that some companies choose to not patent their inventions or they disguise them under the name of an employee. Instead, they prefer to depend on the invention not being imitable because of the need for complementary assets such as brand loyalty, location or inimitable strategic assets such as core capabilities (Haberberg and Rieple, 2008; Reed and DeFillippi, 1990).

TRADEMARKS AND SERVICE-MARKS

A trademark is a visual sign that distinguishes the goods or services of one enterprise from those of other enterprises. Trademarks date back to ancient times when artisans used to put their signature or "mark" on their products. Their use is similar today. In some cases entire brands have been built around the design of the trademark, for example, Chanel in fashion, BBC in broadcasting and Twitter in social media. Valuing a trademark is an interesting challenge, as it is almost impossible to value the trademark separately from the goodwill of the company that it represents (see INTA (2020) for a discussion).

DESIGN RIGHTS

In some countries, designs, which constitute the ornamental or aesthetic aspect of an artifact, are protected under Design Rights laws. To qualify for design right protection, the overall impression of the new design must be different from any existing design. A design may consist of three-dimensional features, such as the shape or surface of an article, or two-dimensional features, such as patterns, lines or color (WIPO, 2022). Protection of works within this body of law can extend to items such as containers, packaging, furnishing, jewelry and textiles.

There are two types of design rights: (1) registered and (2) unregistered. Registered design rights both in the UK and in the EU will give the holder a 25-year monopoly right in the design, although they need to be renewed every 5 years. Unregistered design rights last for 10 years from the end of the year of first exploitation and protect only the shape of a three-dimensional design. In the USA the situation is slightly different in that design rights are termed design patents (Wikipedia, 2022c) and apply to a manufactured item that must be "non-functional and non-obvious". As such more designs are likely to qualify for protection in Europe than in the USA.

One complication is that a design may at the same time be protected by design rights and copyright laws: a design right can protect a look of a product whereas copyright applies to the paperwork that was generated in creating the design. Another complication is that a trademark may also be protected by design rights, although the duration of design right protection is shorter than that of trademarks.

COPYRIGHT

Copyright laws protect an author's property (the term does not just refer to writers but includes musical composers as well as designers and artists) rights to creative works. Copyright does not cover ideas and information themselves, only the form or manner in which they are expressed (Stokes, 2001). Copyright allows an author the exclusive right to use or authorize the use of their work or prevent others from using the work, usually for a limited time. Copyright protects written or literary works, music, photographs, graphic images, sculpture, performances, motion picture and sound recordings, and architectural plans and designs, as well as the buildings themselves.

Copyright does not usually need to be applied for, but lasts for a specific period of time, depending on the type of work and country. Almost all countries have adopted as a minimum standard the Berne Convention (Wikipedia, 2022b), which states that the minimum term of copyright protection is life of the author plus 50 years, but many jurisdictions, including the USA and the EU, have adopted 70 years or even longer. As mentioned above, graphic and industrial designs may have separate or overlapping laws applied to them in some countries.

Although copyright protects authors from illicit copying, there are some areas of leeway. The concept of fair dealing or fair use means that someone may be able to copy some of a work as long as it is a small proportion, not done for commercial purposes and is accompanied by a sufficient acknowledgment. Copyright laws also allow performers (singers and musicians), record producers (record labels and others), broadcasters and cable broadcasters, whose role is to disseminate copyrighted works to the general public, some additional rights called "neighboring rights". For example, a music CD could include the rights of a lyricist and a composer (copyrights), as well as the neighboring rights of the record label and a singer or a musician. This means a potentially complicated negotiation with the different rights' holders if someone wants to upload music from a commercially available CD to an Internet website.

Copying, especially in music, gaming and fashion, although a problem, is also at the same an essential part of the rules of the game. Some schools of thought suggest that making copycat products aids rather than harms the manufacturers of the original item and helps them extend their brand. In fact, imitation or mimesis (i.e., mimicry) is found everywhere in business. But it is particularly prevalent in the CCIs because of the importance of the social-based identity of the (creative) product. One way of measuring whether a product has "caught the wind" is to see how many times it has been imitated. Too identical a copy and lawyers will be citing copyright infringements. But a copy that is just short of a direct imitation, but sufficiently close to be recognizable as an imitation, will help to cross-sell the original products and also help to create a genre or trend that the original product can "ride". Copyright lawyers make a good living (we imagine!) in judging whether a work is a direct (and therefore illegal) copy or simply derivative – a new, original piece of work based on a previously created work. A derivative work enjoys its own copyright protection if it is sufficiently different from the original. For example, a translation of a foreign-language novel and a painting of a sculpture are derivative works.

In some industries copying can be prevented or lessened because of the *complementary assets* that go into making a product or service profitable. Complementary assets are those which work together synergistically to achieve a better outcome (Teece, 2018; Yu et al., 2019). A physical product such as a Zara garment can be easily copied. But what the imitator cannot easily do is replicate Zara's enormous buying power, which allows it to source materials at much lower cost than rivals, its retail locations, where the biggest footfall is to be found and which have been built up over many years, and its skills in reliably making the same item of clothing over and over again. It has also built a brand over time which imitators will not have. This combination of complementary assets allows Zara to achieve profitability levels that imitators cannot match.

On the other hand, copying in some of the CCIs is ridiculously easy and in regions with weak or non-existent IP institutions, as used to be the case in China for example, counterfeiting is rife. New clothes designs are immediately visible to others, and because some of the complementary assets in the fashion industry have been replaced, *disintermediated* or *dematerialized*, by alternative means of distribution (physical retail having given way to online sales), protection from imitation that is conferred by the visibility of physical goods has been weakened.

Anything that is digitizable can be replicated and distributed within seconds. Digital innovations made possible by the Internet, particularly distributed search engines and Peer–to-Peer file-sharing systems, have represented a challenge for copyright policy in some CCI sectors. Piracy of digitized entertainment has become a global phenomenon impacting digitized films, television programming, music recordings and any form of digitized entertainment such as video games. Piracy has so reduced the profitability of digitized sales in some industries that artists have resorted to relying increasingly on live performances to compensate for lost royalty income from copyrighted material.

We return to discussing some of the specific issues to do with IPR in the chapters on the different clusters.

CRITICAL FEATURE 5: ROLE OF THE INNOVATION ECOSYSTEM

Because of the nature of the creative/cultural innovation development process, CCI organizations need to ensure they are connected to resources such as knowledge of the cultural values and movements that their products will signify and be part of. This can be achieved by locating part of the organization in areas that are rich in cultural and creative activity. Cultural or creative clusters, or milieux, are commonplace in a wide variety of CCIs. Having the organization physically situated within such environments helps expose its employees to emerging trends through a combination of visual cues, chance encounters with other creative workers and ease of working with similar organizations nearby. CCI organizations need to work with many different organizations to support the distribution and promotion of cultural works.

But creative milieux also arise because of the industries' dependence on speedily accessing a wide range of physical resources and skills, The creation and delivery of a cultural product or service invariably involves a very diverse range of people with different skills, knowledge and values, which is why the virtual world has not yet been able to fully substitute for physical co-locating, in some of the CCIs at least. So-called agglomeration economies – a geographical concentration of resources and people – configure advantages to the organizations located within them because of three things – specialization, diversity and density (Tao et al., 2019).

Many CCIs are based on project-based organizing principles; a third of the workers in the CCIs are self-employed, moving from project to project, and if they do actually work in a company, it is overwhelmingly likely (95%) to be in an organization that employs fewer than ten people (CIF, 2021). Caves (2000) termed this mixing of people the *Motley Crew*. Complex products such as films or digital games require a vast array of highly specialized people alongside the purely creative or artistic ones, working on technical, administrative and commercial activities that are essential to bring the product to market (DeFillippi, 2015). Thus, there are centers of film production in Hollywood in the USA, Bollywood in India and Nollywood in Nigeria; clothes design in Seoul, New York and Paris; and recorded music in Nashville and London. Fashion, architecture and video games have their roots in drawing and are influenced by the graphic and visual arts and the need to be able to access these sorts of skills. This means that their clusters often arise close to art colleges and universities.

Ecosystem theory brings in an understanding of the wide-ranging sets of available resources, and *potential* resources needed. As creativity draws upon novelty these potential resources are often unknown at the outset. So it pays for CCIs to have tendrils spreading out away from their existing base. These "tendrils" may be in the form of *boundary-spanning* relationships with other organizations in very different lines of business. Or it may be in the less formal form of scouts, people who spend their time traveling the world just to see what is going on.

INTRODUCING OUR TYPOLOGY OF THE CCIs

In this section we introduce and justify our clusters of three different types of CCIs. Although it may make sense for policymakers to identify the economic contribution of the CCIs collectively (DCMS, 2019; arts.gov, 2021), there are few practical and theoretical grounds for regarding these industries as a coherent group. Although all CCIs involve creativity in the development of the product, not all involve cultural aspects; some, such as some types of software, are purely functional. There are also some anomalies in the government-based definitions of, for example, music which are rather vague and nonspecific. Live music performance is very different from the digitized reproduction of recorded music (Miège, 2020; Oakley and O'Connor, 2015), and innovation is different in these different industries. Thus, a single category such as that of "music" is not accurate enough in terms of its industry dynamics or the critical challenges involved; recorded music involves a physical or digitized product, and location decisions as to where the performance takes place are relatively unimportant. In contrast, live music requires the assemblage of performers and audience in a specific, culturally based, place; in this case location is critical.

However, it is not necessarily useful or economic to treat each industry as completely distinct and needing individual consideration. Some industries have critical challenges in common. There is a middle ground between the two extremes, which is the one that we adopt here. We argue that there *are* some similarities between some of these industries, even ostensibly very different ones such as publishing and films, or opera and museums, which make grouping them together justified. Because of their common critical challenges we group the CCIs into three clusters (Figure 2.1).

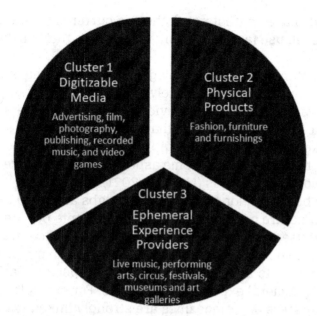

Figure 2.1. The three clusters of the creative/cultural industries.

CLUSTER 1: DIGITIZABLE MEDIA INDUSTRIES

Digitizable media industries include advertising, film, photography, publishing, recorded music and video games. The first cluster is based around the fundamental need to transmit content (words, music, pictures) from the originator, usually via an intermediary, to the consumer in either physical or, more likely nowadays, digitized form.

Critical challenges for companies within this cluster have to do with:

- attracting and retaining artists, authors and developers that can create content that receives favorable attention from social commentators and, in its turn, attracts consumers.
- being able to access and exploit social trends. Product success is often dependent on complementary assets in the wider ecosystem, and sometimes in a different ecosystem altogether. Authors, for example, even if they are not writing directly about celebrity musicians or film stars, need to be aware of developments in these sectors in order to make their writing relevant. Computer games' developers will often use characters from currently popular films or TV

shows, base characters' clothes on current fashion trends and even use famous designers to design their virtual clothes.

- understanding new technologies, sometimes that have been developed in completely different industries or ecosystems. The design of video games' characters' clothes is one of the ways that a new technology, blockchain-based non-fungible tokens (NFTs), is being used to help monetize some aspects of the software development process (Nasdaq, 2021). 3D printers have been developed in innovation labs and used to manufacture cars and airplane components but are now being used in the fashion industry and architecture.

- digitizable media industries act as complementors, and vice versa, to many of the other CCIs, especially fashion and ephemeral experience providers. For example, newspapers and magazines are strongly linked with the fashion industry, about whose products reams of news articles are written daily. In the same way radio or TV broadcasting and recorded music each need each other to succeed. This power of complementors (Nalebuff and Brandenburger, 1997; Brandenburger and Nalebuff, 1996) was proposed as a 6th "force" to add to Porter's famous conceptualization of the five forces that affect the profitability of an industry (Porter, 1979, 2008). Although Porter himself apparently did not approve of this addition to his theory, complementor power appears to us to be extremely important in the CCIs.

Innovation within the media industries has been wide-ranging, embracing technological (the Internet, digitization, sound carriers, recording studios and hardware, printing machinery); social (the use of big data, social media, crowdsourcing); process (online downloading and payment systems); and business models (digital distribution and payment systems, such as PayPal and NFTs).

Technological innovations have been used as the basis for introducing new products and services and product extensions. It has also been applied to the methods of production and distribution; a critically important issue given parallel changes to consumers' buying behaviors. It is this cluster that has seen the most profound move away from physical products (CDs, DVDs, newspapers, books, etc.) to digitized content transmitted electronically over the Internet to another person's computer or phone. Technological innovations have allowed some producers to reach enormous numbers of customers directly, allowing for very high sales to be achieved for successful producers and shifting the balance of power away from the middleman – the publishers or TV broadcasters. Technological innovation has however been double-edged as illegal copies of works can quickly be created and circulated, thus depriving the original producers of the required return needed to support the next product or project.

Although there are many similarities between the different product categories in this cluster, there are also some differences. For example, the film industry is rather different from the music industry in respect of how it monetizes product consumption. Filmmaking has dealt with digitization through streaming services that use their offerings as add-on services to subscribers. These contracts help pay for producer costs, including those of artists. Streaming services for music have allowed musical artists to receive compensation for their performances. But many musical artists depend upon live performances to complement their recordings, and some receive large earnings from this. This personal involvement in the product is also one of the reasons that COVID has severely cost them in terms of performance revenue, losses not compensated by other sources of revenue.

CLUSTER 2: PHYSICAL PRODUCTS[1]

Our second cluster includes fashion goods, furniture and furnishings. These involve the design, making and selling of a physical good. Some definitions of the CCIs that we cited earlier include fashion, some only include fashion design (as part of the design category), and some include the whole fashion industry. We believe that it is right to examine the whole industry as it is an integrated supply and distribution system that involves creativity across much of its activity (retailing is every bit as creative as fashion design), and innovation has been an important feature of the recent transformation of the industry.

Critical challenges in the physical products cluster relate to:

- Location decisions. For physical products, because they are formed from tangible raw materials and because they are sold (still, although becoming less so) in physical stores, the locations of the various activities and the communications between them are key cluster challenges. The need is at one end to situate the organization where it can access knowledge about trends and find designers who are skilled at interpreting these, at the other end to acquire consumers who want to buy these products, and in the middle be located where goods can be manufactured cheaply and reliably.
- Product design capabilities are critically important, whether this is mass-market cheap and cheerful clothing or furniture that is not intended to last or top quality, expensive, products that are intended to become classics. Product designers need to be able to sense and then capitalize on trend knowledge, both within their own industry and others. Some designers are located at a distance from their eventual markets (H&M, for example), although many are located close to their markets where they can respond to local customers' desires. Although technological developments in, for example, CAD/CAM equipment have sped up the design process, and aided interactions with manufacturers some distance away, design is still very much a hands-on process.
- Because they are manufactured, whether by hand or in a factory or workshop, manufacturing capabilities are also critically important. Fashion, especially, is very cost conscious, and some of the biggest innovations and strategic developments in recent years have been the hunt for cost reductions through the use of manufacturing facilities in low-cost countries many thousands of miles away from their eventual markets. A major part of the success of these developments has been new technologies in materials requirement planning, just-in-time manufacturing and real-time IT-based links between shops and manufacturers that allow sales-based responsive scheduling of orders.

- The sometimes-enormous distances between design, manufacturing and sales mean that logistics technologies and capabilities in the transportation of both the raw materials and the finished product are critically important. Many of these technologies are, once again, IT- and Internet-based. Some of the most successful companies have developed deep capabilities in product scheduling. For example, H&M has a different logistics strategy for its high fashion goods and its basics, such as T-shirts; the basics are manufactured in low-cost locations and transported, slowly, by ship. Fashionable items are manufactured much closer to their eventual markets, and sometimes transported by air, at a much higher cost.
- Retail and website design. An integral aspect of many of the biggest furniture and fashion companies, IKEA, Uniqlo and Zara, for example, is to design their stores as an integral part of the customer purchasing experience. These companies sell only their own products in their own stores and can make sure that the brands' values are applied coherently from product to retail environment. This also applies (although arguably to a lesser extent) to the design of these companies' websites, which are increasingly being used to sell their goods. However, website design is critically important in other ways, in attracting customers, building in "stickiness" and making it easy for customers to find their way around the site, and crucially then be able to buy and pay for their items. Developers and suppliers of innovative payment systems such as PayPal have played a critically important role in this process.
- Building complementor links with other industries. These include game developers, who recently have started to use fashion designers to create virtual clothes for games' characters, and most of the media industries that either use or report on product developments and trends in fashion or furnishings.

Innovation within the physical product cluster has been as wide-ranging and profoundly important as in the media cluster. It has embraced technological innovation (the Internet, digitization,

EDI, MRP, JIT, CAD/CAM, 3D printing); social (the use of big data, social media, trend construction); physical (manufacturing machinery, plant layouts); process (online ordering and payment systems); and business models (location of manufacturing and distribution, clothing rental and recycling, online ordering and payment systems, such as PayPal, NFTs and multichannel retailing).

CLUSTER 3: EPHEMERAL EXPERIENCES

Our third cluster includes museums, art galleries, festivals, live music and performing arts. Ephemeral experience providers' "products" do not last beyond the consumer's experience of them with little or no lasting tangible components. Experiences include events put on by performing arts organizations: dance and ballet, live concerts of both classical and popular music, the performance of plays, festivals, and exhibitions at museums and art galleries. Some of the organizations that provide such experiences are extremely well-known arts organizations such as the Sydney Opera in Australia, the Kirov Ballet and Opera in St Petersburg, and festivals such as Comic Con, Sundance, Glastonbury or Coachella. Others, the majority, are small, or even micro enterprises (defined as those with fewer than ten employees), with a very narrow range of offerings and a small niche market, often surviving from hand to mouth from year to year and dependent on handouts from government or generous donors. In fact, the donation (philanthropic) economy plays a strong part in the finances of this sector, far more so than any other.

Critical challenges in this cluster include:

- Bringing the consumer, audience or visitor to a specific place at a specific time. Location and the physical aspects of the performance or gallery space are a key part of the provision. Another part of the challenge for this cluster is to be able to access resources in their immediate environment, and although large famous companies may attract star performers from around the world, technical and support skills are very often located close by. The local ecosystem is important for the organizations in this cluster. This cluster is also dependent on having a sufficient number of paying customers close by who are able to get to and from the experience.

- Selecting and designing the performance content demands both skills and cultural judgment. Specialist resources are required to help generate interest in the event and embed it within a cultural framework or milieu. Listening to music, watching a play or looking at a painting is a social experience that is shared with, and visible to, others. This "public" quality of experiential products means that being part of a tribe of "people like us" forms, at least some, part of the experience. In some venues the audience is expected to be part of the show – circuses for example. But even if this is not the expectation, audiences can gain enjoyment from observing their fellows and being part of the "show", through adopting a clothes "uniform" (black tie) or behaviors, reverential silence or alternatively noisy participation.
- Strong complementor links with some of the media cluster industries (Dalle Nogare and Murzyn-Kupisz, 2021). The larger performing arts organizations have now extended their profit-generating activities into recording or filming their activities and cross-promoting the artist in both performance and recorded forms. There are also complementor links with publishing, notably newspapers and magazines who fill their pages with articles about pop stars or the latest "must-sees".

Innovation in the experience providers cluster relates to the product itself, such as novel types of show or exhibit (Cirque du Soleil in circuses, for example), and in the form of new physical structures such as concert halls with vastly improved layouts and acoustics (the Elbphilharmonie concert hall in Hamburg, for example), the technical capabilities of equipment used in performances (for example, the high-tech equipment used by Cirque du Soleil performers or the highly sophisticated lighting and sound equipment used by the major rock groups in their concerts. Innovation in the museum visitor experience has included "enhanced" and more personalized visitor experiences. Lascaux in France has embraced the innovative use of BigData to identify visitor characteristics and target experiences accordingly (Pellegrin-Boucher and Roy, 2019).

Important innovations have also been seen in the experience providers' business models. Many have developed touring arms, in which the performance is standardized and replicated so that it can be packed up and transported, sometimes across the world. The largest circus company in the world, Cirque du Soleil, has become so because it learned how to standardize what it offers to its globally diverse audiences. This touring of standardized offerings also applies to famous art and museum exhibitions in which some of the world's most priceless objects are transported from their home base – said to be an operational and logistical "nightmare". Apart from the risk of theft as irreplaceable objects move (even anonymously) across city streets, there is a very real risk of damage as sometimes very fragile artifacts are moved. Technological innovations in transportation and security equipment have made these movements possible, meaning that the performance or art can reach a larger audience, increasing the possibility for selling add-on items such as licensed replications of the art work, records or videos of the performance or complementary recordings of the artist or museum visits.

STRUCTURE OF THE BOOK

In the remainder of this book we discuss some of the innovations that have transformed the industries in each of our three clusters. In each chapter we identify some of the most important drivers of innovation in each cluster and provide examples (exemplars) of innovations that respond to these drivers. At the end of chapters 3, 4 and 5 we discuss the implications of COVID-19 for each cluster. We conclude each of chapters 3, 4 and 5 with a comprehensive case study or two that illustrate how many of the drivers for each cluster have influenced the focal organizations summarized at each end of chapter case.

We finish the book with a summary of key transformational innovations likely to persist in a post COVID world.

NOTE

1 Although art and crafts are physical products, they are different from both fashion and furnishings in that few art or craft works are intended to be replicated or mass produced. They are driven by different economic dynamics, in the case of fine art heavily swayed by consumers who wish to buy products that are of the moment and reap profits from the resale market. As a result, we do not include these in this chapter.

REFERENCES

Appadurai, A. (1988). Introduction (p 50). In Appadurai, A. (Ed.). (1988). *The Social Life of Things: Commodities in Cultural Perspective.* Cambridge University Press.

Arts.gov. (2021). US' creative economy coalition. Available from: https://www.arts.gov/ sites/default/files/Research-Art-Works-Milwaukee.pdf. Accessed August 15, 2021.

BBC. (2015). Heavens-Gate from Hollywood disaster to masterpiece. Available from: https://www.bbc.com/culture/article/20151120-heavens-gate-from-hollywood -disaster-to-masterpiece. Accessed April 20, 2022.

Bouquillon, P., Miège, B. and Moeglin, P. (2021). *L'industrialisation des biens symboliques: Les industries créatives en regard des industries culturelles.* PuG.

Bourdieu, P. (1996). *The rules of art: Genesis and structure of the literary field.* Stanford University Press.

Brandenburger, A. and Nalebuff, B. (1996). *Co-opetition.* Doubleday.

Caplanova, A. (2020). *Start-Up Creation: The Smart Eco-efficient Built Environment,* p.81. Elsevier.

Caves, R. E. (2000). *Creative Industries: Contracts Between Art and Commerce (No. 20).* Harvard University Press.

CIF. (2021). Creative industries infographic. Available from: https://www.creativeind ustriesfederation.com/sites/default/files/2019-12/UK%20Creative%20Industries %20Infographic.pdf. Accessed June 18, 2021.

Cnossen, B., Loots, E. and van Witteloostuijn, A. (2019). Individual motivation among entrepreneurs in the creative and cultural industries: A self-determination perspective. *Creativity and Innovation Management,* 28(3), 389–402.

Dalle Nogare, C. and Murzyn-Kupisz, M. (2021). Do museums foster innovation through engagement with the cultural and creative industries?‰ *Journal of Cultural Economics,* 45(4), 671–704.

DCMS. (2019). Creative Industries Economic Estimates - Business Demographics, January. Available from: https://www.gov.uk/government/organisations/department -for-digital-culture-media-sport. Accessed March 3, 2022.

DeFillippi, R. (2015). Project based organizations in creative industries. In Jones, C., Lorenzen, M. and Sapsed, J. (eds.), *Handbook of Creative Industries.* Oxford University Press.

Dziurski, P. (2016). Success in creative industries: A discussion about critical success factors. *Journal of Management and Financial Sciences,* 9(24) 87–100.

Frank, R. H. and Cook, P. J. (2010). *The Winner-take-all Society: Why the Few at the Top Get So Much More Than the Rest of Us.* Random House.

Haberberg, A. and Rieple, A. (2008). *Strategic Management: Theory and Application.* Oxford University Press.

Handke, C. (2018). Intellectual property in creative industries: The economic perspective. In Abbe E. L. Brown and Waelde, C. (Eds.), *Research Handbook on Intellectual Property and Creative Industries.* Edward Elgar Publishing.

INTA. (2020). The licensing and valuation of trademarks. Available from: https://www .inta.org/fact-sheets/assignments-licensing-and-valuation-of-trademarks/ Accessed April 17, 2022.

Karpik, L. (2007). *L'économie des singularités* (Vol. 2). Gallimard.

Loots, E. and van Witteloostuijn, A. (2018). The growth puzzle in the creative industries. *Revue de l'Entrepreneuriat,* 17(1), 39–58.

Miège, B. (2020). Creative industries, a large ongoing project,still inaccurate and always uncertain. In *The Industrialization of Creativity and its Limits* (pp. 151–161). Springer.

Morning Consult (2021). Dolby: What you need to know about the spatial audio format. Available from: aw.cnet.com/tech/home-entertainment/dolby-atmos-what-you-need-to-know-about-the-spatial-audio-format/>. Accessed June 21, 2022.

Nalebuff, B. and Brandenburger, A. (1997). Co-opetition: Competitive and cooperative business strategies for the digital economy. *Strategy & Leadership*, 25(6), 28–23.

Nasdaq (2021). Why fashion.is the next frontier of NFTs. Available from: https://www.nasdaq.com/articles/why-digital-fashion-is-the-next-frontier-of-nfts-2021-04-07. Accessed April 17, 2022.

NI Business Information. (2022). Intellectual property rights in different countries. Available from: https://www.nibusinessinfo.co.uk/content/intellectual-property-rights-different-countries. Accessed April 21, 2022.

Oakley, K., & O'Connor, J. (Eds.). (2015). *The Routledge Companion to the Cultural Industries (Vol. 10)*. Routledge.

Paris, T. (2010). *Manager la Créativité*. Pearson Education.

Paris, T. and ben Mahmoud-Jouini, S. (2019). The process of creation in creative industries. Creativity and Innovation Management, 28(3), 403–419.

Pellegrin-Boucher, E. and Roy, P., eds; (2019). *Innovation in the Cultural and Creative Industries*. Wiley.

Porter, M. E. (1979). How competitive forces shape strategy. *Harvard Business Review*, 57(2), 137–145.

Porter, M. E. (2008). The five competitive forces that shape strategy. *Harvard Business Review*, 86(1), 78–93.

Reed, R. and DeFillippi, R. (1990). Causal ambiguity, barriers to Imitation, and sustainable competitive advantage. *Academy of Management Review*, 15(1), 88–102.

Rosen, S. (1981). The economics of superstars. *The American Economic Review*, 71(5), 845–858.

Schatz, T. (1981). *Hollywood Genres: Formulas, Filmmaking and the Studio System*. Random House.

Stokes, S. (2001). *Art and Copyright* (pp. 48–49). Hart Publishing. ISBN 978-1-84113-225-9.

Tao, J., Ho, C. Y., Luo, S. and Sheng, Y. (2019). Agglomeration economies in creative industries. *Regional Science and Urban Economics*, 77, 141–154.

Teece, D. J. (2018). Profiting from innovation in the digital economy: Enabling technologies, standards, and licensing models in the wireless world. *Research Policy*, 47(8), 1367–1387.

Tidd, J. and Bessant, J. R. (2020). *Managing Innovation: Integrating Technological, Market and Organizational Change*. John Wiley & Sons.

Welkos, R. W. (2004). From the archives: 'Heaven's Gate': The film flop that reshaped Hollywood. *Los Angeles Times*, June 12, 2004. Available from: https://www.latimes.com/entertainment/movies/la-et-mn-heavens-gate-flop-archive-20040612-snap-story.htm. Accessed April 20, 2022.

Wikipedia. (2022a). Copyright lengths. Available from: https://en.wikipedia.org/wiki/List_of_countries%27_copyright_lengths Accessed April 17, 2022.

Wikipedia. (2022b). Design patent. Available from: https://en.wikipedia.org/wiki/Design_patent Accessed April 17, 2022.

WIPO. (2022). What is intellectual property? Available from: https://www.wipo.int/about-ip/en/. Accessed April 17, 2022.

Wohl, H. (2022). Innovation and creativity in creative industries. *Sociology Compass*, 16(2), e12956.

Yu, W., Jacobs, M. A., Chavez, R. and Feng, M. (2019). Data-driven supply chain orientation and financial performance: The moderating effect of innovation-focused complementary assets. *British Journal of Management*, 30(2), 299–314.

Trans-formational Innovation in Digitizable Media

Alison Rieple, Robert DeFillippi and David Schreiber

Chapter 3

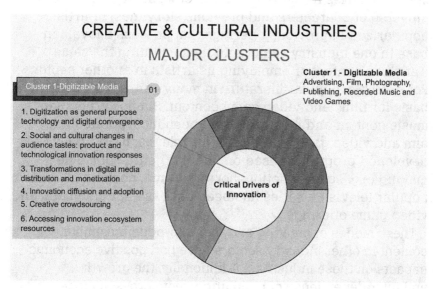

Figure 3.1.   Creative and cultural industries: Cluster 1 Drivers of Innovation.

DOI: 10.4324/9781003207542-3

Introduction

Arguably, of our three clusters digitizable media industries have been the most affected by transformational innovations over the past three decades. This is the result of a number of different technologies that exponentially changed the way we consume and engage with content and its creators.

Digitizable media industries primarily create, promote and distribute creative content to their users. Industries associated with this cluster include advertising, film, photography, publishing, recorded music and video games. Innovations in these industries include novelties in the content (e.g. new formats of songs, movies, games, stories), new artists or genres, new technologies for producing content, such as digital cameras, as well as new forms of content such as online gaming.

Every digitizable media industry has to respond to audience desires for novelty. These industries spend considerable resources in identifying and investing in new content and its artists, whether they be songwriters, game developers, movie/television actors and directors. Media industries have a long history of creating new content by utilizing franchise content (stories from the same universe, such as the Marvel universe of characters and previous storylines) or artists popularized in previous offerings that possess a loyal fan base in one industry sector and then imitating the same franchise content or employing its artists in another sector. For example, popular literature in many genres has been the basis for films and video game content. Similarly, popular music content and its artists have been incorporated into film and video game audio content. Television originally developed programs based on popular genres of movie making (e.g. science fiction, horror, drama, comedy). Similarly, popular television series has been the basis for cinematic and video game offerings.

These modes of creating and then reproducing similar content in other industry sectors have had positive economic impacts on these industries. Additionally, the growth and inter-dependence of popular content across multiple media industries have historically impacted the structure of media conglomerates, which have incorporated diverse media industries. These conglomerates have grown larger by integrating an increasing array of media entertainment industries beyond the scope of their original focus. For example, Disney began as a cartoon production organization and rapidly expanded to include theme parks, television, movies, radio and even cruise lines, and thus they have substantially expanded their impact on innovations developed in each of the media segments where they enjoy substantial ownership. Disney's core businesses import innovative content from other industries, such as their subcontracting of animation and visual effects content from outside contractors and incorporate innovations from these sources in their creative content offerings.

These innovations shaped how value was created and the relative power of different participants to influence what content was made available to consumers. They also shaped how the economic value was appropriated to various industry participants such as content creators, advertisers, distributors and consumers. It is today's transformational innovations such as these that are now creating new opportunities for employment and careers by people who are the producers, technical support, data analysts, marketers and logistics professionals of these industries, and who dwarf in numbers the artists who create content (Hearn, 2020).

This chapter focuses especially on how digitization technologies have transformed how creative content is created and distributed, for example, by streaming, and how these new modes have transformed the processes by which value is created in the digital media ecosystem. Business model innovations resulting from streaming have transformed how artists and distributors can monetize creative content. We will also examine specific examples of product innovations (e.g. eSports) and their market acceptance and transformative impacts on CCI industries, along with process innovations in digitizing the creation and distribution of video content (i.e., video streaming). New business model innovations such as subscription models for monetizing digital content will also be discussed.

We then discuss how changing social and cultural experiences of youth have influenced the evolution of media content, illustrated by the rock and roll music genre.

We then discuss how innovations are adopted by industry in response to the innovator's social capital and the role played by the adopters of the innovation.

We next discuss the role of external communities and more anonymous aggregates (crowds) in creating digital media content for media producers Our analysis will examine the virtues and perils of crowdsourcing creative digital content from these sources.

Finally, we examine the ecosystems of digital media industries and how resources are organized, accessed and coordinated through the relationships between key participants in these ecosystems (Figure 3.1).

CRITICAL DRIVER 1: DIGITIZATION AS GENERAL PURPOSE TECHNOLOGY AND DIGITAL CONVERGENCE

General purpose technologies (GPTs) are technologies that can affect an entire economy (usually at a national or global level). GPTs have the potential to transform preexisting economic and social structures (Lipsey et al., 2005). Digitization of formerly nondigital media-based products and services is an example of GPT.

Mathematician Claude Shannon is credited for laying out the foundations of digitization in a paper "A Mathematical Theory of Communication", written in 1948 and published with coauthor Warren Weaver in 1963 (Shannon and Weaver, 1963). Digitization is best understood as a sequence of innovations that cumulatively contributed over the subsequent decades to the ability to convert technology from analog format to digital format. By doing this, it became possible to make copies that were identical to the original. Digitization was associated with product, process and system innovations, including the transistor, the integrated circuit and the subsequent inventions of the computer, the microprocessor, the digital cellular phone, the Internet and the World Wide Web. All these innovations comprise what is now referred to as the digital revolution (Wikipedia, 2021c).

The ability to digitize media content profoundly impacted the channels for artistic innovation and discovery. New artists enjoyed access to a much larger range of distribution opportunities, and thus barriers to entry were reduced, although not eliminated. Established entertainment stars still enjoyed enormous advantages of favorable promotion of their work, but digitization did make possible the entry of a wider range of entertainment offerings. Digitization of media content and its dissemination also promoted audience exposure to diverse offerings, and they in turn could develop idiosyncratic playlists of their preferred artists and artistic offerings. Hence over time the locus of control shifted from large-scale content creators (e.g. major studios for film, music and video games) to content distribution platforms (e.g. Netflix and Apple Music). These digitized platforms effectively disintermediated (replaced or supplemented) a variety of interim points of distribution such as the radio channel promoter and the movie theater owner. It also provided more direct access to the content of choice by consumers of digital content.

Filmmaking illustrates many of these trends in media entertainment. In late 2013, Paramount became the first major studio to distribute movies to theaters in digital format, eliminating 35 mm film entirely. In 2006, 95% of US cinema screens were analog, and such films were distributed and exhibited from reels of 35 mm celluloid film (Follows, 2018). This was an expensive experience for all involved. Distributors needed to make and ship huge prints, and cinemas had to combine six or so reels together and then disassemble them a few weeks later. The more they were used, the dirtier and more scratched they became, and at the end of the run they were hard to recycle. Digital prints were much cheaper to produce and ship; they could be of higher quality, never deteriorated, were much easier to recycle and had vastly better protections for copyright owners. By 2016 US cinema was almost entirely digital with just 2.2% of screens using analog projection (Follows, 2018).

Multiple transformation changes subsequently arose in the film industry as a result of digital technology convergence (defined as the tendency for technologies that were originally unrelated to become more closely integrated and even unified as they develop and advance): firstly the growth of Internet downloads and video on demand; secondly the reduction of production costs due to the digitization of the whole filmmaking process (especially in ultra-low budget filmmaking); thirdly the digitization of cinema screens, which reduces physical distribution costs and increases the profitability of cinema releases of niche films; fourthly the short-circuiting of the value chain, by producers being able to market and distribute their films directly to the consumer; and finally the long-term growth of the niche markets as a result of web sales and the impact of video stream platforms like Amazon and Netflix.

EXEMPLAR 1A: VIDEO STREAMING BY NETFLIX AND AMAZON PRIME

During the 1990s technological advances in video bandwidth, compression and transfer rates made possible digital transmission of video content to a variety of suitable devices such as televisions, video game consoles and computers. However, it wasn't until 2007 that Netflix (a film and music rental service) introduced a large-scale commercially operational video streaming service, which allowed subscribers to select on demand at any time on any device-specific movies, television programs and music available from Netflix library (Alsin, 2018). This online distribution model was a digital extension of Netflix's previously successful model of film rental that had employed the physical mailing of DVDs of movies to its subscribers.

Other players soon entered the video streaming business. Perhaps the most significant new entrant in the film industry was Amazon, which introduced its Amazon Prime subscription service in 2005 and its own video streaming service in 2011. Both Amazon and Netflix continue to invest heavily in original programming to secure market share, reinvesting profits and increasing debt levels to fund content production. In 2019 Netflix produced 90 movies, including documentaries. To compare, the five conventional film studios left standing – Paramount, Universal, Sony, Disney and Warner Bros. – made about that many combined (Chozick and Barnes, 2019). The reason for this heavy investment is that both Netflix and

Amazon Prime Video need their own intellectual property (IP) to protect against new entrants, particularly cash-rich tech firms such as Facebook, Google and Apple, which have the potential to outbid them for popular titles. Existing filmmaking studios and broadcast network-affiliated video streaming services (e.g., Paramount Plus, NBC's Peacock, Disney) also pose a threat as they control extensive back catalogs and have launched rival services. Netflix appears particularly exposed as it has few alternative revenue streams compared to Amazon Prime, which offers a range of bundled services (video, music service and online delivery services for a wide variety of products) in many territories. Amazon provides a distinctive business model for video-on-demand (VOD) services worthy of closer attention.

Whereas Netflix uses premium content to generate more subscriptions to its streaming service and fend off competitors, Amazon uses every element of the Amazon Prime services, including award-winning content, to generate additional revenues. Amazon Prime's main subscription service provides shipping and delivery benefits and online shopping discounts. Amazon Prime's video streaming content is available free to its Amazon Prime subscribers. Prime Video adds value to the Prime subscription and helps keep people shopping in Amazon's online store. However, the video-on-demand service is also a store in its own right. Additionally, Amazon Prime nonsubscribers may also rent a subset of video content from Amazon. However, these one-off rentals don't include full access to the platform's vast library of originals and licensed content that Prime members enjoy as a free membership benefit (Dixon, 2021).

Amazon Prime Video's business model is a hybrid TVOD (transactional video on demand) and SVOD (subscription video on demand). TVOD is a VOD service that allows consumers to buy content on a pay-per-view basis in the sense that they are charged per video or video package rather than gain access to the entire catalog under the Amazon Prime subscription, which is the SVOD revenue model. Industry sources estimate that about 40% of US Prime members stream video from the service. These sources also estimate that Amazon Prime Video contributes about 60 million subscriptions to the total US SVOD market, making it the second-biggest US service. Finally these sources estimate that Amazon video-on-demand services generate about $2 billion in annual revenues (Dixon, 2021).

Video streaming has introduced a fundamentally new business model insofar as streaming companies have bypassed the historic film industry business model of maximizing revenue through individual film licensing to theaters and have instead created direct customer monetization models whereby customers subscribe to a service that makes available a portfolio of film offerings. Hence revenues depend less on any single film and more on the attractiveness of the service in securing and sustaining subscription membership. Such subscription service models have also emerged in music, video games and publishing and have revolutionized the economics of each industry.

Exemplar 1a: Question for discussion

1. How has media streaming impacted other CCI industries: Publishing? Music? Video games? Any similarities to the streaming of movie video content? Any industry-specific differences?

EXEMPLAR 1B: SUBSTACK.COM – A DIGITAL PORTAL FOR WRITERS AND EDITORS

A significant transformation resulting from digitization has been the availability of alternative digital channels for cluster one industry practitioners (artists, journalists and other content creators of digitized media) to distribute their works. Substack.com is an online platform that provides publishing, payment, analytics and design infrastructure to support subscription newsletters. It allows writers to send digital newsletters directly to their subscribers and to monetize these

Internet-based offerings. Substack.com has built an audience of more than 500,000 subscribers since it started in 2017. As of late 2020, large numbers of journalists and reporters were coming to the platform, driven in part by the long-term decline in traditional media employment opportunities. A *New York Times* article reported that there were half as many newsroom jobs in 2019 as in 2004 (Tracy, 2020). The decline of sports-oriented publications such as *Sports Illustrated*, *Deadspin*, and *SB Nation*, coupled with the onset of coronavirus, led to a surge in sports journalists moving to write on Substack.com in 2019 and 2020 (Wikipedia, 2021e).

Typically, online channels such as Substack provide an alternative promotion and revenue outlet for artists (primarily writers) who have not achieved market access of more popular artists in conventional publication channels. However, the increasing audience reach of such channels has attracted more mainstream popular artists. For example, the comic book publishing sector has seen major artists joining Substack. An early artistic entrant is Nick Spencer, a comic book writer best known for his work for Marvel Entertainment, who served as the liaison between Substack and a group of creators who publish new comic book stories, essays and how-to guides on the platform (Gustines, 2021). This initiative arose during the COVID pandemic, which was keeping many fans out of comic book shops, and the creators were looking for new ways to connect with readers. Substack subsequently signed comics creators including Saladin Ahmed, Jonathan Hickman, Molly Ostertag, Scott Snyder and James Tynion IV. The creators were paid by Substack, but they also retained intellectual property ownership of their works. The company took most of the subscription revenue in the first year; after that, it will take a 10% cut (Gustines, 2021). Mr Tynion, who previously won an Eisner Award, the comic industry's highest honor, for best writer, decided to break away from writing Batman for DC Entertainment to devote time to his creator-owned series and his Substack newsletter.

Typically, Substack content contributors (i.e. authors) can sign up for free to create newsletters postings for their audience. These Substack authors can decide to make subscription to their newsletter free or paid and to make specific posts publicly available to nonsubscribers. Substack provides an easy-to-use digital web site for reaching these audiences of Substack contact consumers but requires the content contributors to identify such audiences from their preexisting digital contact sources. Authors of Substack newsletters choose whether subscriptions are free or paid. As of 2020, the minimum fee for a subscription was $5/month or $30/year, and Substack usually takes a 10% fee from subscription payments. Advertising to users plays no role in revenue generation. In February 2019, the platform began allowing creators to monetize podcasts (Wikipedia, 2021e). In March 2021, Substack was experimenting with a revenue-sharing program in which it paid advances for writers to create publications on its platform; this became a program known as Substack Pro.

The success of digital portals such as Substack will depend on how credible are the artists and writers who enlist in Substack and how successful will these Substack portals be in attracting fans of these artists and generating revenue. One criticism may be that Substack's lack of real-time interactivity will lead more Internet-savvy and engagement-oriented audiences to seek out more interactive websites such as Twitch, which is currently the preferred platform for video game fans and participants in eSports, a new form of video game engagement. How Twitch operates will be detailed in the subsequent eSports exemplar.

Exemplar 1b: Questions for discussion

1. Do you see digital portals such as Substack.com having a long-term future for enterprising creative artists who are shut out of more traditional, high prestige advertising and distribution outlets for their creative offerings?
2. Could you see more established artists utilizing Substack.com even after COVID's eventual decline as a pandemic? Why? Why not?

EXEMPLAR 1C: ESPORTS AS A BUSINESS MODEL INNOVATION

The Internet evolution facilitated the transformation of video games from individual competitions to virtual team–based collaborations that were without geographic boundaries (Figure 3.2). This revolution has also led to the development of a fast-growing video game segment of eSports (Electronic Sports) that has attracted a worldwide audience. eSports is a form of competition using video games, often taking the form of organized, multiplayer games, particularly between players who play the games professionally, either individually or as members of teams. Although organized competitions have long been a part of video game culture, these were largely between amateurs until the late 2000s, when participation by professional gamers and spectatorship in these events through live streaming saw a large surge in popularity. By the 2010s, eSports was a significant factor in the video game industry, with many game developers actively designing and providing funding for tournaments and other events (Wikipedia, 2021d).

These gamers are watched and followed by millions of fans all over the world, who attend live events or tune in on TV or

Figure 3.2   An eSports game. *Source*: ziiinvn/Shutterstock

online. Streaming services like Twitch allow viewers to watch as their favorite gamers play in real time, and this is typically where popular gamers (competitive eSports game players) build up their fandoms. Streaming services and live events have turned casual gamers into serious stars who can sometimes rake in seven-figure earnings from tournament winnings, merchandise sales and massive brand endorsements. Many eSports teams make a majority of their revenue, approximately 90%, from sponsorships and advertising (Miyakoshi, 2019). The audience has also been growing steadily since the introduction of team eGames that players and audiences can interact with.

Because game developers hold the sole intellectual property rights to their titles, they are also the sole entities that determine who has access to a game, and at what quality, making distribution, player and audience access also drastically different from traditional sports. Publisher revenues from eSports do not accrue primarily from sales of the eSports games, which are often available for download for free. However, the publisher does garner revenues from the sales of items purchased by eSports players, who need to have access to tools and resources to be able to make a living competing and working for an eSports team or company. Additional publisher revenue sources include entry fees by nonplayers (fans) for attendance to live eSports competitions, fees paid by players to participate in eSports tournaments, fees paid for use of their game titles by professional leagues and advertising revenue from sponsors of games titles and the brands advertised at eSports competitions.

Game publishers were the early developers of sponsored competition for their game titles. However, professional leagues have proliferated in recent years from a wide array of sponsors. The teams competing in such tournaments are often privately owned by wealthy individuals similar to the ownerships of other professional sports such as baseball, basketball and premier league football (otherwise known as soccer to US audiences). These teams often cover multiple eSports games within tournaments and leagues, with various team makeups for each game. Teams will play a number of games across a season and compete for top positioning in the league by the end of that season. Those that do well, in addition to player salaries and competition-earned prize money, may be promoted to a higher-level league, while those that fare poorly can be demoted to a lower level league. Higher league promotion carries the bonus of expanded status for their team, higher player earnings and prize money and expanded advertising revenue and sponsorships. These economic features of eSports are similar to the organization of professional sports leagues for world soccer.

eSports are played both in live tournaments which can draw live audiences equal in attendance volume to those of popular professional sports such as NBA basketball and world soccer tournaments. However, live attendance figures dwarf in comparison to the number of online viewers of eSports tournaments and professional league competitions. eSports analytic reporting source Newzoo provides annual statistics on eSports attendance. They distinguish two types of eSports viewers: enthusiasts and occasional viewers. They define eSports enthusiasts as people who watch professional eSports content more than once a month and occasional viewers as those who watch professional content less regularly than once a month. For 2020, they reported 220.5 million occasional viewers and 215.4 million eSports enthusiasts, a combined eSports audience of 435.9 million (Geyser, 2021).

Esports are live streamed on free platforms. Viewers who watch eSports comprise a combination of teens and young adults, a demographic that has grown up with YouTube and free media and is largely unwilling to pay monthly subscriptions to watch a game on a streaming channel.

Game developers get to choose which platforms they use for their official broadcasts, and nearly all of them use Twitch, although some of them also use YouTube's live streaming feature via their YouTube channel. This provides Twitch, and subsequently Amazon, with a near global, although free-to-watch, monopoly on eSports entertainment, which even breaks into otherwise closed markets like China, which has its own internal streaming monopoly (Leroux-Parra, 2020).

eSports is a significant economic contributor to video game revenues. The eSports industry is expected to make more than a billion dollars in revenue in 2019 (Miyakoshi, 2019). Moreover, the eSports industry is a global industry, with eSports audiences, tournament competitions and professional leagues found worldwide. The sport is also gaining recognition as a legitimate professional and amateur sport. Universities across the world (mostly China and North America) are offering scholarship opportunities to incoming freshmen to join their collegiate eSports teams. As of 2019, over 130 colleges have eSports-based programs (Morrison, 2018). Finally, major multimedia entertainment corporations (including end-of-chapter case Tencent) have incorporated eSports into their portfolios in expectation of continued eSports industry market growth.

Exemplar 1c: Questions for discussion

1. Can eSports provide a model for other forms of live audience engagement with media? Can there be eMusic or eTalent where singers, musicians or other forms of entertainment talent compete for prizes online and attract both fandom and brand endorsements? There seems to be a precedent in popular television programs such as American Idol and America's Got Talent.

CRITICAL DRIVER 2: SOCIAL AND CULTURAL CHANGES IN AUDIENCE TASTES – PRODUCT AND TECHNOLOGICAL INNOVATION RESPONSES

Much of the competition within digitizable media industries is the attempt to attract and keep consumers' attention to their offerings, whether this is in book, musical or game formats. Such industries are constantly responding to their sense of what audiences will buy and whether there is an emerging zeitgeist of common interests associated with significant segments of their audience, demographic, economic or geographic.

Some audience interests are relatively easy for innovators to anticipate and thus focus their inventive energies on. For example, the benefits of the addition of sound and color to film were obvious early on; the primary barriers to adoption were technology- rather than marketing-based. However, other trends in audience preferences are less technologically driven and come from cultural shifts. In music, innovative genres have arisen among younger artists and audiences that did not involve older audiences who had established earlier preferences for musical forms and entertainers. The importance of youth culture and its role in artistic innovations has resulted in savvy entertainment companies using trend spotters to search the world for emerging cultural trends that might be introduced to larger audiences outside their initial geographic, demographic or economic niches. In this respect, entertainment content can be best understood as a fusion or evolution of earlier forms with occasional innovative disruptions from elsewhere, and in some cases from unanticipated sources.

EXEMPLAR 2A: ROCK AND ROLL AS A SOCIOCULTURAL AUDIENCE AND TECHNOLOGY EVOLUTION

Rock and roll is a genre of popular music that evolved in the USA during the late 1940s and early 1950s and became a staple of the youth generation lasting at least into the 1970s. It transformed recorded music and production and continues in various derivative forms to this day. Its origins lie in black American musical forms such as gospel, jump blues, jazz, boogie woogie, rhythm and blues, as well as from southern USA–based country music (Wikipedia, 2022d). Rock and roll's formative elements can be heard in blues records from the 1920s and in country records of the 1930s. Blues and gospel music were primarily focused in the southern USA and were performed by black artists to primarily black audiences.

The promotion of this type of music was constrained by the social conventions of the time, which racially segregated musical forms, their artists and their audiences. In 1951, Cleveland, Ohio, disc jockey Alan Freed began playing this emerging new music style, referring to it as "rock and roll" on his mainstream radio program. A major contribution by Freed

---

was to expose this previously black audience-focused set of music formats and styles to white youth, whose musical tastes were evolving during the post–World War II era to incorporate more diverse music influences. Gradually, white musicians began to imitate and in some cases integrate elements of these black musical forms, including rhythms, instrumentation and lyrics, into what became known as rock and roll. One icon of the early rock and roll era was Elvis Presley, a white artist whose lively (and some thought overly sexualized) performances of a fusion of rhythm and blues and gospel made him an international celebrity.

The appeal (at least within the younger generations) of rock and roll was partly a product of mass media promotion of popular music. Television shows such as American Bandstand increasingly featured new artists and their music to a live audience of dancing youth. Youth culture during the 1950s and 1960s was becoming big business and the music industry was a prime beneficiary in catering to the music tastes of a growing postwar so-called baby boomer generation. This generation had also been exposed to other significant events arising during their formative years. The Civil Rights movement of the 1950s and 1960s brought issues of race relations into the consciousness of youthful music followers and led to increasing openness to forms of music expression not limited to white musical artists. This created opportunities for more racially diverse sources of artists and art producers.

Over time rock and roll also featured crossover music writers and performing artists whose music appealed to both white and black audiences. An example of this crossover phenomenon occurred in the 1950s and 1960s with the creation of the Detroit sound by Motown Records, founded by black music producer and former auto plant worker Berry Gordy. The Motown label became home to some of the most popular recording acts in the world, including Marvin Gaye, The Temptations, Stevie Wonder, Diana Ross and The Supremes, plus other Motown artists of the era (Wikipedia, 2022d).

There were also changes in the record industry during this time, with the rise of independent labels like Atlantic, Sun and Chess servicing niche audiences with a concurrent rise in the popularity of radio stations that played their music. It was the realization that relatively affluent white teenagers were listening to this music that led to the development of what came to be defined as rock and roll as a distinct genre (Hall, 2014). Hence, the changing demographics of the music listening audience influenced the focus of music recording studios on rock and roll as a lucrative music genre investment.

During the mid-1960s rock and roll underwent international transformation with the so-called British invasion of the USA, Europe and eventually the world, spearheaded by the Beatles. British groups that quickly followed the Beatles included the beat-influenced Freddie and the Dreamers, Herman's Hermits and the Dave Clark Five. Early British rhythm and groups with more blues' influences included the Animals, the Rolling Stones and the Yardbirds (Wikipedia, 2022d). Over the succeeding decades, rock music has morphed into an ever more complex array of musical forms with distinctive artists from throughout the world. Various formats and artists have claimed crossover appeal to worldwide audiences and the fragmentation of popular music (replacing the earlier brand of rock and roll) represents the continuing pattern of fusion and evolution of earlier influences within this music entertainment genre.

Exemplar 2a: Questions for discussion

1. How predictable are artist genre innovations and what contributes to their success and longevity?
2. Are cultural shifts that lead to genre innovation driven organically by youth culture and subcultures or by industry gatekeepers such as agents, managers and record companies?
3. Can you do a genealogy of your preferred current musical genre and artist and identify the roots of their music in earlier art forms and artists? What factors led to their evolution to your current preferred artist and art form?

EXEMPLAR 2B: INNOVATIONS IN MUSIC INSTRUMENTS, AMPLIFICATION AND RECORDING

The development of rock and roll was accompanied by another product innovation, the revolution in electronics and digital technology (Figure 3.3). The rock and roll–focused genre and subsequent "style" was usually played with one or two electric and one bass guitars. The evolution of the electric guitar was followed by other forms of digital instrumentation, such as the digital keyboard and in some cases electronic drum sets. These innovations enabled artists to produce sounds for live performances unmatched by their acoustic predecessors and contemporaries, illustrated by jazz, which was dominated by acoustic instruments such as the trumpet, trombone and sax-ophone while being accompanied by upright bass and piano.

While artists did not create the digital technology, they were the lead users of digitally enhanced instrumentation that was adopted by aspiring rock and roll musicians seeking to recre-ate the sounds of their favorite artists.

Similarly the studio for the creation of recorded music became a laboratory for sound production, amplification and arrangement. One of the most well-known innovations in

Figure 3.3   DAW music editor. *Source*: BeautifulBlueSky/Shutterstock

recording and producing during this era of digital development in the 1960s and 1970s was the "Wall of Sound". Developed by music producers Phil Spector and Larry Levine, the intent was to create an effect that would allow songs to sound strong, full and alive when being played on the radio and jukeboxes of the time. Reverb, echo chambers and other innovative recording techniques led to what the recording industry now calls the loudness wars of the 1980s (Buskin, 2007).

Despite the progression of other production techniques, it was the transition from analog to digital recording software that arguably accelerated genre transformations. The Digital Audio Workstation, known in the industry as "DAW", is an application software used for producing, recording and editing songs and other audio files.

By the mid-1990s, many major recording studios had transitioned from analog to Digidesign's Pro Tools software, the most widely known DAW application at the time. Prior to its widespread use, recordings were done by "analog" means that often required large bulky equipment and consoles to record music. With DAW, recordings became less expensive to produce and therefore more easily accessible to music creators.

Exemplar 2b: Questions for discussion

1. Do you feel the rock and roll genre would have been as transformative in popular music culture without the simultaneous innovations occurring in music instrumentation? Why or why not?
2. What role did innovations in sound recording play in the many iterations of rock and roll since its creation in the 1950s?
3. With the rise of artificial intelligence (AI) and big data, is there any likelihood that these technologies might provide a basis for intentionally evolving new musical forms (genres) and actual popular music based on a synthetic, AI-based genre? There is already evidence of AI producing facsimiles of musical forms imitative of current musical composers. Could this lead to less imitative and more innovative forms of AI-created music compositions and arrangements?

CRITICAL DRIVER 3: TRANSFORMATIONS IN DIGITAL MEDIA DISTRIBUTION AND MONETIZATION

In order for creative content to flourish, it must be exposed to potential audiences. Digitizable media industries have employed diverse channels for content distribution to overcome pre-digital barriers to distribution. In the music industry, the introduction of new musical artists and formats during much of the 20th century enabled radio show programmers, who were often paid under-the-table fees through "payola" schemes (i.e., bribes) to play the work of new artists. Similar bottlenecks in the distribution of innovative artistic content existed in the early decades of filmmaking through the joint ownership of film production and film theaters by large Hollywood studios. It took a US Supreme Court decision (Paramount vs. US, 1948) to break the control of movie studios over distribution by eliminating their ownership of film theaters. Innovation in the video games industry was constrained by the power of gaming platform owners such as Microsoft, Sony and Nintendo to limit users to playing only games designed for their platforms. Finally, the publishing industry limited the ability of new authors to get their work published because of their control over the industry's manufacturing, marketing and sales channels. All of these bottlenecks in distribution by powerful media organizations were transformed by the advent of the digital revolution and the impact of digitization on creative content production, marketing and distribution.

Digital products are not sold through the same channels as physical products or services and therefore need different methods of payment. It is arguable that the mass digitization of media products would not have happened if some means of receiving payments for them had not been developed. Many CCI firms are micro-sized and online payment systems allowed them to extend sales of different types of products and sell to many more countries than would previously have been possible. These complementor products (or rather services) are based around EDI technologies and include credit/debit cards and latterly companies that act as digital "wallets" between buyer and seller. One of these is PayPal, which allows any business or individual with an email address, credit card or bank account to collect and receive payments online. It has played a critical role in enabling content creators to innovate and capitalize off fandom across digital platforms and is widely used by aspiring artists, musicians and influencers that make a living off of platforms like Etsy, Soundcloud, TikTok and Twitch (McKee, 2022). Its services include payment processing, merchant accounts, consumer and merchant credit, fraud prevention and regulatory compliance (Burgelman et al., 2015). The ease and convenience of PayPal registration quickly attracted sellers who were too small to qualify for merchant accounts with credit card companies and thus lacked commercial credit histories.

PayPal not only allows easy online transactions but can prevent them as well. For the music industry this proved to be a critical development in the fight against piracy and other illegal activity in the mid-2010s. Within its user agreements, PayPal has the right to suspend account transactions if the holder is suspected of infringing copyright on a grand scale. By cutting financial transactions to websites that were found to be enabling illegal activities, the IFPI and London authorities were able to make progress in fighting infringers that were doing so on a grand scale.

A large chain of providers and technologies is involved in the process of providing payment systems that are suitable for digital transactions. These include regulators of banks and financial services in every country in which transactions take place; authorized certificate authorities – companies that ensure the security of purchases and data; banks; and computer and smartphone manufacturers; and website designers who are critical in encouraging customers to have an easy experience when they pay for items.

Credit cards and online wallets were profoundly transformational in their time. However, cryptocurrencies have now been invented! We do not as yet know whether these innovations will be significant, and so we discuss these in Chapter 6. But there are indications that they might be, particularly, in the CCIs with their dependence on intellectual property protection and the number of intangible products involved.

EXEMPLAR 3: MP3 TECHNOLOGY AND THE TRANSFORMATION OF RECORDED MUSIC

In 1999 at the hands of Shawn Fanning and Sean Parker, the global music industry would forever be changed. With their invention of Napster and Peer to Peer (P2P) file-sharing technologies, the consumer's consumption and engagement with recorded music would be transformed. This propelled the music industry into a new era of both uncertainty and opportunity. This transformation was made possible through the compression of sound into digital files, which the world would soon recognize as MP3.

Although multiple formats of sound compression were in development at the time, it was the MP3 that gained traction and mass adoption. German psycho acoustic engineers at the Fraunhofer Institute, notably Karlheinz Brandenburg, discovered a way to discard sound information that is inaudible to the human ear, thus shrinking the size of a sound file, which ultimately became a widely accepted format for digitally distributing music.

The invention of the MP3 enabled the distribution of sound files via the Internet, leading to a revolution in the music industry that many were unprepared for. At the time, the MP3 was a perfect example of the innovator's dilemma (Christensen, 1997). MP3 was originally inferior to the superior sound quality of the Compact Disc (CD), but it allowed consumers to pursue the songs they loved without being forced into purchasing the ones they didn't Consumers only really wanted to listen to one or two of their favorite songs that were hits but had to purchase the entire CD in order to access those recordings. After decades of bundling single songs into an album and distributing them as a CD, the MP3, along with vast improvements in Internet bandwidth and accessibility, opened the floodgates to consumer choice and opportunity. It was Napster, the Peer 2 Peer file-sharing service, that first leveraged the MP3 to satisfy consumers' preference for engaging in content in ways they preferred.

Napster and other similar file-sharing services satisfied a market demand for access, but at the cost of industry growth and prosperity for the next 15 years. Consumers had an insatiable demand to listen to music when, where and how often they wanted, but without concern for Intellectual Property rights. The easy access to music and recordings were at the expense of record label, music publisher, songwriter and artist income due to illegal downloading of the songs and music piracy. Sales in the global recorded music industry declined precipitously from its peak in 2001 of $23.6 billion to an industry low of $14.0 billion in 2014 (IFPI, 2021).

With the decline in revenue came industry consolidation, demonstrating that the record labels that were still trying to sell their CDs were competing with "free" music via file sharing and other illegal music distribution practices. This decline was inevitable, and the business model of making, distributing and selling music through CDs was no longer a sustainable distribution practice and business model. Eventually, the recording industry would need to take this "perception of free", in order to meet consumers' perceived value of music, especially in comparison to other creative goods and leisure time competitors, while attempting to sustain a practical industry model.

As this new "perception of free" mentality took hold, industry innovators leveraged this consumer behavior, taking the industry model from one of consumption to engagement with companies such as Diezer, Spotify and Apple Music distributing music files in a consumer friendly and profitable way. Today, organizations such as Tencent out of China and Twitch look to the future by monetizing the concept of "Fandom".

Exemplar 3: Questions for discussion

1. How can the intellectual property owners of music protect their rights against the widespread piracy of digital content? Are there different options available to the artists and content creators than to the music publishers of digitized content?
2. Musical artists have long complained about their loss of income due to prevailing royalty arrangements with music distributors. Some artists (e.g., Taylor Swift) have attempted to develop autonomous web presences where they can directly engage their fan base and

establish independent sources of revenue. Does this form of autonomous engagement seem generalizable to other musical artists and can it compensate for the loss of revenue to artists and distributors due to piracy of recorded music more generally.

CRITICAL DRIVER 4: INNOVATION DIFFUSION AND ADOPTION

Diffusion of innovations theory seeks to explain how, why and how fast innovations spread. In his seminal book on the topic Rogers (1962) proposed that five main elements impacted the process: the innovation itself, adopters, communication channels, time and the social system. The process relies heavily on the innovator's social capital and the role played by the adopters of the innovation. The categories of adopters he identified indicate their relative enthusiasm for the innovation: innovators, early adopters, early majority, late majority and laggards. Moore (2014) adapted this model to examine how innovations in technologically innovative industries were influenced by each type of adopter: innovators are typically found in industries closely related to the innovator's own – enthusiasts who are willing to take risks and have some knowledge about the innovation's technicalities. Their risk tolerance, financial strength and enthusiasm allow them to adopt innovations that may ultimately fail. Early adopters have the highest degree of opinion leadership among the adopter categories. What these early adopters provide is a proof of concept and positive publicity regarding an innovation's potential for adoption. They typically view innovations as an opportunity to gain first-mover advantage through the early adoption of the innovation within their own industry. The early majority category consists of other industry players who now can see opportunities for competing in emerging markets for the innovation. The late majority withhold their adoption of the innovation until it has demonstrated both reliability in its technical performance and an attractive price for adoption. These participants are sometimes imitators who offer less costly versions of the innovation. The laggards are the last to adopt an innovation. These industry participants are typically guardians of a pre-innovation version or rival means of creating value compared to the innovator's offering. The greatest challenge facing most innovators is that of crossing the chasm between the innovators and early adopters and the more discerning and critical audiences of the early and late majority of an innovator's potential market. Laggards are generally regarded as too resistant to be worthy of extensive efforts to convert them to adoption of the innovator's offerings (Moore, 2014).

Digitizable media industries share this common form of innovation adoption. Typically, a media firm introduces an innovation or combination of innovations (technological, product, process and/or business model) embedded in their content offering. If this novel offering attracts commercial (box office sales) and/or artistic success (positive reviews and recognition at award ceremonies), it is common for other firms in the industry to also offer the innovation. In some cases the innovation transforms the industry immediately, as illustrated by the commercial and artistic success and recognition of the 1927 Warner brothers film *The Jazz Singer*, which rapidly transformed filmmaking and viewing from a silent movie to a talkie movie industry.

Other innovations can have a much slower process of adoption and diffusion. For example, the first innovation in the colorization of film was introduced in the late 1890s, but did not break through until the development of Technicolor, a film process that evolved through multiple phases of product improvement between 1915 and 1932. Technicolor eventually attracted interest from the movie studios in the early 1930s. It was the commercial and artistic success of early adopters Disney and Metro-Goldwyn-Mayer Studios, whose animation movie *Snow White and the Seven Dwarfs* and feature film *The Wizard of Oz*, respectively, prompted other film industry producers to adopt Technicolor-based color movies.

However, a major barrier to more widespread adoption was the expense of specialized technicolor cameras, which cost three times that of black-and-white cameras. Printing costs were not cheaper. Eventually the expiration of Technicolor's patent in the

1950s permitted less expensive producers such as Eastman Kodak to lower the price of color film production. Incremental improvements in color film processes, lower production costs and rising competition from television fostered a surge in color film production. Late adopter and laggard studios began to incorporate color film production, ultimately transforming content during the 1950s and 1960s from black and white to color in both the film industry and the emerging television industry.

EXEMPLAR 4: COMPUTER GENERATED IMAGERY (CGI)

A common pattern of adoption is for an innovation that is introduced in another industry to be taken up by media companies (Figure 3.4). This pattern is well illustrated by computer

Figure 3.4   CGI picture of a woman. *Source*: Creative Photo Corner/ Shutterstock

generated imagery (CGI) technologies. The 1980s saw a great expansion of radical new developments in hardware and continuing advances in computer power and affordability. These advances made the creation of computer generated imagery (CGI) both more technically feasible and more affordable. The first cinema feature movie to make extensive use of CGI was Walt Disney's *Tron* in 1982. To create the CGI scenes, Disney turned to the four leading computer graphics firms of the day: Information International Inc, Robert Abel and Associates (both in California), MAGI and Digital Effects (both in New York) (Wikipedia, 2021a).

Computer-based special effects have evolved into a global supplier industry to filmmaking studios, which contract from multiple sources for their visual effects and thus exert their purchasing power to extract value via competitive bidding from multiple visual effects suppliers. The content of visual effects has evolved from simple additions to landscape or physical settings (CGI-generated buildings and physical features) to more complex digital representations of action and even actors.

The technique of performance capture in which human actors had their movements graphically mapped and then applied to digital animations led to humanoid combinations of graphic and human representations of actors. These techniques have advanced further in video games and in online advertising, where actors are completely rendered by CGI and perform in place of human actors. The visual boundary between the real and the virtual has disappeared in a wide array of digitizable media products. Hence CGI has migrated from special visual effects for a narrow genre of filmmaking (science fiction) into an integral dimension of cinematic media content production.

Exemplar 4: Questions for discussion

1 How might advances in performance capture impact the role of human actors in video entertainment? Might simulated actors take on autonomous identities for their audiences within film entertainment much as game avatars have taken a primary role as the performers in video games?

CRITICAL DRIVER 5: CREATIVE CROWDSOURCING

Creative crowdsourcing is a type of participative creative activity in which an organization seeks solutions to a challenging and often creative task from a group of individuals of varying knowledge, heterogeneity and number (Howe, 2008). The rationale for the use of such requests (often referred to as open calls) for solutions is the so-called "wisdom of crowds" phenomenon, which claims that an appropriately diverse crowd of people is capable of generating a larger and wider array of perspectives to solve a creative task than can typically be generated by in-house solution providers (Surowiecki, 2005).

Creative crowdsourcing also depends upon the assumption that volunteer solution seekers are motivated by some combination of the intrinsic appeal of solving a challenging problem and by the extrinsic appeals of social recognition and financial rewards offered. Crowdsourcing may produce solutions from amateurs or volunteers working in their spare time or from experts or small business organizations. The selected solutions become the intellectual property of the sponsor of the crowdsource competition.

Creative crowdsourcing has been widely employed by a variety of CCIs including graphic design, architecture, product design, digital (stock) photography, apparel design, movies, writing, company naming and illustration. It has proliferated with the recent development of web-based platforms where clients can solicit a wide variety of creative work at lower cost than by traditional means (Roth and Kimani, 2014).

In a study of 15 creative crowdsourcing online platforms, Roth and Kimani (2014) identified four different roles that creative crowdsourcing played in the creation of a video advertisement for a client. The first involves idea contests to generate original ideas. The objective of this type of crowdsourcing contest is to generate a high number of advertising ideas in a short period of time (typically a few weeks). The client then reviews these ideas and determines whether any of them are worthy of follow-on development. Often the internal communications department of the client or an advertising agency then works with the crowdsourced idea as input.

A second use of crowdsourcing is for talent and skill identification via a call for pitches. The crowdsourced call serves as a matchmaking service to connect the client to a skilled partner for the execution of a specific project (Lampel et al., 2012). In these situations, the client is looking both for ideas and the person to execute these ideas. Again, this crowdsourcing application is limited to the initial ideation phase of a client project, with the additional expectation of identifying professionals to participate in subsequent phases of the project as employed contractors.

The third, and most common, type of creative crowdsourcing technique is so-called simple contests. This is the most basic approach to crowdsourcing in which a client posts a problem online, a large number of online participants offer solutions to the problem by a stipulated deadline and the winning ideas are awarded some form of compensation. The client then uses the selected solution (Brabham, 2008).

The fourth, and most complex, use of crowdsourcing is to break down the entire production process into stages and incorporate crowdsourcing as stage-based contests. The online creative services company Tongal utilized this process for a client by breaking down its video production process into three phases and designed for each phase a contest, which then provided input into subsequent stages of video development. In the first stage, Tongal asked its crowd to submit ideas based on creative briefs provided by its client. Next the client chose the best ideas and the selected author of the idea received a prize worth several hundred dollars. The client then submitted a call for pitches based on the shortlist of ideas selected at the previous crowdsourced competition. Again, the winning author received a cash prize and the client then sponsored a third crowd contest where the crowd was challenged to provide the actual fully developed video spot based on the previously selected video pitch. At the end of this third contest the client selected the winning video post and purchased the intellectual property of the author to use for their advertising (Roth and Kimani, 2014).

EXEMPLAR 5A: USER-GENERATED ADVERTISEMENTS FOR THE SUPER BOWL

One particularly dramatic application of crowdsourcing occurs each year prior to the American football tournament, the Super Bowl. It illustrates the potential impact of crowd-source competitions for the most expensive and widely watched advertising time slots of sports entertainment. User-generated ads are created by the general public from sponsored advertising competitions as opposed to being created by an advertising agency or the Super Bowl organization themselves.

For the 2007 Super Bowl, the Frito-Lays division of PepsiCo held the "Crash the Super Bowl" contest, allowing people to create their own Doritos commercials. Due to the success of the Doritos user-generated ads, Frito-Lays relaunched the competition for the 2009 and 2010 events. The resulting ads were among the most-watched and most-liked Super Bowl ads. In fact, the winning 2009 ad was ranked by the *USA Today Super Bowl Ad Meter* as the top ad for the year, while the winning ads that aired in the 2010 Super Bowl were found by Nielsen's BuzzMetrics to be the most "buzzed-about" (Wikipedia, 2022a).

Based on the success of the Dorito crowdsourced advertising campaigns, other companies have followed suit. These crowd competitions serve to promote the companies' brand prior to the Super Bowl through their announcements of the advertising contest. For their 2019 Super Bowl ad, the Australian wine brand Yellow Tail took a page out of the Doritos playbook and asked their customers to submit self-produced video segments for their "Tastes Like Happy" commercial. The winning segment – a submission from customer Adrien Colon – was included in the final product (Polkes, 2022).

Creative crowdsourcing and user-generated content are innovative practices that have utilized the power of the Internet and web-based tools to connect companies to both their customers and to creatives who are fans of particular companies and their brands.

Exemplar 5a: Questions for discussion

1. Can you identify applications for crowdsourcing in a non-advertising industry?
2. How might crowdsourcing be employed to help creative industries make product design choices, such as in filmmaking or music production?

EXEMPLAR 5B: GETTY IMAGES – TRANSFORMING A COMMUNITY INTO A CROWD

Many of the online platforms for crowdsourcing make reference to the importance of their creative communities (e.g., Tongal.com). However, crowdsourcing does not require the platform to mobilize a community of people who are individually aware of each other. Crowds are typically anonymous among its individual members, even if they are individually pursuing some common purpose or activity, such as a crowd contest.

However, sometimes an online platform utilizes both communities and crowds in their business practices, and on occasion, a company may shift emphasis from the more intensive, expensive and time-consuming process of building and maintaining a creative community to the more scalable, less expensive and more flexible use of crowds through standardized and sophisticated eCommerce business models and supporting technologies. An example of this community-crowd transformation is in the history of Getty Images, one of the world's foremost publishers of stock photography (pre-produced imagery that can be used in many different applications).

The photographic (still or video imagery) industry has undergone a major transformation over the past several decades due to the availability and proliferation of digital photographic hardware and software as well as advances in Internet-based connectivity and commerce (Angus and

Thelwall, 2010). For example, one consequence of digital photo editing and digital file-sharing software was the empowerment of amateur photographers to autonomously create their own catalogs of imagery and to share within their online communities their images and photographic experiences.

One important development was the emergence of microstock websites, such as iStockphoto, which facilitated photographic file sharing and provided a means for amateur photographers to earn royalties on their photographic contributions. iStockphoto sought to support the engagement of its photographic community by providing free tutorials, discussion forums and even live photo shooting sessions (so-called iStockalypses) where the company provided attractive venues, professional models and directorial guidance to its community members. Although the sponsored events required the payment of a conference fee, the attendees could subsequently earn royalties by providing their imagery to the company. Several studies of the iStockphoto community members revealed that its members' participation incentives were transitioning from an early intrinsic interest in the fun of sharing photos and improving their craft to more extrinsic interests in earning income (Brabham, 2008, Zupic, 2013).

In 2006 Getty Images acquired iStockphoto and incorporated its community of photographers into its own highly automated and sophisticated ecommerce website. This was used for soliciting and selecting imagery for display and promotion in the company's online catalogs. Getty Images was transitioning stock photographers from a community of collaborative artists into a creative crowd of diverse professionals and amateurs, who anonymously posted their imagery on the company website for corporate review and selection.

Getty Images connects with its crowdsourced imagery content providers through Twitter and emails to communities identified by genre, aesthetic and topical specialty. It has largely replaced the personal touch with more automated forms made possible by its sophisticated contributor communications management systems and thus can alert selected categories of content contributors to emerging market demands fitting their historic profiles of contributions.

As the volume of available digital stock photography grew, the earnings of an increasing fraction of photographers who were part-time professionals or amateurs declined. Additionally, the revenue model for photographers was shifting from a Rights Managed (RM) model (negotiation with individual photographers over pricing for imagery) to an ascendant Royalty Free (RF) model of pricing digital imagery that demanded no "rights" tracking and sold imagery that was paid by file size. Hence, the work of stock photographers became commodified. The earnings potential of photographic imagery contributors became more a matter of aggregate content availability than individual photographer reputation and loyal customer base (DeFillippi et al., 2014). However, Getty Images still retains a community of non-crowd-based professional photographers whose aesthetic style and imagery match emerging needs in specific niche markets.

In summary, Getty Images has engaged in a series of innovative transformations of its business model and innovatively adapted to the photographic industry's digital transformations. These innovations have provided an abundance of opportunities for amateur photographers to promote their imagery on Getty catalogs. However, the world of stock photographers now increasingly functions more as a crowd of contestants than as a community of photographers, except for an upper tier of professional photographers.

Exemplar 5b: Questions for discussion

1. What seem to be the major tradeoffs between utilizing creative communities versus crowds in sourcing innovation offerings for an organization's clientele or its own use?
2. Can you identify whether some CCIs would favor either community sourcing or crowdsourcing to externally access innovation?

CRITICAL DRIVER 6: ACCESSING INNOVATION ECOSYSTEM RESOURCES

All digital media industries exist in an ecosystem in which they access resources from other industries. For example, filmmaking was a geography- and technology-centric industry for much of its existence. Developments were sourced from within its own geographically clustered "space", which were directed specifically at film production. If anything, it could be defined as a supply ecosystem (Ketchen et al., 2014) with Hollywood as its geographic core. Within this there was no dominant firm or "orchestrator" (Thomas and Ritala, 2022); instead, a group of large firms built relationships with niche suppliers and collaborators who had their own specific resources and capabilities.

This has begun to change with the digitization of the film product. Now innovative technologies are being developed in other ecosystems (the Internet, software, computer hardware) to which film is appended (Kretschmer et al., 2022). Rather than having exclusive control over the channels of distribution, film companies have to compete for bandwidth and online space with other groups. These include self-generated films on YouTube and other distributors such as Netflix, who are not only broadcasting other genres but are themselves beginning to diversify into film production.

In the digital era, complementors (Brandenburger and Nalebuff, 1996; Wang and Miller, 2020; Fang et al., 2021) are becoming more important, as links to other genres and technologies help to increase sales and profits. Distribution technologies such as video streaming and companies that are based on it, such as Netflix, are complementors to film producers whose sales are now heavily dependent on an industry that they do not own and have relatively little control over. Film production now feeds multiple media content industries, including television and multiple device broadcasting of digitized content (music, film video games), on which it is now dependent. Power has shifted.

EXEMPLAR 6: THE K-POP ECOSYSTEM – A CORPORATE MODEL FOR ARTIST DEVELOPMENT AND MANAGEMENT

Much of the discussion on music ecosystem organiza-tion (project-based, collaborative, spatially co-located) is premised on a North American and/or European model of content organization and governance. More specifically, the North American music industry can be characterized as artist-centric, with the artist as the focal recipient of services that include: business managers overseeing the essential requirements of music production; label executives responsible for recording music release; lawyers for intellectual property and contractual issues; agents for organizing and managing live performances; and creative team leaders and stylists responsible for aesthetic elements of music performance (Elberse and Woodham, 2020). All these elements are separately provided and coordinated, the result being that the artist enjoys considerable autonomy and influence over creative and commercial choices.

By contrast, the creation, distribution and marketing of music performers and their offerings within Asia operate on fundamentally different principles focused on vertical integration and corporate organization and control of the entire artistic enterprise (including the artists). These differences can be observed in the South Korean–based K-pop industry (Figure 3.5), named for South Korean popular music, whose appeal has expanded

Figure 3.5   A K-Pop band. *Source*: Silvia Elizabeth Pangaro/Shutterstock

globally to other Asian countries, as well as Europe and North America. In some respects the K-pop artist relationship to resource suppliers is similar to the old Hollywood studio model of the 1920s–1950s, where studios would contractually control all aspects of their artists' (actors) careers, including their choice of performance roles and their preferred aesthetics and popular image.

The K-pop industry arose with three major label entertainment companies (SM, YG and JYP, referred to as the Big Three) assuming complete control over all elements. The artist was to be recruited, trained and developed to be a component of a so-called idol group whose look, appeal and styling were directed and whose members' personal life was strictly managed under contractual control (Oh and Rhee, 2016).

Key components of this control included:

- Finding and Recruiting Talent: Korean music labels search the world for talent through networks of scouts and open auditions. So popular are the idols featured in K-pop groups that Korean youth spend years developing their singing, dancing and performance styles before appearing at open auditions. Preparations are facilitated by specialized K-pop academies. Casting directors evaluate talent directly or through review of videos of performances available from aspiring K-pop artists. K-pop talent is often recruited globally, with annual auditions held in more than a dozen countries in North America, Europe and Asia.
- Training Talent: One entertainment label estimated that for every 20,000 applications received, they select 30 trainees (Elberse and Woodham, 2020). Indeed it is common for aspiring K-pop artists to audition several times a month at various agencies over multiple years to earn one of those very scarce training slots. Once selected, the trainees sign a contract, giving the entertainment company exclusive control over them. The contract requires a very strict lifestyle while ceding all artistic and creative control over to the company. These idol candidates in training could be as young as nine

or ten years old and are expected to attend training and instruction six days a week. The competition within training is relentless with numerous judged competitions between trainees to separate the winners. If they are unable to make the cut within these competitions, their contracts are terminated. On average, training lasts three years before the surviving trainees make their debuts as idols (performing members of a performing group). One company estimates that only one of every 12 trainees became an idol artist who has their act launched by the company (Elberse and Woodham, 2020).

- Launching Acts: Trainees are organized into idol groups. Each member is carefully selected to fulfill a distinctive performative role and aesthetic element of the ensemble. The teams live together for roughly 18 months in group training prior to their actual performance debut. Idol groups participate in peer evaluations to select one of them as a leader. However, final decisions on group roles are made by the music label's creative team executives, who also select other roles such as lead vocalist, lead dancer, etc. (Elberse and Woodham, 2020).

- Releasing Music: K-pop artists release new music throughout the calendar year under the careful direction of their managers. Most releases are single songs or extended play (EP) albums. Marketing campaigns for new music typically originate with performances on well-known music shows aired by South Korean television broadcast networks. To further promote their music, artists also record music videos and perform live across the country, appearing on popular variety shows, doing events at shopping malls and festivals and participating in fan meetings (Elberse and Woodham, 2020).

- Engaging Fans: K-pop entertainment companies are masters at using YouTube and other social media to raise audience awareness of new artists and their music while encouraging their artists to interact with and engage their fans. They often establish online forums (fan cafes) and official fan clubs whose supporters join by payment of an annual membership fee. These fan activities are intended to foster a closer connection between the artists and their fans. User (fan) generated publicity is encouraged, such as crowdfunding and the rental of billboard-sized advertising in public spaces to populate with fan selfies and notes of idol group support. Fans are also mobilized to go online in support of their idol groups when new music is released and to promote forthcoming concert performances (Elberse and Woodham, 2020). Idols are active on Facebook and Twitter, and fans are provided behind-the-scenes access to idol group members (Zhuo and Austin, 2018). All these activities are carefully monitored and coordinated by the entertainment company managers of their respective idol groups.

Exemplar 6: Questions for discussion
1. Is the K-pop ecosystem model compatible with the North American and European music industries? Is the K-pop model uniquely suited to Asian cultural industries? How amenable are North American and European artists to being managed and controlled by entertainment companies?

COVID'S IMPACT ON CLUSTER ONE INDUSTRIES

The emergence of COVID in China in late 2019 and early 2020 rapidly diffused to become the most deadly global pandemic since the so-called Spanish flu of 1918–1920. While worldwide deaths were in the millions, the economic impact of COVID on industries and economies was equally devastating. The global COVID pandemic devastated cultural and creative industries worldwide, with significant reductions in employment and economic activity due to the cessation of face-to-face venues for both content creation and content consumption.

Conversely, online audiences associated with the consumption of creative and cultural products and experiences increased substantially all over the world due to the impact of COVID-19 (Faustino, 2021). These impacts necessitated not only the cessation of traditional forms of content creation and consumption but also accelerated innovative practices that were less dependent upon physically proximate content creation and consumption. Some trends that preexisted the COVID pandemic were accelerated, such as the use of digital distribution of content (e.g., movies and television) to personal viewing screens and the cessation of content consumption in movie theaters. Other impacts included the creation of new hybrid forms of content creation such as the utilization of digital collaboration tools for the creation of cultural products, such as music. Lastly, the pandemic provided opportunities for experimentation with new venues for content consumption, such as the utilization of drive-in venues for concerts and live entertainment that harkened back to an earlier era.

Even before COVID-19, however, the film industry was experiencing significant change. Present disruptions only accelerated a transformation well underway in movie production, distribution and consumption. One trend preceding COVID was a decline in per capita theatrical film attendance, despite the investment by movie theaters in upgrading audio-visual technology, making seats more comfortable and introducing consumer-friendly subscription offers.

A second long-term (pre-COVID) trend has been consumer preferences for content consumption which increasingly favor streaming video on demand (SVoD). Many SVoD services are now owned or invested in by movie studios. In response to declining demand for theatrical attendance and increasing demand for streaming video-on-demand content, movie theaters made a number of decisions adversely impacting movie exhibitors, including a reduction in the amount of time that movies are shown exclusively in movie theaters and a reduction in the number of movies that Hollywood studios release to movie theaters.

Another trend accelerated since COVID has been the shift of movie production from studios to streaming platforms, which are either creating their own production studios or entering into contractual relations with movie studios to produce on demand cinematic projects selected and approved by streaming company content creators.

While movie theater revenues plummeted during the COVID epidemic, video game revenues demonstrated continued growth and audiences extended their time in game playing while locked out from more physically proximate entertainment pursuits. On the production side, video game companies could utilize remote work for their game development projects and hence did not suffer the suspension of production activities that arose in filmmaking and television. Nor was there need to compromise on the visual elements of virtual offerings insofar as the only viruses of concern in this space were software based. If anything, COVID accelerated the formation of virtual communities of game players whose shared experience compensated for the diminished availability of face-to-face engagement.

In general COVID has sped up the transformation of media industries from physical offerings consumed publicly in shared physical spaces to digital offerings consumed privately in autonomous physical spaces. These trends have had varying impacts on the production process, but the primary impacts have been upon the distribution and consumption of digital content.

END-OF-CHAPTER CASE STUDY: TENCENT

Introduction: Who Is Tencent?

Tencent is a Chinese multinational conglomerate founded in 1998 with ownership interests in over 600 companies worldwide. Tencent is a world-leading Internet and technology company that develops innovative products and services that operates within a multiplicity of industries ranging from technology engineering to cloud and smart industries to interactive entertainment. At the time of this writing most people outside of China have never heard of the company or what they do. Tencent touches almost all Chinese consumers in some way or another through the myriad of technological innovations the company offers. For the scope of this chapter, our attention will focus primarily on the interactive entertainment group and the wide range of industries in which it operates, but with the understanding that the company has leveraged many of its assets to create a market dominance like few have achieved. Tencent is widely known for its involvement in the video game sector, but is actively involved in a number of industries with the creative economy including social media, video games, music, video streaming, comics, television and cinema:

Tencent Games, created in 2003, Tencent Games is a leading game developer, publisher and operator of the largest online game community in China. They are committed to exploring the full potential of games, leveraging the rich IP resources within Tencent, spanning literature, anime, film and television, to create high-quality interactive entertainment experience[s]. Furthermore, *Tencent Games* actively collaborates with overseas game publishers, such as SEA, Netmarble, Supercell and more, to form strategic partnerships and launch new games.

Tencent Video, measured by daily active users, Tencent Video is the leading Chinese online video platform that includes popular films and dramas, variety shows, anime, sports events and news.

Tencent Pictures, is an open platform for high-quality video content. Its directive covers creative, production, distribution, promotion and licensing of IP Content. Six studios make up Tencent Pictures, Dameng, Heiti, Jinhua Yule, Manyu, Qimiao and Dayu. Since 2015, Tencent Pictures have produced and distributed 35 movies and 25 television programs worldwide.

WeiShi, Tencent's short- and mini-video creation and sharing platform, WeiShi provides viewers with access to high-quality original short- and mini-video content.

Tencent News is committed to offering information products that are relevant, engaging and empathetic to users as a trustworthy, youthful and compassionate brand.

Tencent Sports is China's leading Internet sports media platform, dedicated to providing users with the most up-to-date, comprehensive global news content and multidimensional, original sports programming. Currently, Tencent acquired the exclusive rights to broadcast the French Open, Formula One, NBA, MLB, NHL, NFL games and other top global matches to viewers in China.

Tencent Animation and Comics, Tencent Animation and Comics is the most prominent online copyrighted anime platform in China. It acts as a flagship platform for the IP of anime characters as part of the Neo-Culture Creativity Strategy. They currently have 120 million monthly active users, 30,000 online anime works, 900 signed authors, 1,400 signed anime works and millions of views across 1,500 comics and 35 animations. Many IPs have been developed into mobile games. Their most well-known national anime IP titles include "Fox Spirit Matchmaker", "The Outcast", "Love Story of Cat Spirit" and more.

China Literature Limited is a pioneer in the online literature market and operates China's leading online literature platform. The Company owns nine major branded products. Among these, QQ Reading, a unified mobile content aggregation and distribution platform, is the flagship product. Other branded products focus on individual genres and their respective fan bases.

Tencent Music Entertainment, Tencent Music is a streaming music service provider that uses social thinking by incorporating a social community integrated with other Tencent products. In particular, its innovative approach to monetizing fandom through virtual gifting and coordinated product creation has led the industry in social music innovation:

1. QQMusic (Online Music Service Service)
2. KuGou – Music-centric live streaming platform – mass market
3. Kuwo – Online music service focused on select genres, segments
4. WeSing – Karaoke social community with networking features
5. Ultimate Music – Platform that serves smart devices and vehicles
6. Tencent Music Entertainment (TME) Original Productions
7. Tencent Music Program, Liquid
8. Record Label

Tencent Esports organizes and runs eight professional leagues with the Tencent Global eSports Arena. They host tournaments in their Global eSports arena, form national competition brackets

Tencent Kandian provides users a variety of content services, such as articles, images, small videos, short videos, live streams, columns and programs. Tencent Kandian has launched two Apps – Kandian Kuaibao and Kandian Video, together with a WeChat mini program – Kandian Live, focusing on Pan-info stream, 1–3 minutes of PGC horizontal screen short video and info stream live broadcast, respectively.

Source: Tencent.com (2022).

How Did It All Begin?

It all started when co-founder, Ma Huenteng (also known as Pony Ma), partnered with four friends to create a free instant messaging service, later to be known as QQ (The Conversation, 2018). In a very short period of time, QQ grew from a modest one million users in the first year to over 100 million by year three (Shameen, 2018). From messaging, the company expanded into mobile gaming, for which it is widely known today. As the company grew and entered the mobile phone market, it eventually became the center of Chinese modern life, through the introduction and widespread use of WeChat, a multifaceted social platform that allows for gaming, chatting, texting, payment services and many other interconnected lifestyle enhancing platforms (The Conversation, 2018).

Although WeChat acts as the centerpiece of Chinese mobile life, gaming continues to be the focus of the Tencent entertainment division. Tencent Games invested in their own gaming platform in 2017 called WeGames, allowing users to stream, download and host global contests. It has a stake in the two most popular Battle Royale-style games: Fortnite and PlayerUnknown's Battleground (PUBG), together they generated over $10 billion in 2021 with over 350 registered gamers (Iqbal, 2022; Chapple, 2021). In recent years, much like their 10% investment in Universal Music Group in 2021, Tencent has publicly invested in some of the world's most well-known gaming companies, including Riot Games (League of Legends), Funcom, Leyou, Sharkmob, Supercell and Epic Games (Fortnite) (Cuofano, 2021).

By 2022, Tencent had grown into Asia's largest company and one of the world's top five firms, expanding itself well beyond the gaming sector. WeChat, being at the center of almost every

Chinese citizen's life, has over one billion active users and is the "go-to" for chat, games, buying and selling of goods and services, hailing a cab, ordering food, watching videos, playing music and paying bills for users of mobile phones (Shameen, 2018). Its market capitalization has exceeded $540 billion, while its stock has increased more than 3,638% over 10 years (Shameen, 2018), keeping pace with some of the world's largest tech companies like Amazon and Apple.

Culture and Organization

Unlike in the USA or the UK, where most people first became introduced to the Internet through computers, people in China first got acquainted through their mobile devices. Tencent understands the culture in which it was founded better than most. What's more, knowing that most business conversations within this culture are preferred to be done through "Chat" rather than email, Tencent has leveraged this knowledge.

As any successful multinational conglomerate, Tencent is committed to establishing a culture of innovation and success that begins with its most valuable asset, its people. By offering multiple opportunities for training, growth and development, Tencent is committed to the in-house development of its employees and their careers. At the cornerstone of this development is Tencent academy. Established in 2007, this educational institute was created to provide employees broad and comprehensive training that provides opportunity for career development for those who seek it. Having a reputation for being "the most respected enterprise university" (Tencent.com 2022), Tencent academy continues to spearhead a workforce that is well-trained for tomorrow's challenges.

None of this would be possible however without a solid infrastructure. Opening in 2017, Tencent's Binhai Building is a "fully digital and intelligent" structure that serves as its global headquarters (Tencent.com 2022). The innovative and interconnected nature of the building design was purposeful in order to symbolize the interconnectivity that exists between technology, the Internet, it and the people who use it. With the world headquarters first established in Shenzhen China, it has since grown a global infrastructure with office locations in

Beijing, Shanghai, Chengdu, Guangzhou, the USA and South Korea (Tencent.com 2022).

In addition to a state-of-the-art facility and established academy, Tencent sets the tone in other ways that help to establish its culture and identity with its employees and external stakeholders. At the beginning of each new year, Tencent holds what they call the "All Hands Meeting", where employees are brought into the conversation about company strategy, organizational aims and management updates while simultaneously recognizing the work done by outstanding teams. In order to develop a stronger sense of camaraderie, Tencent also prompts what they call "Tencent Culture Day". On November 11 of each year, Tencent's founding day, employees celebrate and dress up in outfits that have been designed internally. They sponsor walkathons to promote health and well-being and a sense of civil responsibility, and they organize various recreational activities including dancing, music, sports, drama and even board games. In addition, they have established Volunteer Programs to foster a sense of social responsibility. They actively encourage a sense of community and mindfulness by participating in public welfare projects that are at the heart of the culture and community that leadership wants to establish.

Furthermore, many employees speak highly of the environment in which they find themselves seeking a career. Employees describe a workplace that is "open and friendly", "flexible", "young", "energetic" and ripe with "growth and advancement". However, there are also accounts of struggling to find work–life balance due to long working hours. Such long hours are viewed as critical to the commitment needed in a well-established, growing and innovative tech firm such as Tencent (Indeed.com, 2022).

Media, Entertainment and Big Data

Since establishing a widely accessible, user-friendly Internet-based entertainment ecosystem, Tencent has enabled its users to do virtually anything they want or need in one single application. Likening its platform to Western culture and its tech platforms, WeChat combines Facebook, Instagram, Twitter, Tinder, WhatsApp, Venmo, Amazon, Apple Pay, your doctor's appointment app and Uber or Bolt all in one. Tencent is growing faster than any other large global company, including Facebook and Amazon (Cantale et al., 2017).

By leveraging this growth, Tencent has accumulated some of the largest amounts of data on earth. The more data the company collects on consumer demographics, behavior, preferences, trends or user's whereabouts, the more it can use this information with AI analytics to mine for better-targeted ecommerce and advertising sales. Not unlike its global counterparts, the intent is to develop better proprietary content that will enhance its services, clicks and user engagement. With a particular focus on its "Fintech" business, which includes WeBank, Tencent Pay and WeChat Pay, the company is able to maximize its ecosystem so that users will seek convenience within its own platform for daily online banking engagement. For example, users of WeChat Pay are able to make payments in any number of ways in which they prefer, from a quick transfer of funds among friends, paying utility bills through QR codes or by setting up payments for in-app purchases. WeBank, one of Fintech's first "inclusive finance" solutions, enables users to borrow money quickly at low cost (Lan, 2020), all within a single Tencent-owned platform.

Furthermore, as a fast-paced tech conglomerate, Tencent has no intention of remaining complacent in its growth prospects and global presence. It has made it a deliberate corporate strategy to invest in many of its competitors around the world. With investment in over 600 companies worldwide, specific interests have been focused on a 5% stake in Tesla, 12% in social media player Snap, while recently doubling its ownership stake in Universal Music Group to 20%, 10% in Spotify and 6% in gaming company Activision Blizzard. Tencent continues an aggressive investment strategy in order to remain a global powerhouse in technology-related industry (Shameem, 2018).

Criticisms and Challenges Ahead

Like most successful organizations, there often comes criticism and challenges that are driven by decisions related to business practices such as social responsibility and ethics. Tencent is certainly not exempt from these issues and in recent years has come under "fire" for their handling of music streaming rights and the social issues that surround the addictive qualities of online social media platforms and gaming.

TME division for years was heavily criticized for the monopoly they had on the music streaming rights in the Chinese music industry. When they entered this marketplace with QQ Music in 2016, they negotiated exclusive licenses with the three major music and entertainment organizations Universal Music, Sony Music Entertainment and Warner Music Group. After a regulatory ruling in 2021, Tencent Music Entertainment began to downplay its streaming services and exclusive control of content and focus its music division on more "unique content" as well as its karaoke services and social entertainment (Frater, 2021). In addition, they will continue to work closely with its label partners while diversifying into content creation while leveraging its internal services like WeChat video to help promote its content with more purpose. And although Tencent will no longer hold this tight control on music rights throughout the country, it raises important questions ranging from anticompetitive behavior to consumer rights.

In addition to the challenges presented to TME, the Chinese state media branded its popular online gaming platform "opium" as addictive, along with other gaming platforms. Certainly not alone in facing these types of challenges in the gaming and mobile phone markets, it is a criticism that the company will continue to face and will need to work hard to combat or find better solutions to combat what is perceived as the addictive nature of its games (Theedgemarkets, 2022).

It should also come as no surprise for a company that collects so much data on its users, that privacy concerns are at the forefront of debate (Deng, 2021). As of late, Tencent is finding itself needing to defend its position when it comes to how its data is being used. Critics point out that Tencent, by its own admission, has been working with the Chinese government to develop an "early-warning system" for predicting the size of crowds and their movement to help quash dissent (Shameem, 2018). This, in and of itself, poses its own issues in free societies, but in cultures where personal freedoms are more limited and more accepted by its people, being keenly aware of the ethical use of data may tarnish an organization's brand and societal good will.

End-of-Chapter Case Questions for Discussion

Q: Are there opportunities for other non-Chinese media conglomerates to imitate the types of cross-media offerings and synergies of Tencent?

Q: How might regulatory laws outside China impact opportunities for other media companies if they intend to pursue an aggressive innovation strategy similar to Tencent's?

REFERENCES

Alsin. A. (2018). The future of media: Disruptions, revolutions and the quest for distribution. *Forbes*, July 19, 2018. Available from: https://www.forbes.com/sites/aalsin/2018/07/19/the-future-of-media-disruptions-revolutions-and-the-quest-for-distribution/?sh=8ce295160b90. Accessed June 6, 2021.

Angues, E. and Thelwall, M. (2010). Motivations for image publishing and tagging on *Flickr*. In *Proceedings of the 14th International Conference on Electronic Publishing*, Hanken School of Economics, Helsinki, pp. 189–204.

Brabham, D. (2008). Crowdsourcing as a model for problem solving: An introduction and cases. *Convergence: The International Journal of Research into New Media Technologies*, 14(1), 75–90.

Brandenburger, A.M. and Nalebuff, B.J. (1996).*Co-Opetition*. New York: Doubleday.

Burgelman, R., Siegel, R. and Lippincott, H. (2015). *PayPal in 2015: Reshaping the Financial Services Landscape*. Nov. 12. Cambridge, MA: Harvard Business School.

Buskin, R. (2007). Classic tracks: The Ronettes 'Be My Baby'. *Sound on Sound*. Available from: https://www.soundonsound.com/techniques/classic-tracks-ronettes-be-my-baby. Accessed August 16, 2022.

Cantale, S., Buche, I., and Barbie, J. (2017). *China's Tencent: Leading the Way in Monetizing Platforms* (pp. 1–13). International Institute for Management Development (IMD). Available from: https://www.thecasecentre.org/products/view?id=148955

Chapple, C. (2021). *PUBG Mobile Grosses $5 Billion After Generating an Average of $7.4 Million Per Day in 2020*. Sensortower.com. Available from: https://sensortower.com/blog/pubg-mobile-five-billion-revenue. Accessed April 24, 2022.

Chozick, A. and Barnes, B. (2019). Paramount Was Hollywood's 'Mountain.' Now It's a Molehill. *New York Times*. January 17. Available from: https://www.nytimes.com/2019/01/17/business/media/paramount-pictures.html

Cuofano, G. (2021). *What Does Tencent Own? Inside The Tencent Business Model - FourWeekMBA*. FourWeekMBA. Available from: https://fourweekmba.com/what-does-tencent-own/. Accessed April 24, 2022.

Christensen, C. (1997). *The Innovator's Dilemma*. Cambridge, MA: Harvard Business School Press.

DeFillippi, R. Hunt, P. C. Dumas and Hung, K. (2014). Crowdsourcing and the evolution of the micostock photography industry: The case of iStockphoto and getty images. In DeFillippi, R. and Wikstrom, P. (eds) *International Perspectives on Business Innovation and Disruption in the Creative Industries: Film, Video and Photography* (pp. 223–246). Northampton, MA: Edward Elgar Publishing.

Deng, I. (2021). *Consumer Watchdog Questions Tencent Over Data Privacy for Personalised Ads*. South China Morning Post. Available from: https://www.scmp.com/tech/policy/article/3155874/consumer-group-questions-tencent-over-data-privacy-policy-wechat. Accessed August 23, 2022.

Dixon, C. (2021) Accounting for Amazon Prime Video's place in the US SVOD industry. *NScreen Media*, April 18. Available from: https://nscreenmedia.com/accounting-for-amazon-prime-videos-place-in-the-us-svod-industry. Accessed January 12, 2022.

Elberse, A. and Woodham, L. (2020). Big hit entertainment and blockbuster band BTS: K-pop goes global. *Harvard Business School Case Study*, 520–125, June 2020.

Fang, T. P., Wu, A., and Clough, D. R. (2021). Platform diffusion at temporary gatherings: Social coordination and ecosystem emergence. *Strategic Management Journal*, 42(2), 233–272.

Faustino, P. (2021). COVID-19 as an accelerator of innovation, management, marketing and cin the creative and cultural Industry. *Journal of Creative Industries and Cultural Studies*, 5, 14–29.

Follows, S. (2018). 48 trends reshaping the film industry: Part 3 – Distribution and exhibition. January 15, 2018. Available from: https://stephenfollows.com/trends -reshaping-film-industry-distribution-exhibition/. Accessed April 3, 2020.

Frater, P. (2021). Tencent music changes focus after regulatory slap, profits drop. *Variety .com*. Available from: https://variety.com/2021/biz/asia/tencent-music-regulatory-slap -profits-drop-1235042781/. Accessed April 24, 2022.

Geyser, W. (2021). The incredible growth of eSports (+ eSports statistics). *Influencer Marketing Hub*. Available from: https://influencermarketinghub.com/esports-stats/. Accessed September 14, 2021.

Gustines, G. G. (2021). Comic book writers and artists follow other creators to Substack. *New York Times*, April 9, 2021. Available from: https://www.nytimes.com/2021/08/09/ business/media/Substack-comic-books.html. Accessed October 15, 2021.

Hall, M. K. (2014). *The Emergence of Rock and Roll: Music and the Rise of American Youth Culture, Timeline*. Abingdon: Routledge.

Hearn, G. (2020). *The Future of Creative Work*. Northampton, MA: Edward Elgar Publishing.

Howe, J. (2008) *Crowdsourcing: Why the Power of the Crowd Is Driving the Future of Business*. New York: Three Rivers Press.

IFPI. (2021) *IFPI issues Global Music Report 2021*. Available from: https://www.ifpi.org/ ifpi-issues-annual-global-music-report-2021/. Accessed June 3, 2022.

Indeed.com. (2022). *Working at Tencent: Employee Reviews about Culture | Indeed.com*. [online] Available from: https://www.indeed.com/cmp/Tencent/reviews?fcountry =ALL&ftopic=culture. Accessed August 23, 2022.

Iqbal, M. (2022). Fortnite usage and revenue statistics (2022). *Business of Apps*. Available from: https://www.businessofapps.com/data/fortnite-statistics/. Accessed April 24, 2022.

Ketchen Jr, D. J., Crook, T. R., and Craighead, C. W. (2014). From supply chains to supply ecosystems: Implications for strategic sourcing research and practice. *Journal of Business Logistics*, 35(3), 165–171.

Kretschmer, T., Leiponen, A., Schilling, M., and Vasudeva, G. (2022). Platform ecosystems as meta-organizations: Implications for platform strategies. *Strategic Management Journal*, 43(3), 405–424.

Lampel, J. Jha, P.P. and Bhalla, A (2012). Test-driving the future: How design competitions are changing innovation. *Academy of Management Perspectives*, 26(2), 71–85.

Lan, S. (2020). *Tencent's Webank: A Tech-Driven Bank Or A Licensed Fintech?* Equalocean. Available from: https://equalocean.com/analysis/2020080414410. Accessed August 23, 2022.

Leroux-Parra, M. (2020). Esports Part 1: What are Esports? *Harvard International Review*. Available from: https://hir.harvard.edu/esports-part-1-what-are-esports/. Accessed June 23, 2021.

Lipsey, R. Carlaw, K. I. and Bekhar, C. T. (2005). *Economic Transformations: General Purpose Technologies and Long-Term Economic Growth*. Oxford: Oxford University Press. pp. 131–218.

McKee, J.(2022). *Powering Payments in the Creator Economy*. FXCintelligence.com. Available from: https://www.fxcintel.com/research/analysis/powering-payments-in -the-creator-economy. Accessed May 23, 2022.

Miyakoshi, K. (2019). The economics of esports. *USC Economic Review*. Available from: https://usceconreview.com/2019/01/04/the-economics-of-esports/. Accessed June 23, 2021.

Moore, G.A. (2014). *Crossing the Chasm*. HarperCollins Publishers.

Morrison, S. (2018) List of varsity esports programs spans North America. Available from: https://www.espn.com/esports/story/_/id/21152905/. Accessed June 28, 2021.

Oh, W. and Rhee, M. (Nov 2016). K-Pop's global success did not happen by accident. *Harvard Business Review.* Nov. 16. Available from: https://hbr.org/2016/11/k-pops -global-success-didnt-happen-by-accident. Accessed July 1, 2022.

Polkes. A. (2022). Why Doritos' marketing strategy made Super Bowl history. Available from: https://www.yotpo.com/blog/how-doritos-wins-every-super-bowl-with-ugc/. Accessed April 12, 2022.

Roth, Y. and Kamani, R. (2014). Crowdsourcing in the production of video advertising: The emerging roles of crowdsourcing platforms (pp. 177–199) in DeFillippi, R. and Wikstrom, P. (editors) *International Perspectives on Business Innovation and Disruption in Creative Industries: Film, Video and Photography.* Northampton, MA: Edward Elgar Publishing.

Shameen, A. (2018). *Tech: How Tencent became an internet giant.* Available from: https://www.theedgemarkets.com/article/tech-how-tencent-became-internet-giant/. Accessed April 13, 2022.

Shannon, C. E. and Weaver, W. (1963). *The Mathematical Theory of Communication* (4th print. ed.). Urbana: University of Illinois Press. p. 144.

Surowiecki, J. (2005). *The Wisdom of Crowds.* Anchor Books.

Tencent.com (2022). Tencent 腾讯. Available from: https://www.tencent.com/en-us/about .html. Accessed April 24, 2022.

Thomas, L. D. and Ritala, P. (2022). Ecosystem legitimacy emergence: A collective action view. *Journal of Management,* 48(3), 515–541.

The Conversation. (2018). How Tencent became the world's most valuable social network firm – with barely any advertising. Available from: <https://theconversation.com/ how-tencent-became-the-worlds-most-valuable-social-network-firm-with-barely-any -advertising-90334>. Accessed April 24, 2022.

Theedgemarkets (2022). How Tencent became an internet giant. Available from: https:// www.theedgemarkets.com/article/tech-how-tencent-became-internet-giant. Accessed February 10, 2022.

Tracy, M. (2020). Journalists are leaving the noisy internet for your email inbox. *The New York Times,* September 23.

Wang, R. D. and Miller, C. D. (2020). Complementors' engagement in an ecosystem: A study of publishers'e-book offerings on Amazon Kindle. *Strategic Management Journal,* 41(1), 3–26.

Wikipedia. (2021a). Computer generated imagery. Available from: https://en.wikipedia .org/wiki/Consumer_neuroscience. Accessed June 21, 2021.

Wikipedia. (2021c). Digital revolution. Available from: https://en.wikipedia.org/wiki/ Consumer_neuroscience. Accessed June 25, 2021.

Wikipedia. (2021d). eSports. Available from: https://en.wikipedia.org/wiki/Esports. Accessed June 23, 2021.

Wikipedia. (2021e). Substack. Available from: https://en.wikipedia.org/wiki/Substack. Accessed January 10, 2021.

Wikipedia. (2022a). Advertising. Available from: https://en.m.wikipedia.org/wiki/ Advertising. Accessed May 12, 2022.

Wikipedia. (2022d). Rock and roll. Available from: https://en.wikipedia.org/wiki/Rock _and_roll. Accessed February 5, 2022.

Zhuo, M. and Austin, R. D. (2018). *Big Hit Entertainment and BTS: K-Pop Reaches for a Global Breakthrough.* Ivey Publishing Case Study.

Zupic, I (2013). Social media as enabler of crowdsourcing. In Bondarouk, T. and Olivas-Lujan, M. (eds) *Social Media and Management (Advanced Series in Management, Volume 10).* Bingley: Emerald Group Publishing.

Trans-formational Innovation in Physical Products

Alison Rieple, Robert DeFillippi and David Schreiber

Chapter 4

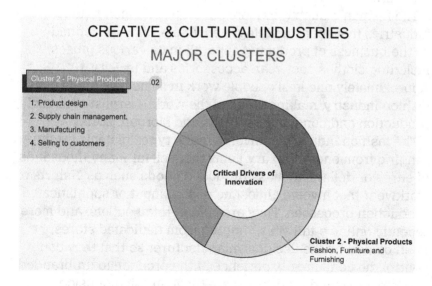

Figure 4.1   Creative and cultural industries: cluster 2 drivers of innovation.

DOI: 10.4324/9781003207542-4

Introduction

In this chapter we focus on transformational innovation in physical products. Although we focus especially on fashion, much of the discussion in this chapter applies to other CCI industries that produce physical products, including furnishing and furniture (defined as the creation of physical products for the home, office and interiors). In addition to the end-of-chapter case study on the fast fashion supply chain, a supplementary case study discusses innovation in the world's largest furniture manufacturer/retailer, IKEA. And although they are physical products, we do not include fine arts such as sculptures or paintings, or crafts, within this cluster. This is because of their lack of replication and the relative importance of resale value.

Despite their common requirements for creativity, innovation and intellectual property development, physical products differ from the media industries discussed in Chapter 3 in the way they are manufactured, sold and distributed (Gong and Hassink, 2017). Although digital technologies have played their role in transforming some aspects of this cluster in recent years, this has not been the only source of transformational innovation.

The fashion industry, or more accurately fashion-related industries that act as an integrated whole,[1] may be defined as the business of producing apparel[2] in its various guises, including clothes, footwear, accessories and jewelry. Approximately one in six people work in some part of the global fashion industry, making it one of the world's largest chains of production and consumption (Ross and Morgan, 2015).

The fashion industry is diverse in the types of items produced, ranging from one-off luxury items that sell for many thousands of euros or dollars, to mass-produced goods such as T-shirts or workwear that involve almost no design input or sophisticated production processes. They are sold in retail outlets, and more recently online e-tail sites, ranging from dedicated stores, often owned by the designer/manufacturer so that they can control the consumer experience of the product, to un-branded supermarkets and markets where the items sit alongside goods made by other manufacturers as well as other types of products.

Fashion has many areas of overlap with other manufacturing-based industries in terms of processes as well as their supply and distribution chains and logistics management systems. But they differ from some other manufacturers because of their need to create and respond to trends and changing consumer tastes.

The creation of a physical product involves a number of different components – design, manufacturing, supply, transportation and retailing (Figure 4.2).

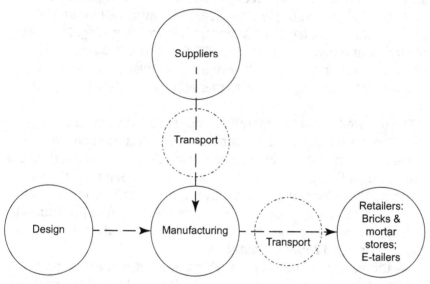

Figure 4.2   The apparel product value chain.

A few large global companies undertake all of these functions in-house; in many other cases these activities are carried out by independent organizations that sell their products to other firms. However, there are normally very close links between these functional areas even if the companies involved are independent.

In this chapter we discuss the four critical drivers of innovation in the physical products cluster. We first discuss the critical role of product design. Design provides both the form and functionality that makes the product and its brand attractive to consumers, and also provides the information that manufacturers then use to make up the product in larger quantities. Innovation in design, like many other things that we discuss in this chapter, has been heavily influenced by digitization, in this case the communications technologies that allow data on which design decisions are based to be transmitted across the world.

We then discuss the management of the supply chain, and how physical goods manufacturers source the raw materials, and then transport them to where they are needed in the manufacturing stage, and then finally to the place where they are bought and sold. This is now a chain that involves many players often located far away from each other in a search for the lowest possible costs. Partnerships in the supply system are nowadays embedded in a complex IT infrastructure. Major innovations have, again, used digital technologies such as MRP, JIT, EDI and ERP systems that allow the exchange of real-time data, and logistics systems that use sophisticated algorithms to manage the efficient transport of goods.

Thirdly we look at the manufacturing process, a critical function in this cluster. The manufacturing function has very close links with both suppliers and (r)etailers and innovation has profoundly affected the communications between the different partners. Developments in ICT have also radically changed the actual manufacturing process such as the design of production layouts, scheduling and the use of AI and automation to improve the process and reduce wastage.

We then discuss the ways in which innovation has shaped the way that physical product companies sell to customers. The way that this is done is now heavily driven by digital-based processes involving big data, VR/AR, AI, social media, electronic payment systems and web-based retailing.

Finally, we comment on the changes brought about by the COVID pandemic and speculate what transformations are likely in the future. The move to online purchasing has been the biggest effect of the pandemic, but there has also been a significant upheaval in the supply chains that involve developing countries, and the start of a reaction against unsustainable practices. What is less certain is the role of 3D printing and electronic payment systems such as NFTs. These are starting to be used but have not yet become truly transformational.

THE CRITICAL DRIVERS OF INNOVATION IN CLUSTER 2, PHYSICAL PRODUCT INDUSTRIES

CRITICAL DRIVER 1: PRODUCT DESIGN

Designing a physical product involves taking an idea, expressing it in the form of a sketch (traditionally on paper, although more recently on computers/tablets), creating a pattern, cutting materials using the pattern and finally making and finishing the product. At each stage there are likely to be many iterations of the idea leading to a prototype that is then refined further.

Critical success factors in product designing include:

1) *Designing desirable items*

Designing desirable items involves being able to design products that consumers want, communicate these designs in a timely way to the product's manufacturer(s) and troubleshoot jointly on any design-manufacturing related problems. In this, communications technologies are critical. These allow design ideas and specifications to be transmitted across the world, as well as enabling almost instant transmission of sales patterns and trends from one region to another, many miles away. CAD/CAM systems (see exemplar below) have transformed the designer's ability to visualize a new product. 3D printing or additive manufacturing (Vanderploeg et al., 2017; Jacobsen, 2017) has similarly transformed design prototyping. 3D printing involves adding molten materials (typically metal or plastics) layer by layer onto a base until the object is formed. It allows products to be made on demand rather than in large runs, using designs that can be downloaded and printed on a local printer.

One of the most successful fashion companies, H&M, has increased its own design credentials by collaborating with some of the biggest names in fashion design, including Versace (a collection that was also endorsed by Prince), Kenzo and many others (Leong, 2021). Karl Lagerfeld was the first to join with H&M to create a range of womenswear and menswear, an "unprecedented" partnership that "sent shockwaves through the fashion world" (fashionnetwork.com, 2016). This innovation made high fashion more accessible at a time when luxury labels were focused on their exclusivity. The entire collection sold out within minutes of release, with some consumers buying 20 pieces of the same item. In March 2021 Irish designer Simone Rocha's limited-edition collaboration with H&M caused China's most popular app, WeChat, to crash as a result of the number of people rushing to get their hands on the items (Williams, 2021).

2) *Differentiating through the creation of brands*

Brand differentiation means developing a style and a discernible identity that then shapes in turn the characteristics of the products' future designs. In some cases the intellectual property involved in the product's design may be exploited through licensing or replication. For example, Zara operates franchised stores in some parts of the world, a form of licensing in which the franchisee agrees to sell the franchisor's products (for a fee) and maintain agreed standards. Another approach might involve a fashion designer agreeing to let other companies, sometimes in very different industries (accessories, home goods and health and beauty aids, for example), use their designs on their own goods. Pierre Cardin licensed his designs to manufacturers of products as diverse as cars or cigarettes. Although heavily criticized by branding consultants, he became one of the wealthiest men in France through it (Friedman and Indvik, 2020).

3) *Using technology to enable product customization*

Exploiting advances in social media and AI to enable consumer participation in product design, resulting in products that are customized to personal tastes (Wilson, 2017). The former era of mass production is becoming the era of mass customization. Some of the most famous examples of this trend include Nike for You, Gucci DIY and Hermès Sur-Mesure.

4) *Exploiting cultural cues*

Designers need to be able to pick up cultural "vibes" relevant to wherever the product is to be sold. For major international companies such as IKEA, Zara or H&M this may be almost anywhere in the world. Many trend-focused physical product companies have to interact with other parts of the cultural ecosystem, borrowing ideas from related industries such as music or fine arts.

5) *Managing IPR*

Designers have to steer a difficult path between being excitingly new at the same time as being recognizable and familiar. It is a challenge to avoid copyright infringement through "passing off", where a design is seen to be a direct (illegal) copy of another design intended to create an association in the minds of consumers between the two items. The problem for many designers is that fashion design does not have the same protection as other creative outputs (as discussed in Chapter 2) because apparel is classified as "functional" and therefore excluded from protection by copyright laws. Some elements of fashion design *are* protected, but with limited effectiveness. The copyright law covers print patterns, trademark law protects items with visibly displayed protected logos, and trade dress trademark laws can protect the visual characteristics of a product, if they are specific to a designer or product.

Some countries have tried to introduce laws to protect fashion design; however, the protection is inconsistent around the world. In the European Union, the Creative Designs Directive and the European Designs Directive protect new designs for three or five years. In the 2017 Supreme Court case, Star Athletica, LLC v. Varsity Brands, Inc., it was ruled that Fashion design can be covered by copyright.

EXEMPLAR 1: DESIGN PROCESS INNOVATION THROUGH COMPUTER-AIDED DESIGN AND MANUFACTURING (CAD-CAM)

For many years the product design process remained relatively stable. The biggest change has come in the last 40 years with the arrival of computer-aided design and manufacturing (CAD-CAM). CAD is a set of software tools that assists product

---

designers to create virtual representations of the artifacts they are designing. CAD created a revolution in designing – what used to take a week can be done within a day. Now it is ubiquitous in physical products industries.

CAD-CAM began life by providing substitutes for prototypes of physical products. The design is displayed in three dimensions, allowing viewing of the virtual object from any angle. Alterations, such as adjusting to different materials, are easier and quicker, saving time and reducing errors. Costs are also less because virtual versions of the design can be viewed without needing to purchase fabric or materials.

More recently technological developments in Cloud-based CAD software have enabled designers to collaborate with manufacturers and other designers in any location in the world. Fashion designers, for example, are often located close to their markets and manufacturers in low-cost countries many thousands of miles away. Cloud-based CAD software is also now found in conjunction with 3D printers allowing consumers to not only design their own items but 3D print them at home, an innovation that is now threatening to transform many manufacturing industries.

Exemplar 1: Questions for discussion

1. What sort of problems do designers face when using CAD systems? How might they overcome these problems?
2. What are the risks of cloud-based designing? How might a designer mitigate these risks?

CRITICAL DRIVER 2: SUPPLY CHAIN MANAGEMENT

The supply and distribution (S&D) function has been transformed over the years by the need to respond to innovations in manufacturing and retailing. The basics of the S&D model have now lasted for many decades until recent developments in online retailing and manufacturing technologies such as 3D printing now threaten to disrupt it.

Before the manufacturing stage is the need to source the raw materials that will go into making the physical good. This sometimes involves a long chain of different intermediary products that goes right back to the basic "raw" material. For example, a finished item of furniture might include wood (grown by farmers, or harvested from natural forests), metal finishings (made from ore mined from the ground) and varnishes (made from oil, also extracted from the ground and then processed). Fashion items are based on fabrics that are made from materials grown on farms (cotton, wool, bamboo, modal) or extracted from the ground (nylon, polyester, acrylic, gold). In some cases the raw materials that designers and manufacturers use are innovative in themselves, requiring consequential changes to the ways that they are distributed and manufactured.

Very few physical product makers undertake all of these stages themselves – a fashion designer does not have the competences, or indeed the desire, to also be a gold miner or oil refiner. There are limits to vertical integration even though it has (mainly in the past) been recommended as a way of taking control of essential inputs.

The lack of vertical integration means that multiple supply channel members have to collaborate in a system in which each company specializes in a specific part of the whole process. Companies that are good at building lasting relationships are likely to outcompete their competitors as they will be able to negotiate good deals and obtain supplies in the right place at the right time (JIT and lean manufacturing depend on it). Partnerships between manufacturers and their suppliers are nowadays typically embedded in IT systems and infrastructure that allow the efficient exchange of real-time data through sophisticated EDI and ERP systems and swift movement of goods.

Sometimes suppliers focus on the invention and development of completely new raw materials, such as nylon in the 1930s, in which case a very close working relationship with other firms in the supply chain is necessary. Because the innovation process is uncertain, a lot of co-development and experimentation are usually required with different inputs from different sources of expertise. Other suppliers might focus on improving existing materials so that they are more robust, and therefore cheaper to operate, more flexible in their possible uses, or more sustainable in their production methods.

Always, there is the issue of how physical goods can be transported from where they are designed and manufactured to where they are sold and consumed, given often unpredictable demand and variable perishability. Costs are a critical driver of success, and innovations have often focused on improving financial performance. Typically, most manufacturing takes place in developing countries where costs are lower, but there are long distances between manufacturing and sales' locations. Innovations in logistics and transportation technologies have been essential in allowing predictable and relatively cheap movement of goods over these distances (Taplin, 2014; Linden, 2016). These innovations include:

- Materials requirement planning (MRP) systems. They tell a company what to order, when to order it and ensure at the other end that goods are delivered to customers at the right time and in the right quantities. MRP programs are essential to JIT systems. These systems were invented by large US and UK manufacturers in the 1950s but have since become ubiquitous in manufacturing industries and are fundamental to the fast fashion business model (see below). MRP systems are dependent on the quality of information they receive in the form of inputted data from partners, and therefore there needs to be high-quality integration with suppliers' and retailers' own computer systems, and some way of deciding which of probably many suppliers will actually fulfill the order.
- MRP data from retailers is dependent on knowing which items have been bought, in what quantities, at which stores and also which have been returned. Barcode tracking software and subsequently radio-frequency identification (RFID) tags are critical to this process, feeding their data into integrated electronic point of sale (EPOS) and manufacturing systems. This means that information about trends and product popularity can be fed into the whole supply system and changes made to orders if necessary. Unlike a barcode, an RFID tag does not need to be within the line of sight of the reader and may be embedded into the tracked object and so can be used in shops to expedite checkout and also to reduce theft by both customers and employees.

Transportation innovations have also played a huge part in allowing products to be distributed economically over great distances. These include developments in containerization and air freight as well as in pallet and box design (see IKEA case study). Containerization has hugely reduced wastage and product damage as goods remain in (sealed) containers until they reach their destination. Electronic tagging allows them to be traced, minimizing inaccurate deliveries, and goods within them are safe from pilfering.

EXEMPLAR 2: H&M'S SUPPLY AND DISTRIBUTION CHAIN

H&M is one of the world's largest fashion retailer/manufacturers and has been so for over 20 years. It has spent years competing with rivals such as Zara (Inditex) for the title of the most innovative supply chain and is (along with Zara) the originator of the fast fashion business arguably model (see the end-of-chapter case). H&M sells its clothes all over the world and manufactures them predominantly in east Asia. This provides an extremely complex supply and distribution chain environment, and H&M has been successful over the years because it manages this extremely effectively.

H&M has to address a number of sometimes conflicting demands simultaneously:

- achieve both low costs and high quality
- adjust volumes and mixes in order to quickly respond to customer demands and changes in trends
- provide products with a high degree of local relevance differentiate between different categories of product flows

H&M's strategic positioning is largely to be a fashion design follower, rather than an initiator. Designers visit major fashion and cultural hubs such as Paris and New York to capture new trends. They also use feedback from store EDI terminals to understand customers' current buying patterns. AI and data analytics software are used to forecast demand in order to both minimize costs and improve local relevance. This forms

---

a "push–pull" type of production model. A number of highly automated logistics centers were also added in 2021 to create additional capacity and increase assortment availability.

High fashion items with a short lead time are manufactured in locations close to where they are to be sold, for example, Turkey, where they can be quickly transported to shops and warehouses. However, less fashionable garments such as T-shirts and jeans which do not go out of fashion quickly are still overwhelmingly manufactured in China, Bangladesh and India (Statista, 2022). This innovative flexible model of distribution (which H&M call their omni model) means that H&M can adjust volumes, channels and mix based on customer demand and/or unexpected events. It works both ways: the company can increase production quickly but can also scale back volume. There is a focus on choosing the most optimal equipment for the product and filling transport units to the maximum, with a ruthless focus on costs. Cheaper transportation costs are achieved by the use of sea and rail rather than the more expensive air freight. H&M outsources its logistics to partners such as DHL and Green Cargo and has strong relationships with shipping company Maersk, which aids in making changes to supply routes. It uses an ICT platform to track items.

H&M's omni model requires suppliers that are equally flexible and adaptable and able to scale up or reduce production at will. H&M's supply chain is built on strong long-term partnerships. It invests heavily in supplier training and development, especially important since suppliers are typically based in countries without a particularly strong corporate governance infrastructure.

H&M's production offices are based near to their suppliers and they manage them closely. This aids the company's knowledge of local laws and ways of doing business. H&M only works with suppliers on its list, which is now published and for which there is a rigorous recruitment and selection process. As part of a response to increasing consumer concerns about sustainability and transparency, the list includes the name, location, product type produced and number of workers employed by each supplier. H&M divides its suppliers into several tiers (H&M, 2022); each tier does business with its immediately adjacent tiers. Tier 1 are the suppliers H&M does business with directly. They make 99% of H&M's products – 602 companies and over 1500 factories in Europe, Asia and Africa. H&M does not normally have a direct trading relationship with Tiers 2–6. Tiers 2 and 3 mills, for example, make fabrics and yarns, processes that can involve environmentally sensitive fabric dyeing and printing processes. The raw materials for these would be produced by suppliers in Tiers 3-6. H&M's supply chains vary according to the product type or materials used. Some are vertical – short with few tiers. Others are horizontal and comprise several tiers (H&M, 2022).

Eight years is the average length of H&M's relationship with a supplier, although some have worked with the company for over 25 years (H&M, 2020). Building close, long-term, relationships with suppliers is an essential precondition for digitalizing the sourcing process through technologies such as 3D sampling or automated production order placement, which require the synchronization of lead firms' and suppliers' IT architectures (López et al., 2021). 3D sampling and automated order placement allow H&M to avoid shipping of physical samples and minimize communication and human errors in the order process (Berg et al., 2017).

Exemplar 2: Questions for discussion

1. H&M uses partners to manage aspects of its supply chain. (a) How do these relationships improve H&M's own performance? (b) What does it need to do to make these partnerships work well?
2. What are the risks of H&M's supply/distribution business model?

CRITICAL DRIVER 3: MANUFACTURING

Manufacturing involves the physical transformation of raw materials into finished goods. In the case of furniture, the raw materials are likely to be wood, leather, plastics and metals, all of which need to be shaped and glued or joined together in some way. In the case of apparel the raw materials are more diverse, including plastics such as acrylics and polyester, natural fabrics like cotton and linen, and materials such as suede and leather, and because of the need to respond to fast-moving trends, more dynamic. Manufacturing provides one of the biggest sources of costs in physical products industries and therefore is one of the areas where innovations in cost reduction can lead to transformational performance. The search for low costs underpinned some of the business model innovations that we discuss later and the widespread movement of manufacturing to low-cost countries such as China, Vietnam and Bangladesh.

The steps in manufacturing include (Suh, 2020):

- Receiving raw materials such as plastics, components or fabrics. These will typically arrive in shipping containers and are stored in a holding area.
- Cutting and machining. These are some of the most important stages because once the materials have been cut little can be done to rectify defects.
- Sewing. In apparel this is an especially labor-intensive process and provides a big source of costs.
- Fitting and finishing.

The manufacturing process itself has to produce items reliably and at the lowest possible cost, given the quality profile desired. Items may be made in larger or smaller quantities, normally identical to one another. The factory may often need to change what it makes when new designs come in, something that may require the retooling of equipment and changes to the layout of the manufacturing plant. Fashion manufacturing is especially complicated because there are frequent changes in style and the requirement in many cases for intricate manual work. Different materials need different manufacturing techniques, and many factories specialize in one type of product or another – there are economies of scale in dedicating production to one method.

Just-in-time Manufacturing

In recent years some of the biggest innovations in the manufacturing process have been "borrowed" from other industries. Taiichi Ohno, from the Japanese car maker Toyota, is generally credited with creating the process and system innovations now known as the Toyota Production System at one of the company's plants in the early 1970s (Economist, 2009). One of the underpinning principles of this business model was just-in-time (JIT) production, in which raw materials are provided to manufacturers in the right quantities and at the right time. This was in contrast to the old model of just-in-case, where inventory was held for every possible eventuality, just in case it was needed. JIT thinking hugely reduces stock-holding costs, meaning that manufacturers do not need enormous warehouses where they store raw materials or hold buffer stocks until they are needed.

JIT systems require immense cooperation between suppliers and manufacturers, meaning that top-notch communication systems (initially manual, but now almost entirely IT-based) have to be in place between suppliers and manufacturers. This is an essential role in the supply chain that we discuss in the next section. Suppliers have to be as agile and flexible as their partners, and trust between the partners is essential. Nowadays EPOS (Electronic Point of Sale) systems can share sales data in real time with their manufacturers and in turn their suppliers so that they can quickly respond to market demand by altering their assembly lines.

JIT principles were used to improve textile production in DuPont's plant in the USA (Billesbach, 1994). Through this the company was able to reduce work in process by 96.0%, working capital by $2 million and the textile production operating budget by more than $3 million. Production quality also improved by 10% (Raj et al., 2017). Another study found that American firms that introduced JIT gained on average a 70% reduction in inventory, a 50% reduction in labor costs and an 80% reduction in space requirements over five years (Economist, 2009).

Although extremely effective (and now virtually ubiquitous in product manufacturing industries), there are risks to JIT systems if transportation fails, something that can happen because of economic or labor market turmoil, rising energy costs (as was happening in October 2021) or because of unplanned weather events like hurricanes and floods.

Another process innovation that has become dominant in recent years is lean manufacturing, a method that also emerged from the Toyota Production System. It incorporates and builds on JIT principles but goes further. A challenge for CCI product manufacturers is how to produce runs of fewer items in short lead times. Mass production helped everyone to cut costs through economies of scale; now the problem is to produce customizable, or short-term orders, and economies of scope are more important (Kumar, 2011). Lean production shows how to cut costs while producing small quantities. Key differences between the two systems are:

Mass production system	Lean production system
Suitable for large quantities	Suitable for low quantities
Stock production	Custom production
High inventory levels	Low inventory levels
High levels of work in progress (WIP)	Low WIP
Higher process waste	Lower process waste

Lean production is critical for the implementation of small-order manufacturing systems in the fashion industry. However, lean manufacturing in furniture manufacturing appears rather more rare (Popescu et al., 2018).

Successful implementation of lean methods significantly reduces production costs, reduces waste, minimizes inventory and buffering costs, reduces over-production, helps to achieve continuous and uninterrupted flow of items and reduces defects. Lean focuses on the removal of many types of waste through (a) using a minimum of raw materials and avoiding scraps; (b) maintaining an ideal supply and demand ratio without accumulating idle inventory; (c) reducing the amount of transportation of materials (or workforce); (d) optimizing energy, time and space utilization; and (e) minimizing defects. This is done through systematic analysis of processes and systems and information technologies to help gather data and undertake the analyses (Jana and Tiwari, 2021).

A number of proprietary methods have come out of this thinking, such as *Six-Sigma*. Six Sigma was implemented first in Motorola and then in General Electric, both large American multinational manufacturers. The sigma refers to a statistical term, a standard deviation; anything that deviates by three sigma from the mean was deemed to need improvement. Another technique is Autonomation, which describes a feature of machine design that has some supervisory functions so that, if an abnormal situation arises on a production line, the machine detects it and signals that production should stop.

USING INFORMATION AND COMMUNICATION TECHNOLOGY (ICT) TO IMPROVE THE EFFICIENCY AND EFFECTIVENESS OF THE MANUFACTURING PROCESS

Numerous innovations in ICT-based processes and systems in recent years have transformed the way that CCI manufacturers function, including:

1. Big data and Artificial Intelligence (AI)
   a. Identification of the causes of product and machine failures, production delays and locating workers and products through smart, networked, sensors
   b. Smart product planning systems to enhance forecasting accuracy
2. Automation
   a. Automatic sewing machines
   b. Intelligent robots, for example, laser cutting machines, buttonhole machines and fusing machines
   c. Machine learning to remove manual intervention at key stages of production
3. Smart production systems
   a. Internet of Things (IoT) and modular sewing systems, SewBots, gripper robot arms
   b. IT-based integration with the supply chain, e.g., using cloud computing
4. Remote-controlled systems
   a. modularization, digitalization, vision-based sewing
5. Computer-integrated design/manufacturing (CAD/CAM)
   a. multi-scale dynamic modeling and simulations
   b. rapid design changes

The most comprehensive of these applications is *intelligent manufacturing*, which comprises three technological paradigms: digital manufacturing, smart manufacturing and new-generation intelligent manufacturing. This highly complex innovative system integrates advanced manufacturing and information technologies. Digitalization adds "brains" to products, networkization allows low-cost and wide-ranging connections among equipment and products, intelligentization (AI and big data) allows products to have "sensing and learning" capabilities, which consequently lead to changes to product functionality and performance (Zhou et al., 2019).

Digitalization technologies include enterprise resource planning (ERP), office automation (OA), manufacturing execution systems (MES) and supply chain management (SCM), all of which can be said to be Industry 3.0 (Kagermann et al., 2013). Smart manufacturing combines digitalization and networkization technologies, such as e-commerce, the Internet of Things (IoT) and online coloration platforms – Industry 4.0. New-generation intelligent manufacturing integrates digitalization, networkization and intelligentization technologies.

Fashion manufacturers are said to have been relatively slow to embrace some of these, preferring instead to depend on cheap labor. According to a report from *Forbes* (Columbus, 2017, 2019) although smart factories have been adopted in 67% of industrial manufacturing, 50% of automotive and transportation production, and 40% of consumer goods production, the "smartening" of the fashion manufacturing sector is so weak that it is subsumed in the report under "others" (Lee et al., 2021). With the exception of sportswear specialist Adidas' Speedfactory (opened in December 2015), Amazon's robo-cutting fabrics for customized orders (Bain, 2017) and China's Kutesmart (see exemplar below) most apparel manufacturing remains at a basic level and few have switched to smart factory systems. Some of the technologies required, such as Big Data and AI, and other smart factory features such as product traceability systems and algorithm-based forecasting, are available only to large global companies; smaller companies have to make do with less complex technologies. It is for this reason that some commentators have suggested there will be an increasing move to consolidate smaller factories into larger, more technologically sophisticated, ones in the near future.

**EXEMPLAR 3: QINGDAO KUTESMART –
INTELLIGENT MANUFACTURING**

Kutesmart, founded in 1995 as Redcollar, is an apparel manufacturer based in China's northern province of Shandong. Having started out as a traditional manufacturer, it now focuses on mass customization, made-to-measure (MTM) and customer-to-manufacturer (C2M) production of men's suits. It developed new cutting machines that resulted in threefold efficiency. After smart logistics and automated storage systems were introduced the logistics department needed 80% fewer staff (Zhou et al., 2019). Since Kutesmart's was a make-to-order model, there was less need to carry inventory with the price mark-downs that would come from mismatches between supply and demand.

Its success was thanks to its innovative C2M business model based around new data technologies (Shih and Huadai, 2017). Kutesmart started by adopting networkization technologies such as the Internet to link customers directly with factories. It then digitized its production processes. In time it was the first apparel manufacturer to implement an intelligent manufacturing system. Kutesmart integrates industry and information, using "production process networking and intelligent management to achieve synchronous production of personalized products" (China Daily, 2017). Unlike traditional manufacturing based on mechanization, mass production, or automation, intelligent manufacturing can fulfill individual customer requirements with product variants in a very small batch size, down to one-off items.

Shifting the old company, Redcollar, to the new rebranded bespoke (specialized) Kutesmart model took 13 years and cost many millions of dollars. The made-to-order operations started as a side experiment in Redcollar's factory. Challenges included maintaining existing operations in parallel with the new approach and developing a bespoke order stream.

During this period the company made a number of transformational changes: they invented methods to measure, such that it took only five days for a person to learn how to measure or fit clothes, compared to the traditional three to five years; they reduced batch size from the typical hundreds or thousands to a batch size of one; and developed an automated patterning system that contributed to low subsequent alteration rates and labor costs. In contrast to a mass manufacturing model the production of one suit took 7 days compared to over 1 month (Shih and Huadai, 2017). Staff were traditionally needed to manually develop patterns at the rate of two patterns at most per day; Kutesmart now produced about 3000 customized clothes per day. Standardizing and reducing the production time for each step also made visible the resistance to change within the organization.

Kutesmart's manufacturing begins only after a confirmed customer order is received, rather than based on demand forecast and inventory (Yu et al., 2015). Another component of Kutesmart's success is the ability to connect to its direct sales platform for customers, disrupting the so-called smile curve (proposed in the early 1990s by Stan Shih, the founder of Acer Inc) in which designers, brand owners or retail channels capture most of the value rather than manufacturers (Blair, 2017). Kutesmart is able to reduce prices by eliminating distributors. Customers could either go to one of the company's brick-and-mortar measurement sites or give detailed measurements online. They chose the type of cloth, styles and stitching. This personalized information was then transmitted via the Internet to the customer-to-manufacturer (C2M) data system. In 2015, Kutesmart launched Magic Manufactory, a smartphone app that allowed customers to order tailored clothes directly from the company.

Kutesmart developed a system for measuring a customer's dimensions and design preferences and then translating these measurements into data that could be used to produce a customized clothing pattern. This pattern was then used as the basis for cutting fabric and assembling it into a suit. The patented method, named "coordinate measurement" (Ying et al., 2018), involved creating axes along the vertebra and waist and measuring 19 sites on the body. The company also developed an automatic pattern-making system that incorporated its knowledge of tailoring as well as a database of over 20 million items of human body data that had been accumulated over the years. The database maintained the measurement records of more than two million customers. Its integration with the CAD and computer-aided process planning systems would allow it to generate trillions of patterns in five minutes that would fit 90% of the body types in the world (Su et al., 2019; Lee et al., 2021). "Automatic pattern making is very complex. Other than big data, there are many rules in the algorithm. A single body measurement value will change 9,666 other values, to ensure that the pattern created fits the customer well" (Ying et al., 2018). The pattern making, which originally took two or three days to complete, now takes only seven seconds.

Kutesmart's mass customization process broke down the process of manufacturing suits into over 300 procedures, automatically optimized and assigned to workers based on their availability and skills. With a newly built ERP system Kutesmart was able to collect real-time production data and generate dynamic data profiles (Su et al., 2019). Its intelligent systems not only captured data from the customers' side but also from Kutesmart's employees, thereby matching workers' skills with particular customers' needs. Every order was entered into the computer system and generated an information code that told workers what to do (Lee et al., 2021). Radio-frequency identification (RFID) tags (Bottani et al., 2009) were attached to items containing details of an order, for example, cuff type, the number of buttons and button type, buttonhole thread and personalization information. This information was called up at each workstation. As an operator removed items from the push conveyor, the RFID tag was scanned and work instructions were automatically displayed.

Big data were used to calculate how and when to change threads and needles, and report real-time tracking information. The pieces were also laid out by computer to minimize waste and also ensure that fabric patterns such as plaids matched. Machines can do it faster and more accurately than by hand. The efficiency of their latest cutting machine is seven to eight times that of human labor in a traditional manufacturing process. Internet of Things technologies including hanger, sorting, identification, configuration, materials, scissors, lifting, storage and matching systems were used to develop a vertically and horizontally connected manufacturing system (Pan et al., 2015; Thoben et al., 2017). For example, Kutesmart maintained a very large stock of fabrics on hand and managed them in real time. Its IoT-based system knew precisely how much of a certain type of fabric was available at any time.

As a result of these innovations, production costs were only 10% higher than mass-produced goods, but customization meant that it could charge prices that were a fraction of comparable items, for example, $77 compared to a Dior shirt of the same quality that sold for $616 (Shih and Huadai, 2017). Since 2014 the company has maintained an annual growth rate of over 50% and net profit margin of over 25%, compared to industry norms of less than 10% (Su et al., 2019). It was listed on the A-share Growth Enterprise Market on the Shenzhen Stock Exchange in 2020.

Exemplar 3: Questions for discussion

1) What is innovative about Kutesmart?
2) What are the competences and/or physical assets required to operate Kutesmart's model successfully?
3) Is Kutesmart impregnable? If so, why? If not, what might be needed to challenge its supremacy?

CRITICAL DRIVER 4: SELLING TO CUSTOMERS

Retailing is another area where there has been considerable innovation in the last few years. Digital technologies have become vital aspects of the sales and distribution function: building up trend momentum via social media; using EDI to communicate with suppliers; electronic payments systems; mobile phone apps; purchasing technologies; augmented reality;

big data; and web-based retailing. Many of these overlap with new technologies elsewhere in the supply chain. For example, innovations in manufacturing and logistics in the 1950s onwards enabled the mass supply of goods that could then be sold in large quantities in much larger stores than had existed previously (Doeringer and Crean, 2006); since then just-in-time manufacturing systems have enabled swift responses to market trends.

For all types of physical product companies, but especially fashion, there has been a shift away from physical stores, "bricks-and-mortar" (B&M) retailing to web-based retailing, e-tailing,[3] although there is some evidence of the B&M retailers fighting back towards a degree of convergence (Langley and Rieple, 2021; Bloomberg, 2020). Many traditional retailers have had to implement Internet-based sales in order to compete and many have adopted a hybrid, multichannel or omnichannel, model in which they sell both in store and online, offer online purchase and pick up in store, or offer to take returns that have been bought online.

Although fashion e-tailers have tended to post lower profits than their physical counterparts (4% compared with 8% at traditional "bricks-and-mortar" retailers) (Amed et al., 2018), since 2016 most clothes shopping has been done online (Williams, 2018) a trend that accelerated during the pandemic (see below). Pure e-tailers Boohoo and ASOS reported annual revenue growth in 2018 of 50% and 20% respectively. Similarly, Zalando has become Europe's leading fashion e-tailer, with revenue growth rates of 24% on average 2014–19. Although less common in furniture than fashion, Wayfair has forged a similar path in online furniture retailing (Hammond and Shih, 2019).

The invention and mass adoption of smartphones has put the Internet into the hands of consumers who can now shop anywhere, anytime (Amed et al., 2018). It has also led to a more informed and powerful customer who can research products online and also draw inspiration from social media (Jude, 2016). This makes online purchasing enticing. The process is also enabled by online payment systems, notably credit cards and PayPal, that provide both convenience and security. More recently e-tailers have started to accept new cryptocurrencies such as Bitcoin.

The ability to produce a wide range of products in a short period of time is another consumer-friendly feature of the top fashion e-tailers. California's Fashion Nova, UK's ASOS and Germany's Zalando design, manufacture and market their apparel within one to four weeks compared to Inditex's five weeks and H&M's a few weeks to six months (Şen, 2008). They can outcompete physical stores because of their ability to supply a wider range of goods (the "long tail") without the need to hold tangible stocks in local shops, and can hold stock in low-cost locations (Acimovic and Graves, 2015). The most successful e-tailers typically have >80,000 product lines with 3,000 new ones added every week. ASOS and Zalando have over 3.2 million visits daily and over 13 million active customers.

ASOS and Zalando have also created innovative business models that included building ecosystems with digital partners. This is in order to gain access to the consumers and technologies they need, including cloud providers and social media companies. Both have adopted a "Get Big Fast" strategy. They built dedicated websites, ramped-up browsing speeds and built data centers in every strategic market, for example, the UK, USA, France, Germany, Australia and Russia. Moving to a cloud-based solution (Microsoft Azure data centers) allowed them to scale up quickly. Innovative technologies have allowed them to expand their social media profile rapidly on each of the major platforms, including Instagram and Snapchat (Karimi and Walter, 2015). By interacting with fashion and lifestyle influencers embedded in built-in communities the e-tailers build brand affinity without spending on advertising. Instead, this social media strategy is a blend of influencer marketing and user-generated content (Caniato et al., 2013). The most innovative retailers, in both categories, have developed important capabilities in mining big data in order to understand customer preferences (Frasquet et al., 2018). They know what has been browsed, bought or returned, and the reasons for this.

One of the big risks for online purchasers is that goods cannot be felt, seen in context or tried on. Therefore, online companies have had to put considerable effort into making the returns process easy. This is helped by innovations in support services, with return labels provided and with numerous locations available where goods can be returned. There are some that think that the returns policy has been a victim of its own success and e-tailers are now suffering from opportunistic behavior on the part of customers. ASOS returns are now 40% of sales (Times, 2020), something that is seen to be unsustainable. In late 2021 Boohoo slashed its earnings projections from 25% to 14%, partly because customers were returning more clothes (Hipwell, 2021). Boohoo is known for its party outfits, which have a higher returns rate. Its mostly younger customers buy multiple outfits to try on for an event and then only keep the one they choose to wear, or even return all the items, treating the e-tailer as a rental service, a trend called "wardrobing". In furniture there has been a recent case (perhaps apocryphal) of a customer ordering four three-piece suites, installing them in their home, and then returning the three that were less to their liking. Returns provide a problem for the e-tailers not only in lost sales, but also because the costs of repackaging and moving the goods back to warehouses or shops are high and the process complex.

One way that e-tailers reduce the risks for consumers is to mimic the real experience through designing a virtual experience on the website. VR's functions include product information and recommendations, purchase functions and product display. Technologies that use algorithms to give accurate size recommendations help customers to buy the right items. This is important in minimizing returns. VR can transmit detailed 3D images that show more realistically the aesthetic and functional aspects of products. After Shopify added AR 3D models, conversion rates increased by up to 250% (Silvestri, 2020). As a result the shopping experience is enhanced through improving the user interface and costs are reduced through minimizing returns. It allows clothes to be shown on a virtual avatar of the customer, based on information that they have provided about their size and shape, and furniture can be embedded in a virtual scene (Xue et al., 2020), or interposed in a photograph of the customer's home. However, there are age differences in consumers' attitude to VR and AR. Those aged 18–34 years are more familiar with AR than their elders and have a much greater desire to experience it. In contrast, 40% of participants aged 35–45 reported negative attitudes related to adopting v-commerce. GenZ and millennials regard interactivity, personalization and social networking as critical, and want fun and enjoyment from their experiences as well as convenience.

Although some futurists had predicted that VR would be retail's disruptive technology and despite a rush to adopt the technology, few have yet gained significant user acceptance (Wang, 2016). There is a limited understanding of the optimal experiences for older, more set-in-their-ways consumers, and VR still needs technical improvement (Xue et al., 2020). The VR presentation of the product needs to be a direct substitute for the physical product. Such facilities are beyond contemporary VR's capabilities.

EXEMPLAR 4: ASOS PLC

The British online fashion retailer AsSeenOnScreen (ASOS) was born in 2000. It is one of the leading online fashion retailers, boasting 23 million monthly visitors, 30% annual revenue growth and retail sales in excess of £3 billion per annum (ASOS.com, 2022).

Its founders had noticed that viewers often wanted to buy objects that appeared in films or on television and the company was created to respond to this unmet demand. It initially offered 150 products, primarily fashion items and housewares but commercially available items rather than the specific ones used on screen. ASOS's focus soon turned to fashion and the brands that celebrities such as Madonna and the Spice Girls might have worn. Concentrating on young consumers aged 16–25 years, the company offered over 85,000 items on its website, many times more than the largest fashion stores, and added several thousand new lines every week. They could move more quickly than physical stores, sometimes placing new products online within hours instead of days or weeks. Half of sales were own-label products designed in-house. Others were merchandise sourced from other fashion brands, including big players such as Gap and Mango (Wells and Ellsworth, 2018). Consumers could navigate easily through a wide range of product categories, price points or designers and order for delivery within four working days. Customers

---

Transformational Innovation in Physical Products

who wished to return a product had to ship it back at their own expense within 14 days (a policy that was abandoned in favor of free returns a few years later). In 2017 it introduced a "try-before-you-buy" service. Customers could select a range of items for delivery and return those that they did not want within 30 days.

To support its fast-growing international sales, ASOS tailored its sites for individual countries and opened a logistics center in the USA. It began to establish partnerships with high-street stores to deliver orders and collect returns. By 2018 ASOS sold more than 850 third-party brands and aimed to support small labels. Every season, it turned over 20% of the brands "to keep things fresh". In addition, ASOS sold its own label, which accounted for approximately 41% of sales. Sixty percent of styles sold on ASOS were available nowhere else (Wells and Ellsworth, 2018).

Social networking was a key part of ASOS's strategy, helping its young customers discover the company on blogs, YouTube and Twitter instead of through advertising. ASOS was one of the first retailers to open a shop on Facebook.

It had more than 20 million followers on social media and published more than 60,000 pieces of fashion-oriented content monthly. A group of ASOS "Insiders" provided styling tips to followers around the world by posting photographs of themselves wearing ASOS clothes on Instagram and including the ASOS product codes in the image captions (Wells and Ellsworth, 2018). ASOS analyzed around 30 million Instagram posts that contained #OOTD (Outfit Of The Day) and #Fashion in order to develop new products.

ASOS aims to "continuously innovate" the customer experience (Journée and Weber, 2017), one example being free shipping and returns to all 196 countries. Behind most of these innovations are digital technologies. They include artificial intelligence (AI) and machine learning; blockchain; AR and VR; IoT including smart TVs; Big Data analytics; robotics and automation; custom manufacturing; drone deliveries; and 3D printing (Rietveld and Eggers, 2018; Ott et al., 2017). ASOS was early in recognizing the potential of mobile phones. By

2017, nearly 80% of ASOS's UK traffic and approximately 70% of UK sales came from a mobile device. In 2017 it made 1,300 technology releases compared to 490 in 2016 (Wells and Ellsworth, 2018).

Size and fit are commonly cited as one of the main reasons for customers returning products as there is a lack of standardization across the industry (Sword, 2020). As a way of addressing this ASOS introduced tools that advise users on what size of garment to select, and, based on past purchase, allows them to view clothes on digital models (amido, 2021), taking account of size, cut and fit. This tool was developed with an Israeli augmented reality start-up Zeekit, an example of one of the many innovations developed through acquisitions or alliances with other firms. They have also introduced chatbots that respond to descriptions of specific items and have developed an app that allows customers to upload a picture of someone and search for a similar outfit from ASOS's offerings.

Exemplar 4: Questions for discussion

1. Are there any risks in ASOS' dependence on social media?
2. AI and big data have become critical elements in online retailers' success. What does ASOS need to do to ensure that it is ahead of the game in these respects?
3. What are the critical success factors that underpin ASOS business model?

COVID'S IMPACT ON THE PHYSICAL PRODUCTS INDUSTRIES

The COVID pandemic has provided a massive shock to the fashion industry and other physical products industries more generally. The digital transformation accelerated and "step-changed" (BOF/McKinsey, 2021b) during the pandemic. It has been estimated that up to 73% of the fashion industry lost value as a result of COVID. Although there were signs by mid-2021 that things were taking a turn for the better, particularly in markets where vaccination rates were high (BOF/McKinsey, 2021b), inequalities in performance that had already been developing were accelerated, meaning that it has become more of a "winner takes all" industry (BOF/McKinsey, 2021b).

Lockdowns changed the way we dress: out went business formal wear and trendy items to be replaced by clothes that are functional and comfortable. Sizes have also been disrupted: 40% of American women and 35% of men are a different size from what they were in 2019. In April 2021 clothing sales in the USA dropped by 79%, the greatest decline in history. The sale of sweatpants, on the other hand, grew by 80% (Aleksander, 2020). Whether this persists once lockdowns become a thing of the past is unknown: working from home may or may not become a permanent feature of working lives. Similarly uncertain is whether online sales will continue to increase, or whether the social and experiential aspects of "real" shopping will force a return to bricks-and-mortar shops.

Variations in countries' healthcare systems and economic resilience mean differences in the consumer markets, operating hubs and sourcing regions that underpin physical products industries. The fashion industry is reliant on an intricate web of global supply chains that have seen unprecedented levels of disruption resulting in shortages of materials, transportation bottlenecks and increasing shipping costs. Future road and rail costs are predicted to be similar to the current sea rates but take half the time; it now costs up to six times more to ship a container from China to Europe than it did at the start of 2019, and up to ten times more from China to the USA (Bof/McKinsey, 2021b). There are potential winners in those that can change their supply chains to take advantage of the developing overland routes between East Asia and Western markets – the "New Silk Road", including the new railway connecting Chongqing in China with Duisburg in Germany.

Another potential beneficiary of the pandemic's disruptions is 3D printing. 3D printers are now found all over the world and can be as small as the size of a laser printer. In fashion its technological development has reached the point where advanced materials can be printed, including leather and fur-like materials (Nazir et al., 2021). This so-called fourth industrial revolution has been predicted to decimate jobs in manufacturing across the globe.

The pandemic massively accelerated the move of fashion companies into digital spaces (Mellor, 2021), including the *metaverse*, in which people work, play, socialize and shop. The use of social media to discover and shop for clothes increased over the course of the pandemic as customers who were unable to visit stores spent more time at home scrolling through their feeds, spawning a new generation of digital innovators:

- Ralph Lauren partnered with South Korean social network and avatar simulation app Zepeto to create a virtual fashion collection, giving users the opportunity to dress their avatars in appearance-altering "skins".
- Gucci has created digital assets for gaming platform Roblox, as well as for Pokémon Go and Animal Crossing (BOF/ Mckinsey, 2021b).
- Social media giants like Facebook, Instagram, Snapchat and YouTube are increasingly building in shopping features such as in-app checkout, sales transactions on live streams or steering customers back to their own websites. Nearly half of US TikTok users say they have purchased a product or service after seeing it advertised, promoted or reviewed on the platform (BOF/McKinsey, 2021a).
- Digital/virtual *influencers*, such as Lil Miquela Sousa or Noonoo Uri.

While Western markets are behind China in rates of adoption, social shopping is growing. GenZ consumers are increasingly focusing on video-based enhanced experiences, for which they are prepared to pay. As a result, many fashion companies are partnering with gaming platforms to design virtual fashion assets. The pandemic has more than ever highlighted the importance of artificial intelligence (BOF/McKinsey, 2021a). Although AI was created many decades ago, but despite its advantages AI-based technologies are not widely used; the costs are high and companies have a limited understanding of AI-based systems and how neural networks work (Giri et al., 2019). But the pandemic has acted as a tipping point pushing companies towards its use. One reason for its increasing prevalence is the data which is essential for learning and product development and is now more widely available through the use of online channels.

How to monetize virtual assets is a problem, which is increasingly being solved by Non-Fungible Tokens (NFTs) and other blockchain-based technologies (Nasdaq, 2021). NFTs are "unique crypto assets whose authenticity and ownership are verified on blockchains and are bought, sold and exchanged in the metaverse, often with cryptocurrency" (BOF/McKinsey, 2021a). In 2021 luxury fashion companies began using NFTs, often via online gaming. Louis Vuitton launched a video game with NFT art that could be acquired by players. Burberry created NFTs within the Blankos Block Party game. The limited-edition Burberry Blanko Sharky B NFT can be purchased, upgraded and sold. The collaboration also includes branded in-game NFT accessories, including a jetpack, armbands and pool shoes.

Blockchain also provides the ability to authenticate virtual assets such as designs. Just like in digitizable media industries, blockchain technology has the potential to reshape the way businesses procure, manufacture and sell fashion, although very little is known of how blockchain is currently used in the fashion industry. Such a technology can be used to store and share product information with both consumers and partners. Digital "product passports", based around blockchain and supported by radiofrequency identification (RFID) tags and QR codes, can help protect against counterfeiting, a big problem in the fashion industry, and in identifying stolen goods. This is an increasing problem because online commerce brings increasing risks from cybercrime and data loss. It is also likely to be a bigger problem in the future because of the increased popularity of second-hand (especially luxury) and recycled items. In providing detailed data on materials, product passports facilitate easier sorting of garments for large-scale recycling.

As consumers are shopping online more frequently, providing valuable data in the process, companies face more threats of cyber-attacks and growing risks relating to data handling. A record number of cyber-attacks took place worldwide in 2020. Retail, including fashion, was the fourth most-attacked industry (BOF/McKinsey, 2021c). Cyber risks include:

- The theft of credit and debit card numbers and the personal and payment data of 4.6 million online customers. With the personalization of customer experience increasingly playing a role in online interactions customers are sharing more personal data than ever before.
- The theft of designs and commercially sensitive information that is stored online. The increasing use of cloud computing, AI and machine learning exposes companies to more cyber risks by widening the scope for attack.
- Distributed denial-of-services (DDoS) or ransomware attacks could lead to entire website or app shutdowns.

Hanging over all of this is the question of who owns our personal data, and who has the right to exploit it, and how.

Finally, one of the biggest potential threats to the fashion industry is the sustainability of its practices and raw materials. Climate change has the potential to impact the fashion industry profoundly. Chronic heat stress could make it impossible to work outdoors or in rooms without air conditioning in some places, including critical regions for cotton production such as India. As weather changes, yields of raw materials could fall. And flooding could jeopardize manufacturing sites in places such as Bangladesh and Vietnam. Fashion is still one of the least environmentally sustainable industries, churning out 2.1 billion tons of CO_2 emissions per year, 4% of the global total. Over 70% of these emissions come from production processes, with the remainder from retail, logistics and product preparation such as washing and drying. Although recycling is gaining ground, less than 1% of used products are currently recycled. However, in addition to the recovery of fibers from used clothes, new more sustainable materials are being developed, including:

- Fabric from kelp, a variety of seaweed or oranges
- Biodegradable glitter made from eucalyptus tree extract
- Leather from apple skins, durable enough to make luxury accessories and dyed and tanned without toxic chemicals
- Biodegradable polyester, a form of biodegradable polyester that can be safely deposited in landfills, wastewater treatment plants and the oceans

- Lab-made fabrics, using technology that has finally reached the point where it can re-program the self-assembly of collagen molecules in the lab and build leather-like fabrics

And finally, just to show that nothing is ever simple in the commercial world, one concern is the environmental impact of the blockchain and cryptocurrency technologies that underlie NFTs, which require huge amounts of electricity to validate transactions: Based on the number of Bitcoin transactions that took place over a 12-month period, some have estimated that the energy usage is something like 123 Terawatt Hours (TWh) or 123 billion kWh – equivalent to the annual energy consumption of Norway! (Moneysupermarket.com, 2022).

END-OF-CHAPTER CASE STUDY: FAST FASHION – SUPPLY CHAIN BUSINESS MODEL INNOVATION

Introduction

Perhaps the biggest change to the fashion industry in recent years was the development of a new business model, the so-called fast fashion movement. This refers to the production of low-price fashionable goods that are intended to be discarded and replaced on a regular basis (Bhardwaj and Fairhurst, 2010). Consumers keep clothing items about half as long as they did 15 years ago, and at the most extreme, replace them after just seven or eight wears (Remy et al., 2016). In this section we will focus on the two main pioneers of the fast fashion model, H&M and Zara who over the years have exchanged the top market share position.

When, or where, fast fashion began is debatable (fashionlaw.com, 2021). It is arguable that it started in the 1960s as young people in cities such as London and New York began to demand regular injections of new clothes that showed their fashionable credentials. Benetton also has some claim to be the originator of the model. However, when Zara came to New York at the beginning of 1990, the *New York Times* used the term "fast fashion" to describe the company's mission to only take 15 days for a garment to go from a designer's brain to being sold in the store (Fashionista, 2016). The throw-away ethos, with which fast fashion is now associated, really took off in the 1990s and early 2000s as Zara, along with its main rival for the title of originator of the business model, H&M,

Figure 4.3   Primark store interior. *Source*: SariMe/Shutterstock

and subsequently Primark (Figure 4.3) and others, developed the
ability to design, manufacture and stock their shops with new
designs multiple times a year, and in some cases several times a
month.

Zara developed up to 24 new clothing collections each year;
H&M up to 16 and refreshed them weekly (Remy et al., 2016).
This was a huge contrast to the previous business model where
fashion companies developed products at most four times a year,
typically associated with the year's seasons. Companies that
were not able to keep up with such a punishing schedule lost
ground, leaving the two dominant fast fashion players the forces
that they remain.

It is a profitable model: fast fashion companies have higher
profit margins than their competitors, helped by mark-
down percentages that are typically only 15% compared to
competitors' 30%: Zara's net profit margin of 10–14% "has been
the envy of mass-market rivals" (Lee, 2019). And the fast fashion
industry grew by more than 21% compared to the fashion
industry as a whole (Statista, 2021a). In 2020 Industria de Diseño
Textil, S.A. (Inditex, Zara's parent company) was the biggest
fashion manufacturer/retailer in the world (second only to
specialist sportswear company Nike) with sales of 20.9 billion

euros. Zara contributes approximately 63% to Inditex's top-line. H&M's sales were 20.2 billion euros.

The Components of Fast Fashion

Fast fashion has only come about because its proponents succeeded in designing and making clothing in a much shorter time than previously and at a much lower cost (Das, 2018; Crofton and Dopico, 2007; Cline, 2012). A number of related innovations were critical in achieving this. Logistics technologies enable goods to be manufactured using inexpensive labor located in low-cost regions of the world and then transported thousands of miles to where they are to be sold.

Cost minimization at every stage of the production and distribution process was fundamental to the achievement of this low-price strategy. H&M and Zara achieved these low costs in different ways. Although Zara is a global company, for much of its existence it has been heavily centralized. It is headquartered in A Coruña, a port in Galicia, one of the less well-off regions of northern Spain. The first Zara store opened in 1975 in the center of the town and its factories were based in the neighboring town of Arteixo.

Complex capital-intensive operations such as computer-guided fabric cutting were undertaken entirely in-house, while labor-intensive operations like sewing were subcontracted to a network of local seamstresses. Zara was usually their sole client, and they worked without any written contracts. This "proximity sourcing" was a deliberate move to achieve superior market responsiveness. Zara also procured more than 50% of its un-dyed fabric from its 100%-owned subsidiary Comditel. The un-dyed fabric allowed Zara to be flexible in terms of color trends. However, not all of Zara's clothing was high fashion, and it sourced some basics such as T-shirts and woollens from lower-cost countries in Asia. It also near-shored moderately fashionable items to nearby countries like Morocco or Turkey, where deliveries were faster, but costs lower than in Spain.

Unlike Zara, H&M from the start chose not to own any factories but sourced its garments from independent suppliers, the vast majority located in Asia. It depended heavily on a state-of-the-art IT network to connect the stores, the production offices and manufacturers. Since they didn't own factories or secure the fabrics in advance, they had to reduce lead times through flexibility and responsiveness in the buying process. Making clothes in Asia allowed H&M to maintain lower prices than its competitors. Finished items were all shipped to distribution centers close to the eventual customer for swift transfer to the stores.

Innovation in the Design Process

Contrary to the previous push-based model of the apparel industry based on forecasting, fast fashion used a "pull" system in which new designs were picked up from catwalks, fashion hotspots or by understanding sales and customer feedback from stores. Fast fashion was based on a strategy of planned obsolescence that involved constantly refreshing collections. Design agility was needed to quickly create near-identical designs, while minimizing copyright penalties. All fashion designers draw inspiration from the world around them and from their competitors; as suggested earlier, copying, or imitating, is endemic in the fashion industry as a whole and is arguably fundamental to the success of both the imitators and the imitated: fast fashion companies have often been accused of crossing the line between being inspired by a design and copying the item. But it is essential to being part of the "zeitgeist". As an example, after Madonna's first concert of her tour in Spain, her outfit was imitated by Zara designers and by the time she performed her last concert some of the audience were wearing near-identical outfits (Kumar and Linguri, 2006).

New Fibers such as Nylon, Polyester and Acrylic

One of the most famous new fibers, nylon, was invented and developed by DuPont, an American chemicals multinational, at their research facility. It was the first man-made fiber developed entirely in a laboratory. The first pair of experimental nylon stockings was then made by the Union Hosiery Company for DuPont in 1937. Nylon was touted as having the strength of steel and the sheerness of cobwebs; the silk that it replaced was prone to snag and run. Its flexible properties mean that it became one of the most dominant materials in both furniture and apparel. Apart from their inherently lower costs, plastic-based fabrics can be used more flexibly than traditional materials like wool or cotton. They can be made into a wide variety of fabrics and styles, important in imitating higher-quality designs quickly. They are also less expensive to manufacture because of their adaptable fibers, fabric sizing and patterns, meaning that there is less wastage and redundancy. They were therefore important in enabling the fast fashion business model to emerge.

Innovations in new fibers and materials typically come from other industries, or in research institutes or universities, without any immediate evidence of how they may be used elsewhere. Polyester, spandex, lycra and Teflon, for example, were developed in other industries. This means that fashion companies who think they may be able to use these new materials need to build good relationships with organizations with very different cultures and ways of working. This process is likely to involve considerable investment, both in money and time, in research and development.

Manufacturing, Logistics and Supply Systems

As discussed earlier, there have been many innovations in both the manufacturing process and the ways that goods are transported to the factory and then to the retailer. All of them were essential to the low-price, swift replenishment aspects of the fast fashion model. Just-in-time methods were fundamental to the ability to source materials and manufacture items on a demand basis. A whole system of new technologies underpinned this, from Radio-Frequency Identification (RFID) tags that collected inventory data which could then be shared with suppliers, through EPOS (Electronic Point of Sale) technologies that measured sales and (just as importantly) returns, to centralized manufacturing execution systems via cloud computing (Shao et al., 2021), new technologies are everywhere. Once the finished items have left the factory, robotic fulfillment solutions and automatic storage and retrieval systems (ASRS) in distribution centers and logistics innovations such as containerization and innovative transportation methods (also see the IKEA case below) allowed the swift and accurate transfer of items to the stores, reducing wastage and improving the accuracy of deliveries, all of which reduced costs.

Store Design

Fast fashion companies own their own stores which were critical to remaining visible and enticing customers. Displays were changed regularly, and store layout, shop-fittings and visual merchandizing used new psychological theories to persuade customers to buy items (Ettis, 2017; Khan, 2018). Store locations were generally on busy, prestigious, city center shopping streets with the highest footfall. Stores rarely restocked even popular items in an attempt to lure consumers back for "fresh" products. Customers were tempted to buy them immediately in case they were not there the next time they visited the shop, a practice known as manufactured scarcity (Chu, 2005) or "see now, buy now" (Das, 2018; Petro, 2018).

Manufacturing items in short runs also prevented the accumulation of inventories (Cachon, 2020). In some cases, stores ran out of stock; however, this was not viewed as a negative as consumers were then encouraged to buy often and find something new every time they went into the shop. As Zara's founder Amancio Ortega said "We want our customers to understand that if they like something, they must buy it now, because it won't be in the shops the following week. It is all about creating a climate of scarcity" (Kumar and Linguri, 2006). The limited production runs also ensured that customers knew that their garment was unlike many others. As a result consumers bought many more items than they would have done previously.

The Future of Fast Fashion

However, the fast fashion business model is arguably under threat. Although the trends are maybe not as clear as some have predicted, there are indications that the appetite for disposable fashion is coming to an end and that consumers are choosing to buy fewer, higher-quality clothes that are longer lasting (Amed et al., 2018). Smartphone apps allow the resale or renting of clothes, allowing the more sustainable reuse of clothes while allowing the fashion-conscious consumer to update their wardrobe regularly. The increasing focus on sustainability suggests that goods that are made from plastic and end up in landfill may become less desirable; many fast fashion items are hard to recycle and wastage from throw-away items is estimated to be contributing more to climate change than sea and air travel combined (Russell, 2019; Smith, 2018). In addition, the fast fashion production processes create environmental and social impacts, such as the pesticides used in farming cotton, fossil fuels that are used to make synthetic materials and unhealthy conditions for workers in sweatshops. Untraceable subcontracting led to PR disasters like Dhaka's Rana Plaza garment factory which collapsed killing 1,134 and injuring many more, affecting the brand image of the companies whose clothes were being made there (Kavthankar and Perepu, 2017).

Due to automation, manufacturing is no longer such a labor-intensive activity, and production costs have gone down. In the process, the advantage H&M had in terms of offshoring became less significant, "warp-speed, low-priced clothing is now ubiquitous and sales have moved online. H&M, the founder of fast fashion, is now too slow" (Cline, 2018). Similarly, Zara's vertical integration appears to be less important now that the bulk of Zara's sales are from around the globe (Kumar and Linguri, 2006). And the advantage that H&M and Zara had in their skilled trend spotters and designers was being replaced by innovations in predictive analytics and AI software.

In addition the historical fast fashion market leaders are being outcompeted by companies who can match, or even beat, their product turnaround times with much less need to hold local inventory (Gustashaw, 2017; Danziger, 2021). Many of these companies sell their goods almost exclusively online or who have, more successfully than either Zara or H&M, converted their operations to sell online. Although H&M started selling online in 1998, it did not invest as much as some competitors in moving to online shopping (Martin, 2018). Online visits to H&M's website grew by only 22% between 2014 and 2017, while Zara increased by 71% and Uniqlo by 470% (Kumar and Perepu, 2020). Online stores such as PrettyLittleThing, Boohoo and ASOS are now ahead of H&M in terms of price and speed, and Shein, a Chinese company that sells its goods online and mainly in the West, has become the largest fast fashion retailer in the USA (Earnest Research, 2021; BOF/ McKinsey, 2022). Between January and June 2021 the fast fashion market in the USA grew 15% and Shein by nearly 160%, compared to H&M (20%) and Zara (11%).

Shein's dominance points to the continuing rise of digital and the company's *mobile-first* strategy. Its founder Xu Yangtian had no tailoring experience when he founded Shein in 2008. Instead, he was a specialist in search engine optimization. This expertise gave him an understanding of how to draw shoppers' attention in the digital world combining social media with online shopping and a revolutionary approach to manufacturing. Where Zara launches about 10,000 new products a year, Shein produces 6,000 fresh "stock-keeping units" every day. Although some are quickly discontinued, its permanent virtual wardrobe numbers 600,000 individual items. Shein has achieved this through combining the fashion supply chain with on-demand manufacturing technologies originating in massive Chinese companies such as Alibaba. Algorithms are used to identify trends, and thousands of websites are trawled for inspiration. Designs are then manufactured in batches as small as 100 items. With all sales coming through its app, managers have a real-time view of the performance of each item, and manufacturing is either ramped up or abandoned (Economist, 2021).

End-of-chapter case questions for discussion

1) What innovations might threaten the dominance of fast fashion companies?
2) Is the management of alliances more or less important for fast fashion companies compared to "slow" fashion companies?
3) Would there be any advantages to the fast fashion companies integrating their manufacturing aspects within their own organization?

SUPPLEMENTARY CASE STUDY: IKEA – BUSINESS MODEL INNOVATION IN FURNITURE AND FURNISHINGS

Introduction

The founder of the world's largest furniture manufacturer/ retailer IKEA, Ingvar Kamprad (1926–2018), began his entrepreneurial career at age five, when he bought matches in bulk and sold them individually to neighbors for a profit.

He remembered the "lovely feeling" of making money on his purchase. As he got older, he branched out, selling Christmas cards, fish he had caught, and berries he picked. "From that time, selling things became something of an obsession: the desire to earn money, the surprise that you could buy anything so cheaply and sell it for a little more" (Huy et al., 2011). As he left home at the age of 17 for the School of Commerce in Göteborg, he announced he was going to form a trading firm and IKEA was born. IKEA was an acronym of his initials, his family farm Elmtaryd, and county, Agunnaryd, in Småland, southern Sweden. Its brand colors, blue and yellow, derive from the flag of Sweden.

Within the next few years, IKEA developed into a mail-order business selling a variety of consumer products, including home furniture made by subcontractors. This soon became the primary focus of the company. In 1955 it began to design its own furniture, in 1956 it introduced self-assembled furniture sold in flat packs.

Since then IKEA has expanded both in terms of product scope and international presence (Figure 4.4).

It is now the largest furniture company in the world, and one of the top three retailers, with 422 stores and a presence in all the major markets (Forbes, 2021). Its product range includes furniture, lighting, rugs, textiles, utensils, kitchens and

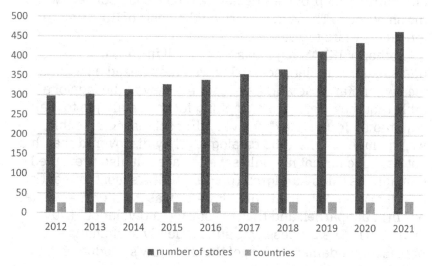

Figure 4.4   Number of IKEA stores and countries worldwide from 2012 to 2021.

bathrooms, glassware and just about any other item that can be found in the typical home. It has been estimated that one in ten babies in Europe was conceived in an IKEA bed. In the UK, almost 10% of furniture spent was on IKEA goods. By the time he died in 2018, Kamprad was one of the richest men in the world, with an estimated net worth of $58.7 billion (Bloomberg, 2018).

The Big Idea

When IKEA was founded, furniture was seen as an expensive long-term investment. However, this left young people just starting to move into their own homes without much choice. Kamprad had a simple vision: "To offer a wide range of well-designed, functional home furnishing products at prices so low that as many people as possible will be able to afford them" (IKEA, 1976). IKEA furniture was expected to last for a few years, then be replaced as the consumer bought new furniture to go with a new house or to fit the needs of a growing family. By creating repeat business for furniture, IKEA built the foundations of its future growth.

Its first store was an old joinery bought for a song, that Kamprad converted into a "showroom". This novelty allowed visitors to walk around and compare items and was an instant success. Over the next few years thousands of people from all over Sweden would visit the "furniture showroom". The coffee and buns that it provided became a coffee shop concept within the showroom. These ideas formed the basis of IKEA's store format for years to come.

Another of IKEA's big ideas was to sell furniture un-assembled in flat packs. This was recognized as a good idea when Kamprad and a colleague removed the legs of a table that they were photographing for the catalogue to make it fit into their car. "Max", the very first self-assembly table, was included in the 1953 catalogue. They discovered that this flat-package format not only saved space but also prevented damage. As Gillis Lundgren (probably IKEA's most influential designer) said "Then one fine day – or was it a night? – we had our first flat parcel, and thus we started a revolution" (Huy et al., 2011). The process was subsequently systematized and became a fundamental part of the company's product design and distribution strategy.

In 1958 the company opened its first store in Småland selling home furnishings. At a size of over 60,000 square feet, it was at the time the largest furniture outlet in the world. The store was an instant success, bringing in 70 million kronor in revenue in its first year. The rush on opening day was apparently so great that a store manager allowed customers into the warehouse to pick up the products themselves. IKEA capitalized on this idea and future stores included a self-service area where customers would pick up their purchases. A parallel initiative included tags on the furniture in the showroom which gave detailed information about the product but also where the item could be located in the pickup area. The customers then assembled the items at home, using basic DIY skills.[4] Both the customer and IKEA won with this arrangement: IKEA reduced costs in manufacturing, transportation and storage, which were passed through to customers in the form of lower prices.

Other subsequent initiatives were related to store design, for example, a supervised children's play area and a self-service restaurant, to accommodate family visits, but also to steer customers through areas where they might be inspired to buy the products displayed there. The intention always was to make customers feel at home and emotionally comfortable (Tantanatewin and Inkarojrit, 2016).

These initiatives have remained an integral aspect of the company's product, store and logistics design to this day. They have underpinned IKEA's growth by transforming the furniture market into one where its operating model appears to hold all of the advantages (Rose, 2015), and yet, even to this day, it has almost no comparable competitors despite a business model that seems from the outside easy to copy.

Culture and Organization

IKEA's culture is rooted in the values of its founder and its origins in Småland, historically one of Sweden's poorest districts, of thrift, frugality and a strong work ethic. Kamprad described it as "the art of managing on small means ... cost-consciousness to the point of being stingy; humbleness, undying enthusiasm and the wonderful sense of community through thick and thin" (IKEA, 1976). The obsessiveness about costs allowed them to charge low prices, typically 25–50% less than competitors' similar products. For many years, despite his wealth, Kamprad preferred to live a simple life, driving an old Volvo and living modestly in a house in Switzerland furnished with IKEA furniture.

IKEA's culture appears to have been a curious mixture of obsessive attention to detail, informality and creativity. Kamprad's extraordinary attention to detail was legendary. In a group of 600 items, he would ask about a particular product, know its price, its cost and its source, and expected others to know it too. He did not seem to believe in delegation, bypassing formal structures to talk directly with front-line managers, especially designers and those in the purchasing group. Doing the rounds of a new store, Kamprad is said to have made points that covered 19 pages of notes – from the store's design to the size of the price tags and the placement of posters (Bartlett and Nanda, 1996). IKEA's motto, "Retail is detail" (IKEA, 2018), was another indicator of expected behavior.

Paradoxically perhaps, informality and lack of hierarchy were the order of the day in the company. Once a year the company celebrated Anti-Bureaucracy Week, in which all executives and managers spent at least a week working in stores and warehouses, and generally got a feel for the retail experience (IKEA, 2018). Except for senior executives, no titles were used, and everyone called each other by their first name and used familiar forms of address ("du" in German rather than "sie", and "tu" rather than "vous" in French). Everyone was a "co-worker", whether they worked in a store or in the corporate HQ. Everyone ate at the stores' public cafeterias. And casual dress was the norm, although this had not always been the case. Until the late 1960s, Kamprad wore smart suits and drove a Porsche. He was rather formal in manner and colleagues thought him rather restrained and introverted. This all changed in the early 1970s, and in came casual clothes, an ordinary car and greater interaction with co-workers. Although this coincided with the sweeping changes taking place in society, it was also suggested that the transformation may have been a conscious decision of a leader who wished to embody IKEA's values of thrift and tight control on spending.

IKEA's management structure was flat, with only four layers separating the CEO from the warehouse clerk or shop assistant.

This was partly to get away from status and convention. But a senior executive had another view: "This environment actually puts pressure on management to perform. There is no security available behind status or closed doors" (Bartlett and Nanda, 1996).

One of the ways that pressure was put on his colleagues was to search for creative solutions to problems. Kamprad himself was revered as a visionary. "He consistently turned problems into opportunities and showed us how it is not dangerous to be different" (Bartlett and Nanda, 1996). Kamprad had written "Only while sleeping one makes no mistakes. The fear of making mistakes is the root of bureaucracy and the enemy of all evolution". Thus initiative and experimentation were strongly encouraged. IKEA was described as an empowered organization, with its staff an integral part of the innovation process. By substituting a general strategic direction instead of formal goals store managers were given the freedom to set their own path. Instructions from headquarters were replaced with general guidelines on how to recognize opportunities. Young corporate entrepreneurs would buy land, build and set up a store, and quickly move on to the next one. The pace was said to be breathtaking, with "unbelievable confidence in its people". This experience created IKEA's future leaders.

By 1973 IKEA had 1,000 employees and an international presence and Kamprad had become concerned that the company's culture and values might be lost. In 1976, he set out his philosophy in a book that every recruit received titled "Testament of a Furniture Dealer" (IKEA, 2018). This became an important tool for disseminating IKEA's culture throughout the organization. Examples from this work include:

- To create a better everyday life for many people by offering a wide range of well-designed, functional home furnishing products at prices so low that as many people as possible will be able to afford them.
- We have great ambitions. We know that we can be a beneficial influence on practically all markets. We know that in the future we will be able to make a valuable contribution to the process of democratization outside our own homeland too.

- The main emphasis must always be on our basic range – on the part that is "typically IKEA". Our basic range must have its own profile. It must reflect our way of thinking by being as simple and straightforward as we are ourselves. It must be hard-wearing and easy to live with. It must reflect an easier, more natural and unconstrained way of life. It must express form, and be colorful and cheerful, with a youthful accent that appeals to the young at heart of all ages.
- "Throw-away" products are not IKEA. Whatever the consumer purchases shall give long-term enjoyment. That is why our products must be functional and well-made. But quality must never be an end in itself: it must be adjusted to the consumer's needs.
- The true IKEA spirit is still built on our enthusiasm, from our constant striving for renewal, from our cost-consciousness, from our readiness to take responsibility and help out, from our humbleness in approaching our task and from the simplicity of our way of doing things.
- Profit is a wonderful word! Let us start by stripping the word profit of its dramatic overtones ... Profit gives us resources. Let us be self-reliant in the matter of building up financial resources.
- You know what it takes to do that: we must offer the lowest prices, and we must combine them with good quality. If we charge too much, we will not be able to offer the lowest prices. If we charge too little, we will not be able to build up resources. A wonderful problem! It forces us to develop products more economically, to purchase more efficiently and to be constantly stubborn in cost savings of all kinds. That is our secret. That is the foundation of our success.
- Wasting resources is a mortal sin at IKEA. It is not all that difficult to reach set targets if you do not have to count the cost ... Expensive solutions to any kind of problem are usually the work of mediocrity.
- Daring to be different is one of the most important criteria behind the IKEA success. It's the thinking behind some of the most significant aspects of our business idea. Here are some examples: while other furniture retailers were selling manufacturers' designs, we started to make our own designs. While furniture dealers set up shop in the center

of town, IKEA was building large stores out of town. While others turned to furniture factories to help them make tables, IKEA got them made by door manufacturers. Whereas others sell their furniture assembled, IKEA lets customers assemble it themselves

- The fear of making mistakes is the root of bureaucracy and the enemy of development … We must allow people to get things wrong now and again. We have to encourage initiative and dynamism, give young co-workers responsibility and constantly remind people that missed opportunities result in indirect expenses which may sometimes be a good deal higher than those incurred directly. But … The right to make mistakes does not give you the right to do a bad job.

Co-workers were also invited to the headquarters in Sweden for training and to absorb the company's cultural values, and IKEA "ambassadors" were placed in key positions to act as role models and spread the cultural message. Although earlier days had seen experimentation and new store layouts, eventually the design became set in stone: store managers wishing to alter any part of the "concept" would have to ask permission.

Product Design

At the heart of IKEA's success are its products. Ingvar Kamprad called it "our identity" and set up clear and detailed guidelines on profile, quality and price. While leaving flexibility for fringe products, he decreed that IKEA's essential products for the home should be simple, durable, and well designed, and priced to be accessible to young people and low- and middle-income earners who wanted stylish design at low cost.

The stores carried over 20,000 products, of which 12,000 were core items that were sold in all stores. IKEA almost never sold others' products but designed and made its own. Decisions on the entire IKEA product range were made in Älmhult, the spiritual heart of the company. Design was done in teams, including a product developer, an engineer and a designer. IKEA had a group of about 20 in-house designers and 100 to 200 freelancers. At times, the company worked with famous designers, but more as an opportunity to learn than as a marketing tool.

Apart from continuous improvements to existing products, IKEA launched about 2,000 to 2,500 new products every year – and withdrew about the same number. IKEA's obsession with costs permeated its design. "Any designer can design a desk that will cost 5,000 kronor. But only the most highly skilled can design a good, functional desk that will cost 100 kronor" (IKEA, 2018). The need to engineer costs out of the design meant that product development was a slow process, sometimes taking three to five years. Every product design started with a target price, split by price points from the low-cost, through low, medium and high price. This enabled the design team to look for gaps based on price and style.

In recent years IKEA has been a big user of the novel 3D printing technology to build its prototypes. 3D printing tends to be less expensive than traditional manufacturing methods, being both more flexible and less wasteful of raw materials. In designing for cost, the company was also obsessed with packaging, often redesigning products just to reduce the size of its packaging, reducing the cost of transportation in the process. Such cost reductions often led to big increases in sales. The concept of self-service flat-pack furniture was unique when introduced by IKEA. It has effectively "disintermediated" the assembly stage from its supply chain. Instead, it outsources this stage (and the associated costs) to the customer. Some have even suggested that IKEA's customers liked having to make up their furniture – even when the end result was rather wobbly. But to help deal with the long-held belief that IKEA furniture is impossible to assemble easily, there are now robots that can do the job for customers (Burdick, 2018).

IKEA also looks for technologies and components that can reduce costs, improve quality or allow new designs. They pioneered the use of pine rather than oak and undertook numerous projects to improve coatings in conjunction with its suppliers. The basis of IKEA furniture is particle board, which also allowed IKEA to minimize the package dimensions of its furniture.

Store Design

Rather than conform to the service-intensive sales processes that were typical, IKEA applied self-service and cash-and-carry concepts to furniture retailing. In the early 1960s a new store was built on the outskirts of Stockholm in the newly built suburb of Kungens Kurva, with a floor space of 31,000 square meters, the largest in Europe at the time. Traditional furniture shops were small and mainly located on the high street, but this store was built on cheaper land outside the city, easy to reach by car and with plentiful parking. Car ownership was rising and customers could take their purchases home themselves. Closing at 7 pm meant that customers could shop after they finished work for the day. Kamprad's intention was to "create a unique ambience that makes IKEA not just a furniture store, but a family outing destination that can compete with the entertainment park and the zoo for family time" (Bartlett and Nanda, 1996).

This new store opened to queues of 18,000 people. Chaos resulted. There were too few checkouts and too few staff. Processing the traditional handwritten orders took a long time, as did fetching goods from the stockroom. Because of the lines at checkouts some customers took their goods and left. Having chased a customer into the car park to collect payment, the store manager decided to open the stockroom so customers could collect their own goods. This spontaneous initiative, rather than conscious planning, launched IKEA's self-service model. The Kungens Kurva was destroyed by fire in 1970 and replaced by the largest IKEA store at 55,200 square meters. Ideas that had emerged over the previous years were put into the store's new design, becoming recognizably what is still the IKEA model. Although in the early days IKEA store managers were encouraged to experiment with new ideas, this had led to a certain amount of wheel reinvention and variability so that as IKEA matured the spirit of experimentation was foregone in favor of a more standardized approach, the "IKEA Concept". This involved the development of standard store designs. In every store there were five or six areas called studios which displayed the best-selling products and defined the traffic flow (Ettis, 2017; Khan, 2018) that took customers through the store in a four-leafed clover pattern to maximize their exposure to the products (Figure 4.5).

Wherever IKEA opened a store, imitators sprung up. In 1987 a California-based retailer called Stör began copying IKEA's format: ready-to-assemble furnishings, product designs,

Figure 4.5   IKEA's store layout. *Source:* ZikG/Shutterstock

and store features such as a ball-filled children's play area. IKEA filed a lawsuit against the company, claiming copyright infringement of the store layout and advertising. Stör was forced to change. It was acquired by IKEA in 1992. No other competitor has been able to match IKEA's cost and quality standards.

After leaving its retail format almost unchanged for more than 40 years, in 2015 IKEA moved in a limited way into online services and launched "click-and-collect" stores. These did not have a standard format and were typically about 5–10% of the size of a traditional store. The stores had a limited range of products on display for immediate pickup but mostly acted as a point to collect products that were ordered online. Many had a restaurant. Some of the click-and-collect stores would charge a collection fee, with different rates from store to store. In the UK, for example, fees ranged from about £5 for a small item to almost £20 for a large order. Home delivery would cost up to twice as much. By 2016, IKEA had opened 22 click-and-collect stores in 11 countries (one exception being the USA).

Supply Chain Management

Below IKEA's quirky surface lies a company that is highly effective at aligning its various operations. IKEA's growth has been achieved through an integrated model of a strong concept and product positioning, in-house design and supply chain management. However, its start was not as easy as it could have been. When IKEA started to exhibit at the local trade fairs, anonymous letters and articles started to appear in the press, criticizing IKEA for selling imitations and undercutting prices. In 1950, Kamprad and IKEA were both banned from attending trade fairs. Kamprad fought back, using a range of tactics to circumvent the ban. Competitors also tried to stop manufacturers from selling to IKEA. Kamprad later described spending "many tear-filled nights" coming up with new solutions. An observer commented: "This hurt him tremendously and probably made him eager for revenge" (Huy et al., 2018).

Throughout the 1950s the boycotts and sanctions continued. Kamprad responded by buying from a few loyal independent Swedish furniture makers and then looked further afield. Kamprad flew to Poland (at that time a Communist country and part of the Soviet Union) and secured suppliers to produce the chairs. The prices were very low; often less than 50% of a Swedish comparator. Polish manufacturing soon accounted for more than 50% of IKEA's products. This was an early example of IKEA's willingness to work with its suppliers to improve standards. The Polish production lines were outdated, inefficient and sometimes dangerous. In contrast to the then practices in Germany and Britain to buy in small quantities and pay a sizable premium for expedited delivery, IKEA set up high-volume fixed contracts with its suppliers. It would order goods that weren't immediately needed and keep them in stock in large warehouses. And when the Berlin Wall fell and the worth of the Polish zloty collapsed, he saved his manufacturers from default by paying them higher prices than their contracts stipulated (Van den Steen and Galor, 2016).

In order to fulfill its low-price business model, IKEA has had to create a supply chain that could undercut competitors while maintaining quality (Lutz, 2015). IKEA of Sweden is the Älmhult-based business unit that has overall responsibility for the development, purchase, manufacturing, distribution and marketing of each product. It electronically monitors sales and shipping patterns worldwide. Its influence extends to raw materials suppliers. The vast majority of IKEA's products are made by outside suppliers: IKEA currently has about 1600 in over 70 countries (IKEA, 2022). Usually IKEA was their main customer. IKEA has established many joint ventures with companies to tackle specific product and technical development issues. Some can involve up to 20 firms. It also allies with companies in supposedly difficult countries in order to access low-price sources. They also sought out non-traditional suppliers that had surplus capacity. This was a unique operating model, challenging suppliers to produce goods they had little experience of. For example, IKEA contracted with a ski manufacturer to produce tables and a shirt factory to supply it with cushions. There is now a greater use of Chinese suppliers, not simply because of lower production costs, but also because of their increasing technical capabilities.

IKEA also introduced an innovative unit load carrier that allowed it to transport different unit load dimensions and address different market needs. This allowed it to increase space utilization in its transporters by more than 40% (Hellström and Nilsson, 2011).

Finances and Performance

Furniture retailing remains highly fragmented worldwide, with small manufacturers and distributors catering to the demands of their local markets. However, it is a huge market (Figure 4.6).

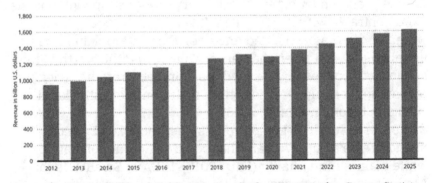

Figure 4.6   Revenue of the global furniture market by country in $m. *Source*: Statista (2022)

Transformational Innovation in Physical Products

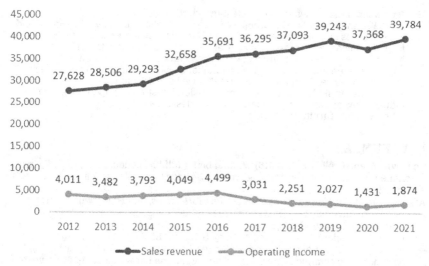

Figure 4.7   INGKA Group (IKEA) financial performance 2012–2021 €m. *Source*: IKEA annual reports 2012–2021

As of 2021, IKEA is not only the largest furniture retailer brand in the world with huge profits (Figure 4.7), but it is also among the leading retail brands globally, valued at nearly 18 billion euros in 2021 (Statista, 2021c). It is a privately owned company that has a complex corporate structure of trusts that protects the company from potential takeovers and succession issues. The structure also has the benefit of reducing the taxes that IKEA pays in each country it is in.

In 2020, there were more than 800 million customer visits to IKEA's stores, and nearly four billion visits to the company's online webpage (Statista, 2021b).

Supplementary case study questions for discussion

1) What innovations might change the furnishing industry?
2) What aspects of IKEA's culture contribute to its innovativeness?
3) What is the future of IKEA without Ingvar Kamprad?

NOTES

1   See Haberberg and Rieple (12, section 3.3) for a discussion on how to define an industry
2   Apparel covers a multitude of types of clothing, jewelry and footwear. Not all of this is fashionable–functional workwear such as dungarees or overalls, for example. However, most of the issues that we discuss in this book refer to items that have a high IP content, and for this reason we use the shortcut "fashion" in this chapter to refer to the apparel industry.

3   A number of the biggest and/or fastest-growing retailers and e-tailers (e.g., Amazon
.com, VIP shop, and The Hut Group) sell clothes but also sell many other goods and
in most cases do not manufacture their own goods. Similarly, some of the largest
fashion companies by market capitalization (e.g., Louis Vuitton, Gucci or Chanel)
have fewer sales than the largest fashion companies by revenue. Some of the
biggest e-tailers focus specifically on functional sportswear and have fewer less
cultural influences than the companies that we have selected.
4   Sometimes the skills needed were not as basic as customers hoped. An entire
industry has arisen over the years that provides assembly services for IKEA (and
other flatpack) furniture.

REFERENCES

Acimovic, J., and Graves, S. C. (2015). Making better fulfillment decisions on the fly in an
online retail environment. *Manufacturing & Service Operations Management sustain*,
17(1), 34–51.

Aleksander, I. (2020). Sweatpants forever. *New York Times*, August 6. Available from:
https://www.nytimes.com/interactive/2020/08/06/magazine/fashion-sweatpants
.html. Accessed May 12, 2021.

Amed, A., Balchandani, M., Beltrami, A., Berg, S. H., and Rölkens, F. (2018). The state of
fashion 2019: A year of awakening. McKinsey & Company. Available from: https://
www.mckinsey.com/industries/retail/our-insights/the-stateof-fashion-2019-a-year-of
-awakening. Accessed February 12, 2020.

Amido (2021). ASOS. Available from: https://www.amido.com/case-studies/asos.
Accessed March 5, 2022.

ASOS.com (2022). Trading statement. Available from: https://www.asosplc.com/news/
trading-statement-four-months-ended-31-december-2021/. Accessed March 5, 2022.

Bain, M. (2017). Amazon has patented an automated on-demand clothing factory. *Quartz*,
April 19, 2017. Available from: https://qz.com/963381/amazon-amzn-has-patented-an
-automated-on-demand-clothing-factory/. Accessed November 29, 2021.

Bartlett, C A and Nanda, A (1996). *Ingvar Kamprad and IKEA*. Harvard Business School
Case Study.

Berg, A., Hedrich, S., Lange, T., Magnus, K. H., and Mathews, B. (2017). The apparel
sourcing caravan's next stop: Digitization: McKinsey Apparel CPO Survey 2017.
Available from: https://www.mckinsey.com/~/media/mckinsey/industries/retail
/our%20insights/digitization%20the%20next%20stop%20for%20the%20apparel
%20sourcing%20caravan/the-next-stop-for-the-apparel-sourcing-caravan
-digitization.pdf. Accessed November 19, 2021.

Bhardwaj, V., and Fairhurst, A. (2010). Fast fashion: Response to changes in the fashion
industry. *The International Review of Retail, Distribution and Consumer Research*,
20(1), 165–173.

Billesbach, T. J. (1994). Applying lean production principles to a process facility.
Production and Inventory Management Journal, 35(3), 40.

Blair, D (2017). Kutesmart sews up tech-based biz model in traditional industry. *China
Daily*, June 19.

Bloomberg (2018). i Ingvar Kamprad Ikea's Swedish billionaire founder has died.
Available from: https://www.bloombergquint.com/business/ingvar-kamprad-ikea-s
-swedish-billionaire-founder-has-died. Accessed August 27, 2021.

Bloomberg (2020). Firm and industry performance database (proprietary). Accessed
February 13, 2021.

BOF/McKinsey (2021a). The year ahead: Building brands with a metaverse state of mind.
December 6. Available from: https://www.businessoffashion.com/articles/technology
/the-state-of-fashion-2022-bof-mckinsey-metaverse-virtual-nft-gaming/. Accessed
January 31, 2022.

BOF/McKinsey (2021b). The state of fashion 2021. Available from: https://www.mckinsey
.com/~/media/mckinsey/industries/retail/our%20insights/state%20of%20fashion
/2021/the-state-of-fashion-2021-vf.pdf. Accessed November 18, 2021.

BOF/McKinsey (2021c). The state of fashion 2022. Available from https://www.mckinsey
.com/~/media/mckinsey/industries/retail/our%20insights/state%20of%20fashion
/2022/the-state-of-fashion-2022.pdf. Accessed January 4, 2022.

Bottani, E., Ferretti, G., Montanari, R., and Rizzi, A. (2009). The impact of RFID technology on logistics processes of the fashion industry supply chain. *International Journal of RF Technologies: Research and Applications*, 1(4), 225–252.

Burdick, A. (2018). The marriage-saving robot that can assemble IKEA furniture, sort of. *The New Yorker*. Available from: https://www.newyorker.com/science/lab-notes/the-marriage-saving-robot-that-can-assemble-ikea-furniture-sort-of. Accessed April 12, 2022.

Cachon, G. P. (2020). A research framework for business models: What is common among fast fashion, e-tailing, and ride sharing?. *Management Science*, 66(3), 1172–1192.

Caniato, F., Moretto, A., and Caridi, M. (2013). Dynamic capabilities for fashion-luxury supply chain innovation. *International Journal of Retail and Distribution Management*, 41(11/12), 940–960.

China Daily (2017). Kutesmart sews up tech-based biz model in traditional industry. Available from: https://www.chinadaily.com.cn/business/2017-06/19/content_29792872.htm. Accessed December 12, 2021.

Chu, P (2005). Excellence in European apparel supply chains: ZARA. MIT-Zaragoza International Logistics Program Executive Summary. Available from: https://dspace.mit.edu/bitstream/handle/1721.1/101918/2005_2_Chu.pdf downloaded. Accessed November 6, 2021.

Cline, E. (2012). *Overdressed: The Shockingly High Cost of Cheap Fashion*. London: Penguin.

Cline, E (2018). H&M's woes mean fast fashion is getting worse, not better. *Los Angeles Times*, April 05.

Columbus, L. (2017). Smart Factories Will Deliver $500B In Value By 2022. *Forbes*, July 30. Available from: https://www.forbes.com/sites/louiscolumbus/2017/07/30/smart-factories-will-deliver-500b-in-value-by-2022/?sh=4061eb042d22. Accessed November 26, 2021.

Columbus, L. (2019). Smart factories will boost global economy $1.5T by 2023. *Forbes*. November 17. Available from: https://www.forbes.com/sites/louiscolumbus/2019/11/17/smart-factories-will-boost-global-economy-15t-by-2023/. Accessed November 26, 2021.

Crofton, S., and Dopico, L. (2007). Zara-Inditex and the growth of fast fashion. *Essays in Economic & Business History*, 25, 41–54. Available from: https://scholar.google.com/scholar?hl=en&as_sdt=0%2C5&q=Crofton+%26+Dopico+2007+&btnG=. Accessed July 29, 2021.

Danziger, P. N. (2021). Uniqlo intends to become the world's top fashion retailer by distancing from H&M and zara. *Forbes*, February 17.

Das, Sushree 2018, *'See Now, Buy Now' A Sustainable Model for the Fast Fashion Industry?* Bangalore: Amity Research Center.

Doeringer, P., and Crean, S. (2006). Can fast fashion save the US apparel industry?. *Socio-Economic Review*, 4(3), 353–377.

Earnest Research (2021). Shein now leads fast fashion. June 24. Available from: https://www.earnestresearch.com/data-bites/shein-leads-fast-fashion/. Accessed November 7, 2021.

Economist (2009). Just-in-time. https://www.economist.com/news/2009/07/06/just-in-time

Economist (2021). Shein exemplifies a new style of Chinese multinational. October 7. Available from: https://www.economist.com/business/shein-exemplifies-a-new-style-of-chinese-multinational/21805217. Accessed February 19, 2023.

Ettis, S. A. (2017). Examining the relationships between online store atmospheric color, flow experience and consumer behavior. *Journal of Retailing and Consumer Services*, 37, 43–55.

Fashionista.com (2016). Fashion history lesson: The origins of fast fashion. https://fashionista.com/2016/06/what-is-fast-fashion. Accessed November 10, 2021.

Fashionlaw.com. (2021). https://www.thefashionlaw.com/resource-center/fast-fashion/. Accessed November 10, 2021.

Fashionnetwork.com (2016). H&M scores success with designer collaborations. https://ww.fashionnetwork.com/news/h-m-scores-success-with-designer-collaborations,697734.html. Accessed November 10, 2021.

Forbes (2021). IKEA. Available from: https://www.forbes.com/companies/ikea/?sh=697d20cd2ad0. Accessed August 15, 2021.

Frasquet, M., Dawson, J., Calderón, H., and Fayos, T. (2018). Integrating embeddedness with dynamic capabilities in the internationalisation of fashion retailers. *International Business Review*, 27(4), 904–914.

Friedman, V., and Indvik, L. (2020). Pierre Cardin, fashion designer, 1922–2020. *Financial Times*, December 29. Available from: https://www.ft.com/content/f4de70be-6a55-43fa-97d9-981660e50543. Accessed November 21, 2021.

Giri, C., Jain, S., Zeng, X., and Bruniaux, P. (2019). A detailed review of artificial intelligence applied in the fashion and apparel industry. IEEE online. Available from https://ieeexplore.ieee.org/stamp/stamp.jsp?tp=&arnumber=8763948. Accessed January 3, 2020.

Gong, J., and Hassink, R. (2017) Exploring the clustering of creative industries, *European Planning Studies*, 25(4), 583–600.

Gustashaw, M. (2017). Uniqlo is going to start producing clothing at zara speeds. *GQ*. Available from: https://www.gq.com/story/uniqlo-fast-fashion-speed-zara-competition. Retrieved October 15, 2021.

H&M (2020). Annual report. Available from: https://hmgroup.com/wp-content/uploads/2021/04/HM-Annual-Report-2020.pdf. Accessed October 15, 2021.

H&M (2022). Supply chain. Available from: https://hmgroup.com/sustainability/leading-the-change/transparency/supply-chain/ Accessed June 29, 2022.

Hammond, J., and Shih, A. (2019). Wayfair: Fast Furniture? Cambridge MA: Harvard Business Publishing Case Study.

Hellström, D., and Nilsson, F. (2011). Logistics-driven packaging innovation: A case study at IKEA. *International Journal of Retail & Distribution Management*, 39(9): 638–657

Hipwell, D. (2021). Boohoo falls to five-year low as shoppers return more party wear. Available from: https://www.businessoffashion.com/news/retail/boohoo-falls-to-five-year-low-as-shoppers-return-more-party-wear/. Accessed January 14, 2022.

Huy, Q., Jarrett, M., and Duke, L. S., (2011) *How IKEA's Strategy Was Formed*. INSEAD.

IKEA (1976). The testament of a furniture dealer: Perspective from Ingvar Kamprad. Available from: https://ikeamuseum.com/en/digital/the-story-of-ikea/the-testament-of-a-furniture-dealer/. Accessed June 4, 2021.

IKEA (2018). Testament of a furniture dealer: Ingvar Kamprad. Available from: https://www.inter.ikea.com/en/-/media/InterIKEA/IGI/Financial%20Reports/English_The_testament_of_a_dealer_2018.pdf. Accessed August 29, 2021.

IKEA (2022). Let's grow together: Become an IKEA supplier. Available from https://about.ikea.com/en/work-with-us/for-suppliers. Accessed June 1, 2022.

Jacobsen, R. (2017). The shattering truth of 3D printing. Wired. Available from: https://www.wired.com/2017/05/the-shattering-truth-of-3d-printed-clothing/. Accessed November 13, 2019.

Jana, P., and Tiwari, M. (Eds.). (2021). *Lean Tools in Apparel Manufacturing*. Woodhead Publishing.

Journée, R., and Weber, M. (2017). Co-creation of experiences in retail: Opportunity to innovate in retail business. In *Managing Complexity* (pp. 391–404). Cham: Springer.

Jude, G. (2016). Innovation in retail. *Telstra*. Available from: https://www.telstra.com.au/content/dam/tcom/business-enterprise/campaigns/retail-innovation/retail-innovation.pdf. Accessed January 3, 2020.

Kagermann, H., Lukas, W.-D., and Wahlster, W. (2013). Industrie 4.0: Mit dem Internet der Dinge auf dem Weg zur 4. industrial Revolution - vdi-nachrichten.com. March 4, 2013. Available from: https://web.archive.org/web/20130304101009/http://www.vdi-nachrichten.com/artikel/Industrie-4-0-Mit-dem-Internet-der-Dinge-auf-dem-Weg-zur-4-industriellen-Revolution/52570/1. Accessed December 12, 2021.

Karimi, J., and Walter, Z. (2015). The role of dynamic capabilities in responding to digital disruption: A factor-based study of the newspaper industry. *Journal of Management Information Systems*, 32(1), 39–81.

Kavthankar, A and Perepu, I (2017). *Zara: Future Ready?* IBS Center for Management Research.

Khan, H. (2018). How to create retail store interiors that get people to purchase your products. Shopify, Customer. Available from: https://www.shopify.co.uk/retail/120057795-how-to-create-retail-store-interiors-that-get-people-to-purchase-your-products. Accessed January 3, 2020.

Kumar (2011). Implementation of Lean Manufacturing System in Apparel Industry. Research Gate. February. Available from: https://www.researchgate.net/ publication/352808466_Implementation_of_Lean_Manufacturing_System_in_ Apparel_Industry. Accessed March 20, 2022.

Kumar, K. B. S., and Perepu, I. (2020). *Hennes & Mauritz (H&M): High Cost of Fast Fashion, Hyderabad, IBS.*

Kumar, N., and Linguri, S. (2006). Fashion sense. *Business Strategy Review*, 17(2), 80–84.

Langley, P., and Rieple, A. (2021). Incumbents' capabilities to win in a digitised world: The case of the fashion industry. *Technological Forecasting and Social Change*, 167, 120718.

Lee, H. L. (2019). How agility put Zara ahead in fast fashion. *Financial Times*, December 10, 2019.

Lee, S. E., Ju, N., and Lee, K. H. (2021). Visioning the future of smart fashion factories based on media big data analysis. *Applied Sciences*, 11, 7549.

Leong, Z. W. (2021). Karl Lagerfeld, Balmain and more: 10 Best H&M collaborations with fashion designers, March 16. Available from: https://www.tatlerasia.com/style/ fashion/sg-hm-iconic-fashion-designer-collaborations. Accessed November 10, 2021.

Linden, A. (2016). An analysis of the fast fashion industry. Available from: https://pdfs .semanticscholar.org/b2de/106e5e0f33478eea88c4592cf0fb63bae7eb.pdf. Accessed December 21, 2019.

López, T., Riedler, T., Köhnen, H., and Fütterer, H (2021). Digital value chain restructuring and labour process transformations in the fast-fashion sector: Evidence from the value chains of Zara & H&M. *Global Networks*. Available from: https://onlinelibrary .wiley.com/doi/full/10.1111/glob.12353. Accessed July 10, 2022.

Martin, K. (2018). H&M admits 'mistakes' in handling shift to online shopping. *Financial Times*, January 31.

Mellor, S. (2021). Fast-fashion giants Zara and H&M are recovering from the pandemic at very different speeds. September 15. Available from: https://fortune.com/2021/09/15 /fast-fashion-zara-inditex-hennes-mauritz-pandemic-recovery-earnings/. Accessed November 10, 2021.

Nasdaq (2021). Why fashion is the next frontier of NFTs. Available from: https://www .nasdaq.com/articles/why-digital-fashion-is-the-next-frontier-of-nfts-2021-04-07. Accessed April 17, 2022.

Nazir, A., Azhar, A., Nazir, U., Liu, Y. F., Qureshi, W. S., Chen, J. E., and Alanazi, E. (2021). The rise of 3D Printing entangled with smart computer aided design during COVID-19 era. *Journal of Manufacturing Systems*, 60, 774–786.

Pan, G., Pan, S. L., and Lim, C. Y. (2015). Examining how firms leverage IT to achieve firm productivity: RBV and dynamic capabilities perspectives. *Information and Management*, 52(4), 401–412.

Petro, G. (2018). How 'see-now-buy-now' is rewiring retail. *Forbes*. Avail31.

Popescu, D., Dragomir, M., Popescu, S., and Neamțu, C. (2018). From smart products to smart manufacturing in emerging economies: Challenges and insights from the furniture industry. DEStech Transactions on Engineering and Technology Research. Available from: https://www.researchgate.net/publication/323899808_FROM _SMART_PRODUCTS_TO_SMART_MANUFACTURING_IN_EMERGING_ECONOMIES _CHALLENGES_AND_INSIGHTS_FROM_THE_FURNITURE_INDUSTRY/citations. Accessed December 12, 2021.

Raj, R., Ma, Y. J., Gam, H. J., and Banning, J. (2017). Implementation of lean production and environmental sustainability in the Indian apparel manufacturing industry: A way to reach the triple bottom line. *International Journal of Fashion Design, Technology and Education*, 10(3), 254–264.

Remy, N., Speelman, E., and Swartz, S. (2016). Style that's sustainable: A new fast fashion formula. McKinsey Inc. Available from: https://www.mckinsey.com/business -functions/sustainability/our-insights/style-thats-sustainable-a-new-fast-fashion -formula. Accessed November 13, 2019.

Rietveld, J., and Eggers, J. P. (2018). Demand heterogeneity in platform markets: Implications for complementors. *Organization Science*, 29(2), 304–322.

Rose, D. (2015). IKEA: Redefining the market to achieve success. December 8, 2015. Available from: https://digital.hbs.edu/platform-rctom/submission/ikea-redefining -the-market-to-achieve-success/. Accessed December 12, 2021.

Ross, M. (Producer) and Morgan, A. (Director). (2015). *True Cost [Motion Picture]*. United States: Untold Creative. Available from: https://truecostmovie.com/about/. Accessed November 27, 2021.

Russell, C. (2019). Could this be how we make fast fashion sustainable? *Forbes*. Available from: https://www.forbes.com/sites/callyrussell/2019/08/27/could-this-be-how-we-make-fast-fashion-sustainable/#3180eda21e8f. Accessed March 7, 2020.

Şen, A. (2008). The US fashion industry: A supply chain review. *International Journal of Production Economics*, 114(2), 571–593.

Shao, X. F., Liu, W., Li, Y., Chaudhry, H. R., and Yue, X. G. (2021). Multistage implementation framework for smart supply chain management under industry 4.0. *Technological Forecasting and Social Change*, 162, 120354.

Shih, W., and Huadai, N. (2017). *Data-driven Manufacturing: The Kutesmart System*. Boston: Harvard Business School.

Silvestri, B. (2020). The future of fashion: How the quest for digitization and the use of artificial intelligence and extended reality will reshape the fashion industry after COVID-19. *ZoneModa Journal*, 10(2), 61–73.

Smith, K. (2018). When will the fashion industry take sustainability seriously? https://edited.com/blog/2018/05/fashion-industry-sustainability/. Available from https://edited.com/blog/fashion-industry-sustainability/ accessed February 18, 2023.

Statista (2021a). Apparel Report 2021. Available from (proprietary). https://www-statista-com.uow.idm.oclc.org/study/55501/apparel-report/. Accessed June 1, 2022.

Statista (2021b). Gross profit of INGKA Group (IKEA) worldwide from 2009 to 2020 (in million euros). Available from: https://www.statista.com/statistics/241801/gross-profit-of-ikea-worldwide/. Accessed June 1, 2022.

Statista (2021c). IKEA's brand value worldwide from 2016 to 2021. Available from: https://www.statista.com/statistics/980112/brand-value-of-ikea-worldwide/. Accessed June 18, 2022.

Statista (2022). Revenue of the furniture market worldwide by country. Available from: https://www-statista-com.uow.idm.oclc.org/forecasts/758621/revenue-of-the-furniture-market-worldwide-by-country. Accessed June 1, 2022.

Su, N., Qiu, D., Sun, J., and Zhang, L. (2019) *Kutesmart: The Digital Transformation of Apparel Manufacturing*. Tsinghua School of Economics and Management and Ivey School of Business Foundation.

Suh, M. (2020). Automated cutting & sewing developments. *Textile World*, March 26. Available from: https://www.textileworld.com/textile-world/features/2020/03/automated-cutting-sewing-developments/. Accessed December 6, 2021.

Sword, A. (2020). ASOS trials new AR solution to help customers choose sizes and fits. *Strategy and Innovation - Internet Retailing*. January 15.

Tantanatewin, W., and Inkarojrit, V. (2016). Effects of color and lighting on retail impression and identity. *Journal of Environmental Psychology*, 46, 197–205.

Taplin, I. M. (2014). Global commodity chains and fast fashion: How the apparel industry continues to reinvent itself. *Competition & Change*, 18(3), 246–264.

Thoben, K. D., Wiesner, S., and Wuest, T. (2017). "Industrie 4.0" and smart manufacturing-a review of research issues and application examples. *International Journal of Automation Technology*, 11(1), 4–16.

Times (2020). Serial returners give fashion retailers an online headache. Available from: https://www.thetimes.co.uk/article/serial-returners-give-fashion-retailers-an-online-headache-x33zd676r. Accessed January 7, 2020.

Van den Steen, E. and Galor, A. (2017). *IKEA*. Boston, Mass. Harvard Business School Case Center.

Vanderploeg, A., Lee, S. E., and Mamp, M. (2017). The application of 3D printing technology in the fashion industry. *International Journal of Fashion Design, Technology and Education*, 10(2), 170–179.

Wells, J.R., and Ellsworth, G. (2018). *ASOS PLC*. Cambridge, MA: Harvard Business School Press.

Williams, G. A. (2021). Fairytale ending for Simone Rocha's H&M Collab. *Jing Daily*, March 11. Available from: https://jingdaily.com/hm-simone-rocha-collaboration-china-crash/. Accessed December 20, 2021.

Williams, J. (2018). How smart technology is disrupting the fashion industry. Available from: https://magazine.startus.cc/how-smart-technology-is-disrupting-the-fashion -industry/). Accessed January 3, 2020.

Wilson, D. (2017) Could advances in AI in fashion design signal beginning of the end. *South China Morning Post*, September 24. Available from: https://www.scmp.com/ lifestyle/fashion-luxury/article/2112355/could-advances-ai-fashion-design-signal -beginning-end. Accessed November 8, 2019.

Xue, L, Parke, CJ and Hart, C (2020). How to design fashion retail's virtual reality platforms. *International Journal of Retail & Distribution Management*, ahead-of-print. DOI: 10.1108/IJRDM-11-2019-0382

Ying, W., Pee, L. G., and Jia, S. (2018). Social informatics of intelligent manufacturing ecosystems: A case study of Kutesmart. *International Journal of Information Management* 42, 102–105.

Yu, W., Jacobs, M. A., Chavez, R., and Feng, M. (2019). Data-driven supply chain orientation and financial performance: The moderating effect of innovation-focused complementary assets. *British Journal of Management*, 30(2), 299–314.

Zhou, Y., Zang, J., Miao, Z., and Minshall, T. (2019). Upgrading pathways of intelligent manufacturing in China: Transitioning across technological paradigms. *Engineering*, 5, 691–701.

Trans- formational Innovation in Ephemeral Experiences

Alison Rieple, Robert DeFillippi and David Schreiber

Chapter 5

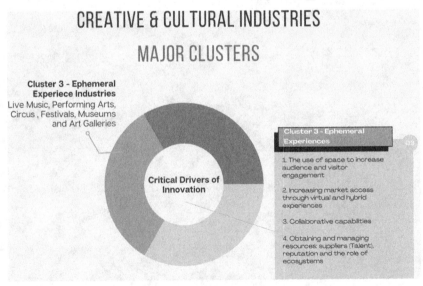

Figure 5.1   Creative and cultural industries: Cluster 3 drivers of innovation.

DOI: 10.4324/9781003207542-5

Introduction

Ephemeral experience providers (EEPs) are organizations whose products are almost wholly focused on providing the consumer with an experience that is time-limited (ephemeral). These products (or more accurately, services) are those in which a consumer (viewer, audience member, listener), participates in the experience. Without the consumer there would be no product. The experience is "of the moment" and not any other time.

We are aware that all consumables have some experiential elements to them. Pine and Gilmore (1999) asserted that economic activity has been transitioning from a focus on the purchase and consumption of products, to services and, finally, to experiences. This is seen in the design of the "shopping experience", or in restaurants such as the Hard Rock Cafe, where the ambience and environment are just as much a part of the restaurant service as the food itself.

Cluster 3 industries include museums, art galleries, festivals, live music and performing arts. In most of these industries an organization provides a spatial setting and an administrative and technical infrastructure that enables the provision of artistic and/or aesthetic offerings. In some industries (festivals, live music and performing arts) the experience comes from a live performance provided by an artist or artists. In other Cluster Three industries such as art galleries and museums the experience comes from the visitor engaging with artifacts selected and displayed by a curator, who is not likely to be directly part of the experience. Cultural tourism offers its audience of visitors (i.e., tourists) the means to navigate and interpret particular experiences that are rooted in the physical locale of the experience offerings. In each the experience is likely to be different, from excitement, to pleasure, to learning and many others.

Ephemerality in each of these cases refers to the fact that the experience does not last – once it has happened it has gone. However, this ephemeral moment may be embedded in a series of other engagements that the consumer has with the experience or experience creator, for example, Internet-mediated services to theater or museum subscribers or event attendees. Some of the more ingenious methods employed to deepen and sustain audience engagement are featured in our examples of innovation in these industries that we describe below.

Many EEPs, including theater or opera productions, create an artificial setting in which imagination helps to create the experience. Some tourism destinations, for example, theme parks such as Disney World or MGM Universal, feature artificial physical settings designed to provide a specific set of experiences catering to the preferences of its target clientele. Other EEPs, for example, museums and art galleries, provide a curated gallery of aesthetic experiences for its audience to encounter. Similar processes underpin EEPs' use of VR and AR technologies to mimic or enhance the "real" experience. All these experiential service providers are attempting to achieve audience engagement and loyalty (Pine and Glimore, 1999).

Experiences that can be reproduced at scale and acquired in a process that is separated in both space and time from the creation of the experience are categorized as another cluster (Chapter 3, Digitizable Media). This may include a live recording(s) of a band's song while on tour or in a recording studio. We also recognize that some aspects of an experience, the videoing of a live performance, for example, may be captured and reproduced (and, indeed, this is where some of the most powerful innovations have taken place recently).

This chapter will focus initially on the role of spatial design and technology innovations to transform the sensory experiences and resulting engagements of consumers within diverse Cluster Three industry settings. Next we will examine how ephemeral experience providers have devised innovative mechanisms for providing their audiences with virtual experiences and opportunities for engagement. We then turn to the role of collaborative capabilities between EEP in aggregating their individual resources to collaboratively enhance what they provide to audiences. We conclude our discussion of innovation drivers with a review of the complex array of actors who participate in Cluster Three ecosystems and the challenges posed to the leadership of key actors governing these ecosystems (Figure 5.1).

Transformational Innovation in Ephemeral Experiences

THE CRITICAL DRIVERS OF INNOVATION
IN CLUSTER THREE INDUSTRIES

Critical Driver 1: Using Environmental Features to Increase Audience and Visitor Engagement

The environment is a crucial component in the way that experiences are put on and felt – experienced – by the consumer. It is where the experience takes place. The environment creates the conditions for positive emotions to come about so its design, and the elements within it that allow for customer interaction and engagement, has been the subject of considerable innovative effort.

Engagement is the emotional, behavioral and cognitive interactions between an artist and their audience, observable in applause, tears, laughter and other visible responses (Ford and Mandviwalla, 2020; Bowman et al., 2021). Historically, the engagement of audiences through improvements in sensory experience is well illustrated in the history of film. Movie theaters have typically played a passive role in transformational innovation. The most dramatic innovations in the sensory experience of film viewing in theaters (sound, color, 3D, special effects) were occasioned by innovations in Cluster One film production companies and their suppliers. The record of movie theaters as sites of transformational innovation is quite spotty with many innovations failing to transform the movie viewing experience of its audiences. An example of unsuccessful innovation can be seen in the 1950s through 1960s efforts by several entrepreneurs to introduce Smell-O-Vision and its rival AromaRama into the cinematic experience of film audiences. In this instance the innovation was a product offering that needed to be installed in each movie theater and the emission of fragrances was synchronized to arise at specific junctures in the movie where fragrance might enhance the visual experience. Unfortunately for its innovators, the audience response to Smell-O-Vision and AromaRama was underwhelming and movie theater exhibitors quickly decided that the market response did not justify further investment. Aroma-based innovation never became part of the cinematic landscape. A 2000 Time reader survey listed Smell-O-Vision in the "Top 100 Worst Ideas of All Time" (Drobnick, 2006).

A more transformational innovation in cinematic audience engagement has arisen with the emergence of large-screen IMAX theaters which integrate more immersive film viewing experiences with IMAX projectors capable of rendering full visual and sound immersion through complementary innovations in film shooting and sound production. However, the original innovation contribution was from the Cluster One sector, where a filmmaker introduced a production process that enabled filmmakers to record and project images in much larger formats and much higher resolutions than conventional systems allowed (Pisano, 2010). Movie theaters are making further investments in immersive audience experience with the introduction of 4DX technology that includes motion seats and atmospherics. Seats that vibrate, move up and down, side-to-side and the use of fragrances, heat, rain, fog and wind effects are simply the beginning of how theaters continue to innovate (Sharp, 2012).

Although some EEPs, such as circuses, exhibitions and some types of festivals, take their performance or exhibition space with them wherever they go, for many EEPs the location is fixed. The type of physical space needed varies with the nature of the EEP and therefore the facilities available in any location matter. Traditionally, art galleries and museums have been limited by their building's fixed physical boundaries, and most are limited in their location by the need to be near and/or accessible to economically sustainable numbers of customers. This is why many are located in large conurbations. Within these constraints innovation has been improving consumers' experiences through, for example, better design of layouts and new curation practices (Armstrong, 2021; Dare, 2019; Nogare and Murzyn-Kupisz, 2021).

More engaging programming is helping to attract audiences to, for example, classical music performances and museum exhibits (Ángel Marín, 2021). However, many of the innovations in this cluster are driven by technological advancements developed elsewhere that enhance the performance or exhibits, notably sound technologies, lighting, wearables, AR and VR. Concert halls or opera houses have benefited from state-of-the-art acoustics that make sound clearer and that allow it to penetrate distant or hidden parts of the venue (Jaffe, 2005; Galiana et al.,

2016). Architects and space designers have also used new knowledge of physical parameters to evoke emotional and behavioral responses from their audiences, such as intimacy or warmth (Armstrong, 2021).

In fact, attending a live performance is a multi-sensorial experience in which many variables interact to influence the consumer's perceptions or emotions (Bowman et al., 2021). Besides acoustics there are components such as temperature, lighting, comfort or the architecture of the venue. There can be associative benefits from attending a concert in an emblematic or prestigious auditorium. Although its acoustics are relatively poor, Milan's "La Scala" opera house has an atmosphere and historical "presence" that overcomes most perceptions of poor acoustics (Galiana et al., 2016). This is an example of the subjective nature of perception (Ohnishi et al., 2001), which has implications for the designs of concert halls and layouts, which need to take account of the intended audience's characteristics and biases.

Theater and opera houses have also long depended on the power of visual effects (mechane, deus-ex-machina, limelight, trapdoors, etc.) to enhance the plot or to stimulate reactions from the audience. Nowadays these effects are almost wholly provided by electronic means; digital innovation has helped theaters to reach new audiences and has been a source of new theatrical experiences (Bakhshi et al., 2010). Digital innovations of the visual aspects of performance include holographic projections, lighting, amplification, video, or augmented reality (Ford and Mandviwalla, 2020; Alsop, 2021), and even robots (Bulut, 2018; Jochum, 2013).

In theater the use of computer-generated images can now provide a dialogue between the visuals and live actions. These images can be used as a part of the scenography and can be integrated with the live actors. Projection techniques include 3D holographics, Pepper's Ghost techniques (4D art) and video projection on cyclorama or canvas. These can be real time or recorded using cinematic techniques. An example is the "Adding Machine" project at Bradley University in Illinois which some time ago (in March 2007) merged real-time performances with the virtual to put actors from Florida and Canada on the stage in Illinois without their having to leave their university campuses.

The production also involved virtual scenery, broadcast and recorded video, and avatar performers (Bakhshi and Throsby, 2009). Another example is Vivid Sydney, the largest festival of its kind in the southern hemisphere, which has used AV technology to bring about huge changes. The festival's previous use of slide projection has evolved to become laser projection (Innovate, 2022), which has allowed for greater complexity of color combinations for architectural projections: lasers have overcome the brightness problems of old technologies, which made it difficult to achieve colors like deep reds, blues or purples. Unlike the relative simplicity of the old ways these new technologies require the bringing together of disparate groups of artists and AV professionals such as electrical specialists, artists, sculptors, architects and industrial designers.

Digital engagement refers to how people use and participate in online activities and content, such as following a performance through live streaming or on social media. This can give valuable feedback to EEPs concerning what their audiences will like or dislike. The Royal Opera House Covent Garden (ROH) was able to leverage the strong subscriber base that they have on YouTube to take on board feedback of a performance of The Nutcracker, which they applied to a subsequent 360○ VR production of Nabucco (Atkinson and Kennedy, 2018). In this the viewer is surrounded by the chorus, is positioned within them and can pivot around 180 degrees to study each of the performers' faces. It also reveals the conductors and behind-the-scenes personnel in the rehearsal space, and then the audience in the opera house itself. Here the behind-the-scenes production becomes part of the spectacle to deepen the audiences' enjoyment and engagement. In this use of feedback the future content of live performances is shaped. Such a mix of activities can be synergistic and recursive – success in one stream of activity leads to success in the other. It is an ongoing debate as to whether this will lead to less adventurous offerings, as EEPs react to what audiences already like, or more innovative as the technology enables new insights and visions of what can be done.

In order to ensure the sustainability of the performing arts in a "mediatized" culture in which technology and televisuality dominate human communication and culture, arts companies need to "speak" the same language as the era (Bakhshi et al., 2010). Hence the use of digital technology to engage audiences is a tangible manifestation of the wider cultural economy. An example of this is VR which can enhance the core features of the experience through audience immersion and/or visual spectacle. This uses four main technologies: game engine platform, motion capture system, telepresence platform and the VR headset itself. A "live" audience wearing VR headsets can experience in different ways the characters and locations in a play. VR is also being used as a tool through which to develop actors' performances. For example, one director took the cast through a VR version of the historical period on which the play was based as part of the pre-rehearsals' characterization process (Bakhshi and Throsby, 2009).

Digital technologies are also transforming the processes of engagement through facilitating and enhancing co-creative projects (Walmsley, 2019) into an "innovation community" which brings together different artists, practitioners and skill sets. These are examples of an "open source" approach to culture, where cultural products are increasingly "ripped, mixed and burnt" into different products (Bakhshi and Throsby, 2009).

EXEMPLAR 1A: INNOVATIONS IN THE PERFORMING ARTS

Anyone who has recently attended a live popular music concert or play can attest to the effects of amplification or lighting (Figure 5.2). Flood, spot, fresnel or strobe lighting and LEDs have made lavish atmospheric lighting a reality. LED lighting in particular provides a multitude of low-heat and energy color options.

Lighting, when enhanced through the use of cell phone apps, can enhance the mood and the interactivity the audience has with the performance. Links to these special apps can be as simple as replacing the cigarette lighters that were once the staple of the rock concert of the 1980s to an in-sync pattern that adapts to the rhythm of the song being played. Some pop bands provide radio-wave frequency wristbands

---

Figure 5.2 Concert lighting. *Source*: Tatsiana Amelina/Shutterstock

for their fans. Within these bands are small LED lights that are programmed to react to certain songs or notes that are played. It enables the wearer to feel more included in the concert experience and not simply a witness to the artists on stage (Jochum, 2013; Hall, 2022).

The use of smartphones, wristbands and other wearables has also enabled more interactivity and control of content between the popular music concert-goer and performer. Wearable clothing with sensors allows the concert-goer to experience vibrations and other sensory enhancements connected to the songs being played. Smartphone apps allow fans to procure "setlists" by using voting systems or social media during the show, allowing artists to respond in the moment to requests and the crowd's energy. Having "a say" or control over the experience continues to be a big draw for many popular music concert-goers and can be an effective way to keep them engaged.

Audio technologies have also enhanced performances. For a long time the studio production of rock music used technology such as multi-track recording techniques and richly layered sound textures to create a richer sound than could be achieved in a live concert. This poses a problem for live artists who want to provide their audiences with the same sort of quality music that they have come to expect from recordings. Pioneers of enhanced live performances included tapes of their studio recordings or overdubs. More recently, digital sampling, MIDI and live looping devices that can create onstage versions of tracks have dominated.

In addition to innovations in lighting and audio design, sensory technology and interconnectivity, the performing arts experience is seeing innovation in the use of virtual and augmented reality. Recent developments in hologram technology have prompted some concert promoters to secure rights from famous dead artists in order to capitalize on the power of nostalgia (Marinkovic, 2022; Vietoris, 2018). For example, in 2012 rap artist 2pac was brought back to 2-D life using Pepper's Ghost' technology during a Snoop Dog's performance at Coachella. Country legend Roy Orbison was rendered in hologram as well, both performances providing the illusion that the person was actually there. This AR technology is still in its infancy but is developing fast. Even legacy artists are adopting the technology: Abba has recently announced a series of holographic concerts using "ABBAtars" (holographic avatars) to take the stage.

Exemplar 1a: Questions for discussion

1) Emotions are a critical part of any experience. How should EEPs ensure that their audiences or visitors experience positive emotions and not negative ones?
2) Augmented reality (AR) and virtual reality (VR) technologies are some of the most common ways that live performance is enhanced. What are the skills involved in using these technologies? What risks are involved in their use?

EXEMPLAR 1B: INNOVATIONS IN BUILDING DESIGN AND ACOUSTICS – THE ELBPHILHARMONIE, HAMBURG: DESIGN OF A CONCERT HALL

Even classical music performances are being enhanced through radical designs of concert halls. One of the most renowned of recent times is the Elbphilharmonie in Hamburg which, in addition to using the most sophisticated acoustics that allows the quietest sound to be heard throughout the concert hall, also brings together performers and audience in a way that is very different from the normal "us and them" design of concert halls. Performers, instead of looking out on to the audience, can find that they are sitting immediately in front of a spectator who can hear every mistake they might make! This may be alarming for the performer, but engages the audience in the performance in ways that have rarely been done before (Figure 5.3).

Figure 5.3   The Elbphilharmonie large hall. *Source*: Yarchyk/Shutterstock

The building itself is spectacular and acts as a magnet to the arts ecology that has emerged in the area. The new glass construction resembles a hoisted sail or wave, resting on top of an old brick warehouse, symbolizing Hamburg's seafaring culture. Every panel in the structure curves and has a print that is unique to that section. This specially developed dot grid offers practical protection against the sunlight and creates a pleasing aesthetic (Figure 5.4).

The complexity of the design and its location in Hamburg's historical docks resulted from years of discussion between the architects and the City's authorities, leading to delays and massive cost increases. Yasushia Toyota from Japan was

Figure 5.4   The Elbphilharmonie. *Source*: Stefan Lauk/Shutterstock

responsible for the acoustics; Hamburg's Parliament speci-
fied that the general contractor must comply with Yasushia
Toyota's requirements, something that apparently caused a
few problems! **(Kampmanngroup.com, 2022).**

Similarly protracted negotiations have accompanied other
proposals for new "statement" arts venues in London and
are an indication of the complexity involved in attempting to
develop new initiatives in the so-called "built environment" in
performing arts.

Exemplar 1b: Questions for discussion

1. The building of a major new arts center such as
   the Elbphilharmonie involves numerous different

stakeholders with very different skills and ways of working:

a. List as many of the different stakeholder groups as you can.

b. For each of these groups write a short paragraph or two characterizing their culture, working practices and power bases.

c. Considering the mix of stakeholder groups and their different sources of power where would you foresee any problems developing? How would you go about dealing with these problems if you were in charge of the project?

EXEMPLAR 1C: TECHNOLOGICAL INNOVATIONS IN MUSEUMS AND ART GALLERIES

Museums have traditionally offered limited opportunities for audience engagement with their cultural artifacts (Figure 5.5). Ubiquitous "guards" are the gatekeepers of any

Figure 5.5   VR being used in a museum. *Source*: Yarchyk/Shutterstock

Transformational Innovation in Ephemeral Experiences

intimate physical contact with the museum's displays. Most museums engaged in unidirectional (expert to audience) lectures by either live guides or via audio programs linked to digital devices made available to museum attendees. Hence a new arena for innovation has emerged from neuroscience research which has led to experimentation with new modes of audience engagement. Such innovations in engagement are motivated in part by evidence of a steep decline in visitor participation and engagement with museums and art galleries, in the USA at least (NEA Research Report #58 January 2015). Another concern was the demographic profile of visitors: nearly 84% of people who visited a US art museum or gallery at least once in 2012 had at least some college education and these attendees were predominantly female and non-Hispanic white (NEA Research Report #58 January 2015). The age of first experience with art galleries and museums was also closely related to US educational attainment, with over 70% of college graduates reporting they visited an art museum or gallery as a child, compared with 42% of adults who have only a high school diploma (NEA Research Report #58 January 2015).

So museums appeared ripe for change. One particularly relevant set of technology innovations that are being used include artificial intelligence, augmented reality and virtual reality (AR/VR/XR). Artificial intelligence based on large data sets of museum usage is making possible the deployment of algorithms that can create new museum programs or exhibits (Agyeman, 2019). An example of the way that AI is used to identify the drivers of visitors' emotional engagement with artifacts is Bologna's Civic museum. The museum placed video cameras around their galleries to monitor visitors' behavior. However, rather than simply tracking which works of art they were most drawn to, the technology made use of galvanic response sensors to identify the emotional response of visitors to the galleries' offerings and surroundings. The information gathered is used to redesign museum layouts, including which exhibits are put on show and which ones are removed or placed in less prestigious settings.

AR/VR/XR is another set of technologies that are playing a role in replacing the standard visitor experience (Han et al., 2021; Cuseum, 2020). These are truly interdisciplinary and are emerging from a number of interrelating industries involving the work of theater, film and game practitioners alongside psychologists, physicians, computer scientists, technologists and programmers. Museums provide a fertile industry arena for AR/VR/XR applications. The National Museum of Singapore has run an immersive installation that focuses on 69 images from the William Farquhar Collection of Natural History Drawings. These have been turned into three-dimensional animations with which visitors can interact. Visitors download an app and can then use the camera on their phone or tablet to explore the paintings (Coates, 2021). The AR/VR technology is said to be likely to transform museum visitor experiences to the same extent as AR/VR has expanded video game players' experiences during game play (Agyeman, 2019).

However, what was once the job of curators could be automated (Charr, 2021) and a major barrier to implementation could well be the resistance from museum professionals who are neither trained in use of such technology nor inclined to support initiatives that threaten to replace their expertise.

Developments in neuroscience are also changing the design of museum exhibits. Neuroscience has emerged as an important scientific discipline for understanding how the brain functions to influence cognitive processes related to attention. It is now possible to analyze brain activity to discover neural explanations for consumer behavior. Today, the nascent scientific field of neuroaesthetics explores how artistic and aesthetic experiences register in the brain (Bidgood, 2017). Although initially slow to apply neuroscience principles, there is now evidence that the arts in general and museum practice in particular have begun to apply neuroscientific theories and methods previously used in consumer research (Dooley, 2019). Museums and galleries have traditionally focused only upon the visual stimulation provided for their attendees. By contrast neuroscience suggests that a wider array of sensory stimuli can augment the visual stimulation of art gallery exhibits and increase audience engagement (PEM, 2021). Engagement occurs when one's attention is directed in a way that elicits an emotional response and leads to the formation of a memory (PEM, 2021). Emotional experiences attract more attention, are processed faster and remembered better. It is the level of arousal – of emotional intensity – that is key to forming a memory (PEM, 2021).

In the Peabody Essex Museum (PEM) in Salem, Massachusetts, established in 1799 and one of the United States' oldest museums, neuroscience is transforming the museum's artistic, visitor and community engagement. PEM introduces itself on its neuroscience website as the only art museum in the world that employs a full-time neuroscientist, who works closely with museum staff as they plan exhibitions (Gay, 2017). The museum is designing multisensory experiences that involve smell, sound, taste and emotions. In an effort to build shows that engage the brain, PEM has tried breaking up exhibition spaces into smaller pieces; posting questions and quotes on the wall, instead of relying only on explanatory wall text (Bidgood, 2017). In its 2018 Rodin exhibition, professional dancers were integrated into the galleries to draw visitor attention to human form, posture and movement. Elsewhere, PEM's Asia in Amsterdam exhibition introduced unexpected multisensory and interactive experiences, emphasized emotive storytelling and integrated Attention Systems logic into the design and layout (PEM, 2021).

The museum's Neuroscience Initiative employs a mixed-methods approach to measuring visitor engagement and uses techniques that access both conscious and unconscious behavioral and emotional responses to their museum experience. These methods include mobile eye-tracking, where research subject volunteers wear a pair of mobile eye-tracking glasses and the resulting data is captured on a computer in the form of a video. This kind of data is extremely useful in revealing what kinds of design decisions draw visual attention. A second method involves galvanic skin response (GSR), which measures the electrical conductivity of the skin, is governed by the brain and reflects the extent of emotional arousal, or the intensity of an emotional experience. Subject volunteers wear two electrodes to their skin and their museum experience emotional arousal and intensity of emotional experience can be monitored in real time (Asher, 2020).

Exemplar 1c: Questions for discussion

1. How might neuroscience be employed in other ephemeral experience settings to create audience engagement and enjoyment?
2. What sort of data might be used by museum and art gallery curators to help them design better exhibitions and gallery spaces?
3. What new skills are required by museums' and art galleries' staff in order to manage and apply AI and AR/VR technologies in their organizations?

Critical Driver 2: Increasing Market Access Through Virtual and Hybrid Experiences

The mixture of personal, virtual and hybrid experiences isn't a new concept in the CCIs. For some time offerings for live performances have ranged from direct experience by physical proximity, to amplification of sound (remote speakers) at a distance to the performance space, to visual and auditory broadcasting of an event. These applications were originally offered as a means to increase audience capacity for especially popular experiences. What is different now is that the provision of virtual experiences has accelerated, notably during COVID lockdowns when live performances were either prohibited by health regulations or rejected by virus-hesitant audiences. Virtual experiences have been made possible by improvements in online streaming technologies (see Chapter 3), and the invention of online, mobile and wearable technologies that provide visual and auditory access to physically remote experiences.

Consuming live performing arts is an experience that is shared with others, something that is mostly lost in recordings and online distribution (Ford and Mandviwalla, 2020). Attendance at a performance co-creates an emotional bond between audience and performers, an "artistic exchange" that adds something to the experience of attending a concert. However, it is limited to the small number of consumers who can physically be present. Other channels provide different engagement mechanisms for high-cultural art forms that result in different types of interactions, therefore different types of value for different and wider groups of stakeholders, meaning that many EEPs' lives are very much more complicated than they used to be.

Many live artists also record their performances, whether this is music or plays. As we said earlier this recording may be considered as a separate "product" (which we discuss in Chapter 3). Most EEPs find it hard to survive on live performances alone and are engaged in a hunt for additional revenues (sell more tickets, raise more funds, increase subscriptions and season tickets) and/or increase non-live performance income (sell recordings, live-stream performances in theaters or on radio channels, and customer engagement (special events and loyalty programs). Some of the most innovative EEPs are those that have combined many of these to create a new business model, with the performance at the center but not necessarily the biggest earner. It acts as the hook onto which everything else attaches.

The arts sector has witnessed a sharp global rise in digital projects, not least the proliferation of live streaming or "simulcasting" (Towse, 2013) dating from the days when New York's Metropolitan Opera live-streamed a production of Mozart's *The Magic Flute* in 2006. Despite the ongoing debate about whether live streaming is cannibalizing live audiences or not (Walmsley, 2019), it is now a commonplace feature of EEPs' business models. Another early example of widening access was the Welsh National Opera's decision to make music and video files of their performances available for download (Bakhshi and Throsby, 2009).

By contrast to "normal" performing arts, a festival may occupy a space that spans multiple locations and times and may cover a larger overall territory than static models. These festivals often have their roots in a particular spatial setting that provides a place identity for its participants, but many carry this origin-based identity around with them as they move from place to place. An emerging organizing principle for events such as festivals is hybrid event planning. In the case of festivals, the hybrid model is one in which the festival event is planned to provide both real-time experiences that can be experienced directly by event attendees and virtually experienced by non-attendees to the physical location of the festival. Design and program choices facing the hybrid festival planners include the following:

- creating programming, content and experiences to meet the needs of both a live and virtual audience, without privileging either type
- the blending of the live and virtual experiences together, so both live and virtual audiences achieve equal engagement and experience
- selecting a technology portfolio comprising a mix of web-based casting, communication and engagement apps which drive engagement and build long-term digital communities and social media integration, to optimize the concurrent delivery of live and the virtual experiences (Han et al., 2021)
- giving the growing virtual audience a voice, to shift the traditional focus from the live to the virtual audience
- deciding whether to create exclusive or shared content for live and/or virtual audiences or to use the same content for both (Marketing Interactive, 2021)

Art galleries and museums are going through similar transformations (Trunfio et al., 2022) in the search for new audiences, for example, through:

- the digitization of collections or the increase in the depth of their engagement with existing audiences
- online access to collections and databases
- online exhibitions (text, image, audiovisual)
- virtual exhibitions (including 360-degree room views)
- virtual museums using real and imaginary exhibition and gallery spaces

A fundamental challenge for EEPs in these cases is to manage their intellectual property rights, and copyright, in particular, to maximize the economic returns from their assets. An example is the dispute between the UK's National Portrait Gallery and Wikimedia over the latter's allegedly unauthorized use of digitized images of works that are under the gallery's copyright (Kennisland, 2010).

EXEMPLAR 2A: HYBRID MODELS OF VIRTUAL AND PHYSICAL EXPERIENCES – THE SUNDANCE FILM FESTIVAL

The Sundance Film Festival (formerly Utah/US Film Festival, then US Film and Video Festival) is an annual film festival organized by the Sundance Institute. It is the largest independent film festival in the United States. It takes place each January in Park City, Utah, Salt Lake City, and at the Sundance Resort (a ski resort near Provo, Utah), and acts as a showcase for new work from both American and international independent filmmakers. The festival has evolved since its inaugural 1978 Utah film festival from a low-profile venue for small-budget, independent creators from outside the Hollywood system into a media extravaganza for Hollywood celebrity actors, paparazzi and luxury lounges set up by companies not affiliated with Sundance.

The COVID virus pandemic devastated film festivals, with many organizers canceling their events and suffering enormous losses in attendance. Their historic sponsors similarly lost tourism-related revenue. Some turned to virtual festivals in lieu of their live formats typically associated with place-based festivals. Sundance, however, chose a different path by transforming its 2021 edition of the festival into a hybrid festival experience. The entire 2021 program was available on festival.sundance.org to passholders and ticket buyers across the USA and in selected international territories. The festival organized physical screenings for each film in its lineup, as well as drive-in options in Los Angeles and Park City. More than 25 arthouses around the country, from Alabama to Puerto Rico, partnered with Sundance for screenings and events. Its full slate of talks, as well as the New Frontier, XR

---

and emerging media programs were made available online around the world. The program was accessible through a custom-built virtual platform, with screenings using the Shift72 player that's become an industry standard for virtual film festivals (Kohn, 2020). Promising directors were still on hand to showcase their work, but viewers were able to watch them from the comfort of their living rooms (Webster, 2021). The hybrid edition of Sundance 2021 reached an audience 2.7 times larger than the 2020 non-hybrid edition in Utah, with over 600,000 audience views (Sundance Institute, 2021). The commercial success of the hybrid festival and the persistence of the COVID pandemic led Sundance to organize its 2022 festival as a hybrid festival and to build upon the lessons learned from its inaugural hybrid offering.

Proponents for hybrid film festivals argue that these types of festivals attract new audiences and provide new online employment opportunities for film festival service providers. On-demand films mean on-demand captioning, on-demand screenings, flexible viewing and new viewing opportunities for vulnerable, housebound and geographically distant audiences (Mistek, 2021). Hybrid festivals also provide additional employment opportunities to service distributors, sponsors, tourism agencies and audiences, and the multi-locational strategy of Sundance 2021 distributed these benefits to a much wider array of locales than would be the case with a single site festival.

Hybrid festival supporters also point to evidence suggesting that online arts participation is likely to increase audience participation in non-online art events (Mistek, 2021). The ability to live-stream festivals provides a second opportunity to engage fans of the artists who are participating in live festivals, and some festival organizers are employing the live-streaming technology to provide virtual opportunities for festival fans unable or unwilling to participate in the live festival activities.

Many new media tools are available to participants, artists and organizers to engage with each other both during the festival and during the intervals between festivals. Websites like Facebook can facilitate engagement and provide links to associated facets of festival offerings, such as associations that are related to the thematic scope of the festival and to ancillary digital media services that can provide follower access to artists and artifacts. RFID wristbands provide participants rapid entry so they can skip long lines and digitally access various festival amenities. Virtual reality and augmented reality hardware can enrich the festival experience.

However, criticisms have arisen over the impact of hybrid film festivals such as Sundance on reducing the communal experiences of shared presence and identification with fellow co-participants in festival events and rituals. These experiences help create a shared identity among film festival attendees that powerfully shapes the impact of such festivals on their ongoing engagement with future festivals. A final criticism is that online participants may be relegated to a second-class citizen status due to the limited access afforded to virtual participation. These access barriers are often magnified due to the complexity of online ticketing and the limitations imposed by virtual event viewing systems, which was a criticism of the Sundance hybrid festival (Mistek, 2021).

The ongoing dilemma for the festival sector is whether virtual forms of engagement that were initially accelerated during the COVID pandemic have enduring benefits that can be preserved and incorporated into hybrid models of festivals without diminishing the territorial benefits to locales that host physical festivals. Also, can hybrid festivals avoid creating a divide between festival attendees who enjoy access to industry artists and professionals and online attendees who enjoy only remote engagements that are more limited and controlled by virtual festival managers?

Exemplar 2a: Questions for discussion

1. As wearable technology advances in providing mobile and virtual substitutes for previously manually operated services, what types of digital support skills will need to be employed by festival organizers and to what degree will they supplement or substitute for more traditional on-site services?

2. The festival experience is likely to vary with the type of CCI industry on which the festival focuses. Those that are already highly digitized, for example, digitizable media industries, have audiences and professionals already adapted to online venues for engagement. Physical products industries are familiar with online retailing. What elements should be incorporated into festivals to give (a) digitizable media industries and (b) physical products industries the best experiences?
3. As COVID (hopefully) recedes as a health threat, do you see a return to physical festival live attendance and the demise of virtual festivals? What about hybrid festivals?

Critical Driver 3: Collaborative Capabilities

Cluster Three industries are dependent on a wide group of other people for their programs, their inputs and their products (Donelli et al., 2021). This is not unique to this cluster – we have already described the wide set of inputs that go into the making of films and other CCIs, and many other industries have important dependencies built into their value chains. But EEPs are peculiarly reliant on artists, costume designers, musicians, composers, technical specialists, designers and architects among many others. And their customers often have a much deeper relationship with the EEP than, say, a toothpaste or car manufacturer's customers do.

EEPs also need to have very strong relationships with collaborators due to their dependence upon technology providers, creative artists, commercial, nonprofit and governmental institutions and philanthropic communities. Some have characterized this as a "virtual reality production ecosystem" in which diverse organizations all join together in an innovative project (Atkinson and Kennedy, 2018).

Collaborations allow organizations to focus on what they do best and not get distracted by having to do things that others do better. Museums and art galleries, for example, may need to liaise with many other organizations, often across international borders, in order to put on the types of displays that will attract crowds. In Chapter 3 we discussed a number of industries whose products, once digitized, had to be distributed and sold through media that were not owned or controlled by them, involving Internet providers, digital networks and online payment services. In Chapter 4 we saw how H&M collaborated with many famous designers in order to improve its product portfolio but also its brand identity, signaling that its products were authentic and high quality – not simply "cheap and cheerful". And many EEPs are dependent on funding from charitable trusts and government grants. All of these require collaborative arrangements, sometimes simply contracts to provide a specific service, but more often than not some sort of agreement to improve the joint product or service, or even invent a new one. Managing these relationships requires considerable skills:

- to find suitable partners in the first place
- to negotiate an appropriate mutually beneficial fee or contract
- to manage the partnership without it failing to achieve the desired outcomes

All inter-organizational partnerships have the risks of learning races and culture clashes. Learning races, in which one partner learns from their collaborator how to do something faster than the other one does (Khanna et al., 1994), can mean that one organization obtains, or even steals, resources such as know-how or relational capital, from their partner, leaving the loser without any basis for continued collaboration. Colliding cultures, where one organization does not do things in the same way as the other or share the same values, can result in a lack of understanding and the breakdown of the relationship (Labaronne and Tröndle, 2021; Gander et al., 2007).

Creative organizations are stereotypically said to be informal and with antipathy to bureaucracy, driven by artistic visioning and not so much by financial performance (although there are those that assert this is an outdated way of labeling CCIs) (Amans et al., 2015; Knardal, 2020). In contrast, some of the organizations that EEPs have to collaborate with, such as software developers, charitable trusts and government bodies can be very detail-oriented, "rational", risk-averse and have very different time scales and ways of doing business (Sassi et al., 2019). Different organizations even from within the same sector can have very different cultures and ways of operating (Byrnes, 2019). Because many CCIs are project-based organizations (DeFillippi, 2015), product development or marketing collaborations are frequent and heterogeneous. They can be between regular partners or involve rare relationships. They can be between small, new outfits and large, maybe rich and famous, institutions. Such institutional complexity means that EEPs with relevant and flexible collaborative capabilities are likely to be more successful (Labaronne and Tröndle, 2021).

EXEMPLAR 3: CONDO AND ART GALLERY COLLABORATIONS

Although art galleries are typically characterized as stand-alone enterprises, the combination of reduced art gallery attendance and increased availability of online art viewing and transaction options has spurred this sector to engage in new forms of collective action and collaboration. For many smaller single-venue galleries, the art gallery's traditional ecosystem is no longer working. Midsize galleries, amid a spate of closings, point to rising rents and declining foot traffic. These challenges have resulted in more pressure for galleries to present their work at art festivals, which require a tradeoff between the advantages of access to more diverse art audiences and the added logistical and exhibit costs of showings at festivals.

One innovative solution – Condo – was launched in 2016 in London. Condo hosts art dealers' work in conjunction with their visiting colleagues to create and install exhibitions that intermingle artists from participating art gallery rosters or take place in discrete gallery spaces adjacent to current exhibitions. This emphasis on collaboration extends to how editions of Condo are assembled. The local organizers identify host galleries, who are then asked to select their top five galleries from a pool of out-of-towners. The organizers use that information to pair them accordingly. Condo's innovative model for collaborative sharing of gallery art and gallery exhibition space in the London inaugural launch has been followed by Condo-sponsored collective art exhibitions in other locations. These include Condo New York, Condo Mexico City, Condo São Paulo and Condo Shanghai (Greenberger, 2018).

The common attraction of the Condo model is that, unlike the alternative of art festival participation, it is designed by art galleries to help them help each other by aggregating their offerings and venues in underused urban spaces. At a time when smaller galleries are struggling with the cost of attending fairs, Condo represents an attractive financial model. Unlike a fair, where booth rentals can run into the thousands, Condo's fee tops out at around $850, which covers a participant's share of an opening night party and of producing a Condo brochure. As with fairs, the galleries pay any installation costs associated with their presentation. Shipping charges depend on what a gallery chooses to bring, but expenses for things like on-site fabrication, handling and installation can be defrayed with help from the host gallery (Greenberger, 2018).

A second example of collaboration among art galleries involves the acquisition of artworks in competition with auction houses. Historically, auction houses enjoyed scale and reputation advantages in bidding for valued art collections to sell to their high-end buyers. However, some recent events suggest that art galleries are finding ways to pool their resources in competing for collections to offer to high-end art buyers. In February 2020, three major auction houses, Christie's, Sotheby's and Phillips, were outbid by a collective collaboration between three mega-galleries – Pace, Gagosian and Acquavella – for a collection of over 300 artworks valued at nearly half a billion dollars (ARTnews, 2020). Although this collaboration was between the largest and most affluent of art galleries, the successful collaboration is further proof that art galleries of many shapes and sizes are finding situations where there are benefits to collective activity.

Exemplar 3: Questions for discussion

1. Collaboration among competitors in the same industry is fraught with risk, especially for the less established and weaker partners in such alliances. (a) What are the greatest risks to small organizations of collaborations with famous galleries? (b) What are the risks to larger and more established galleries of collaborating with less prestigious galleries?
2. How can art festivals maintain their value as venues for art galleries to present their work? How can digital technology lower costs and expand the reach of art galleries and their festival venues for exhibition?

Critical Driver 4: Obtaining and Managing Resources: Suppliers (Talent), Reputation and the Role of Ecosystems

EEPs require a complex organizational architecture to address the range of issues involved in putting on experiences. These include the management of intellectual property including licensing and merchandising operations, the search and selection of artistic talent to deliver the promised experience, scheduling and programming (PACA, 2019), marketing and promotion of the artists, financial management of the typically diversified funding sources (private, public and philanthropic), and operational management of the day to day activities arising during an event, including security crowd management, site logistics and media coverage (Dziurski, 2016).

The complexity of coordination challenges for EEPs is matched by the complexity of leadership and governance challenges. Some EEPs are led and governed by a single entity, who can subcontract out to partners the various elements of the experience provision. However, other EEPs may be organized as private joint ventures, where there is shared ownership and leadership, or as public-private partnerships, where governmental actors may play leadership and governance roles in alliance with their nonprofit or for-profit partners. Often there is a need for special coordinative roles and skills to broker the relations between the various partners and assure that cooperation and coordination arise with tolerable levels of friction between parties. Similarly, there can be specialized roles for curating diverse artists into a coherent experience. A unique human resource challenge for EEPs includes the recruitment, placement and management of volunteers who provide essential venue supportive roles to supplement the contributions of EEP employees. Artistic organizations have found that mobilizing EEP fans into co-creators of the EEP event can energize the fan base as well as provide welcome support for cash-strapped organizations.

Ephemeral experiences are typically organized as project-based ventures, where temporality of resources (artistic, technological, financial and administrative) requires the faster and more flexible capabilities associated with project-based organizing (DeFillippi, 2015). Capabilities such as this can be regarded as strategic resources or assets, contributing to long-term sustainable success (Haberberg and Rieple, 2008; Labaronne and Tröndle, 2021). It is fair to assume that virtual production ecosystems, as introduced above, will continue to be a common pattern for Cluster Three industries. Such ecosystems provide the environment in which competition for critical (rare) resources including artists (the "talent"), locations and technical know-how takes place. Performers in this cluster may be considered to be strategic resources without which the organization is unlikely to survive or thrive in the long term.

Typically, arts organizations, especially those that are large and well-established, are located in cosmopolitan areas and their extended districts have great advantages in fostering the creative collaborations they need, compared to organizations in less populated areas. The larger successful organizations have grown their ecosystems alongside their own growth in a synergistic process. Although digitization is changing the nature of some EEPs' ecosystems, the fact that many have a physical presence means that co-location with the principal source of their resources is still common. Creative "milieux" such as Hollywood, Nashville (Porter et al., 2012) and Shanghai (He and Huang, 2018) are places where visibility stirs competitiveness and improvement and provide opportunities for income generation (vital for future innovation and investment) as well as learning from peers. Such ecosystems provide an ecology of opportunity if spare resources can be brought together in a synergistic way. An example is the music ecology in London. London has over the years accrued a large number of classical (and pop) musicians. It had at the last count over 20 classical orchestras, including five major symphony orchestras. Not all of these provide full employment for their musicians, and many earn additional income through freelance work. When these musical resources meet other spare ecosystem resources such as, in this case, recording studios, a new industry is born – film music recording. London is now probably the world's leading center for this activity, supplying many Cluster One industries[1].

For EEPs, reputation is a critical resource in attracting artists (or curators in the case of museums and art galleries) as well as funders such as customers, charities or government agencies. In contrast, public failures of a project can undermine the careers of artists and the production organizations associated with it, making resources subsequently harder to come by. Some EEPs' "products" are one-off events at a specific location. These pose challenges for consumers and their willingness to part with money, because of their novelty and the need for organizers to predict and cope with first-of-a-kind challenges such as logistics, workflow and audience behaviors. The more repeatable the EEP's offerings, the greater the likelihood that key partners will work with them, providing benefits from the economies of repetition to all parties (Davies and Brady, 2000). Reputation comes from being good, but also from being visibly good. Here social media is playing an increasing role. Reputations have traditionally accrued over time as a result of repeated success with consumers or positive evaluations by artistic gatekeepers such as critics. Nowadays reputation is increasingly driven by "likes" on social media platforms such as Instagram, Twitter or Xiaohongshu (Hausmann and Poellmann, 2013). The use of online media tools such as Facebook, WhatsApp and TikTok provides a variety of engagement opportunities for EEPs with their fans during and between shows or events.

One of the biggest challenges facing many EEPs is recruiting and managing the philanthropists that sponsor and fund artistic ventures in return for some recognition of their contributions. Large-scale EEPs may need to devote considerable organizational resources to both create and sustain a philanthropic funding base and mediate the diverse expectations for recognition and influence over their charitable contributions.

**EXEMPLAR 4: ORGANIZING A MUSIC TOUR –
TRANSFORMATION FROM STUDIO-CENTRIC
TO ARTIST-CENTRIC ECOSYSTEM**

Organizing a music artist's concert tours is an important feature of the live music industry, and it is a complex organizational undertaking. However, the vast majority of performing artists rely upon ad hoc collaborations between the tour promoters, booking agents and local partners and are subject to a lesser degree to the influences of the previously dominant music labels and recording studios who have contractual relations with these artists and are anxious to promote the artist's recordings and protect the brand image and reputation of the artist and, by extension, the affiliated music studio. The once pervasive control exercised by music labels and recording studios over recording artists has diminished considerably since the advent of digital music distribution, and today's music artists are more akin to savvy music entrepreneurs with a relatively high degree of professional autonomy (Tschmuck, 2016). Such flexible, negotiated relationships between artists and music studios stand in sharp contrast to the Asian model of studio control of K-Pop music artists (detailed in exemplar six of Chapter 3).

Despite the increasing reliance of the music industry on streaming platforms for recorded digital music distribution, live tours by music artists are still predominant and a major source of revenue for the performer. Even though streaming revenue was expected to grow to $23 billion by 2022, the live music industry was projected to reach $31 billion in 2022 (Pastukhov, 2019).

The following roles support and collaborate with the performing artist and his or her tour team in planning, organizing and implementing a music tour (Pastukhov, 2019):

- *Business Manager.* The business manager's role is to build and coordinate the artist's team in all aspects of the artists' ventures, including the concert tour business.
- *Booking Agent.* The booking agent's role is to book the tour and sell the shows to the local talent buyers, finding the venue and negotiating the price.
- *Promoters.* Multiple types of promoters participate in the tour team to fund the tour and buy the shows. Tour promoters contract musicians to perform a series of concerts, paying for rehearsals, audiovisual production, covering travel expenses and so on. Once the show is ready, tour promoters, working closely with the artist's booking agent, either rent venues themselves or subcontract the shows to the local promoters, who are affiliated with the performance spaces, where artists will tour. Local promoters are typically responsible for ticket sales and local marketing at each performance venue. Artists frequently participate in promoting their performances through postings on their social media platforms.
- *Tour Managers.* Tour managers travel on the road with the artist's crew and oversee the extremely complex logistics of assembling and overseeing the technicians who set up each tour performance (e.g., assemble the stage, set up the lights and the sound system) and similarly disassemble the required tourist physical elements for re-use and transport to the next physical venue of the planned tour.
- *Music Labels and Music Publishers.* Although recording and publishing industries are not typically directly engaged in the live music performance business, music tours often follow the release of an album and thus collaboration with the intellectual property owners of this material helps to promote the new work. Hence legal agents for the music label and/or publisher also play a role in planning for live performances.

In the North American and European live performance sectors, the feature artists for these tours play a critical role in engaging these tour service professionals to ensure that the tour's content, promotion and execution are aligned with artistic priorities. As such, live performance planning can be fraught with difficult negotiations and conflicts between the various parties surrounding this artist-centric ecosystem.

Although the touring industry in North America and Europe may be characterized as an artist-centric ecosystem, there is some evidence that entertainment conglomerates such as Live Nation and AEG can provide one-stop touring services to selected clientele, such as high-end performing artists. These conglomerates both produce the concert tours and either own or establish partnerships with a network of performance venues for the tour (Pastukhov, 2019). These conglomerates, including Live Nation, also serve as a general business partner to artists and support their activities regardless of whether they concern live concerts, merchandise, licensing, or distribution and promotion of recorded music to consumers (Wikstrom, 2022). However, these conglomerates negotiate with the performing artist and not the recording studio or music label, and thus the ecosystem's artist-centric character is retained.

Exemplar 4: Questions for discussion

1. How has the emergence of social media and online fan-following platforms impacted the promotion of live concerts?
2. How has the emergence of video and audio live casting of tour performances expanded the array of stakeholders involved in artist performances and complicated the relationship between the collaborators in these hybrid events?

COVID'S IMPACT ON CLUSTER 3 INDUSTRIES

COVID-related lockdowns have had a massively disruptive effect on EEPs. With their reliance upon in-person (and often large) audiences, it became one of the most economically impacted of all the clusters during the pandemic. Virtually all live events, from concerts and theaters to festivals and museums, were impacted, with some sectors nearly coming to a halt altogether. Live Nation, the world's largest promoter of events, reported a decline of 90% (Tschmuck, 2020) during this time, while nearly 90% of museums, or more than 85,000 institutions worldwide, closed their doors (UNESCO, 2020).

Many EEPs responded by providing virtual offerings and in some cases special exhibits outdoors that could conform to local COVID safeguards. Patterns of cultural consumption and production are evolving towards an increasingly digital landscape (Khlystova et al., 2022), and some EEPs were able to capitalize on this, using multiple social media and Internet platforms that enabled them to engage with their audiences and visitors virtually. Clips from past performances gave a taste of what might be available from the full experience, but also provided experiences in their own right. Many performers put on virtual concerts, transmitted on Internet platforms such as Facebook Live and YouTube Live which were recorded and then available on demand. Lockdowns also stimulated new ways of creating and producing artistic works using technologies such as Zoom, Douyin, Twitch or TikTok and then distributed and promoted through social media such as Facebook, Instagram, WeChat and Kakao.

In some cases strong virtual connections to audiences developed which have persisted and strengthened after lockdowns came to an end. These experiences have sensitized experience providers to the potential benefits from continuing engagement with their audiences that is not related to their physical attendance at shows or exhibits.

END-OF-CHAPTER CASE STUDY: CIRQUE DU SOLEIL

Introduction

Cirque du Soleil (CdS) (French for Circus of the Sun) is a Canadian performing arts company whose principal business is to provide live shows that are a hybrid of circus, acrobatics, theater and dance (Figure 5.6). It is the biggest producer of theatrical shows in the world (APN, 2018) with 2018 sales of C$850 million, head and shoulders above the rest of the circus industry in size and economic performance.

Figure 5.6 Technological innovation in Cirque du Soleil: the Wheel of Death.
Source: Cirque du Soleil 2022. Credits: Photos: Matt Beard; Costumes: Marie Chantale Vaillancourt

CdS was formed in 1984 by a troupe of street performers in a small town outside Quebec City in Canada. Their intention was to reinvent the concept of the circus, which had barely changed since the 1800s, to avoid the exploitation of performing animals and to blur the traditional boundaries between the different performing arts. This ambition was encapsulated in the company's mission statement: "to invoke the imagination, provoke the senses, and evoke the emotions of people around the world", still current in 2022 (Cirque du Soleil, 2022) – the name "CdS" symbolizes the notion that "the sun stands for energy and youth", and these terms are still used as guiding metaphors within the organization (Cirque du Soleil, 2022).

Although it began in Canada, CdS soon expanded abroad for the first time when putting on its first big show, We Reinvent the Circus, in Los Angeles in 1987. Since then it has grown rapidly. In 1984, 73 people worked for the company; between 1984 and 1989, CdS performed only one show at a time. By 2013 at its peak it had 5,000 employees, including 1,300 performers, and performances on five continents. Some of its shows are now held in permanent locations, such as Las Vegas, Hangzhou or Berlin, others are in a touring big top – "le grand chapiteau" – and yet others take place in suitable arenas or theaters, such as London's Royal Albert Hall. Montreal has remained the location for corporate offices, living, training and performing facilities.

For most of its existence CdS has been owned and managed equally by Guy Laliberté and Daniel Gauthier. Laliberté had responsibility for most of the creative production and Gauthier for the business side, especially external partnerships and financing. Laliberté retained a strong artistic and visionary presence despite the subsequent recruitment of other artistic and musical directors. This created a degree of brand predictability and product coherence. From almost the outset its identity has been explicitly non-national. This is evidenced by the recruitment of performers from all over the world and epitomized by the role of music in the shows. Each uses a live band and singers, with specially composed music in a Latin-sounding mock "language" that transcends cultural boundaries and allows the shows to transfer seamlessly from country to country.

Product Innovation: The Shows

CdS puts on relatively expensive, high-quality, family-oriented shows. All have a considerable "wow" factor, with tumblers, acrobats and clowns performing in often very extravagant costumes, and some acts put on hugely thrilling displays such as high-wire acrobats or contortionists. CdS's strategy shifted its focus to the creation of a brand-new entertainment genre (Kim and Mauborgne, 2015). It is difficult to find direct competitors. Its theatrical performances appeal to an audience above and beyond that of traditional circuses, bridging the excitement of a circus and the creative richness of the theater; the audiences for these shows are willing to pay a much higher price. Because CdS adds an aesthetic component to the performers' acts they need to be both athletic and artistic.

The technology that CdS uses in the shows is also highly innovative, developed specially for the specific acts by in-house designers and technologists, working closely with the artists themselves. A lot of the effects are the result of very carefully programmed automation that has been adapted from its industrial roots and made to work in the theatrical space (Venables, 2013).

Custom-designed rotating frames carry flying performers across the roof space, operated by a variety of different control systems. Although the complex automation sequences are programmed using advanced software, they always have to be able to synchronize with the performers' live movements. One show, *The Beatles Love*, has more aerial performances than any other Cirque show, and at the beginning there are 18 people flying in the air at one time. After a year of rehearsal of parts of the show in Montreal, the team moved to Las Vegas and started working in the performance space of the theater. It was there that the creative team started working out the balance between technology and physical performance: it took a further eight months of rehearsals in the theater before the show opened (Venables, 2013). Other shows are similarly complex. For example, the show "O" (O being a phonetic representation of the French word for water) includes synchronized swimming and a 1.5 million cubic foot tank of water. Performers could be seen rising mysteriously from below the surface of the tank, or diving out of sight, never to be seen again.

Over time CdS started to diversify into different types of arenas. In 2016 CdS made its first venture onto Broadway, re-choreographing a show's acrobatic sequences in order to fit into the smaller space. And in 2017 CdS took to the ice with an arena-sized spectacle "Crystal". The company's costume and props department created its own version of hand-and-foot grips that allowed the acrobats to do handstands or tumbles without slipping. The search for performers with particular skill sets also took the casting department to places it had never been previously. Some performers came from the competitive skating world, and others were found among young skateboarders who might be found at city parks: as Fabrice Lemire the artistic director for touring shows said: "We had to be very open-minded and think ahead in identifying the skill set we wanted and be open to what the skaters and the skating world had to teach us" (Eberson, 2018). In order to develop its acrobats into skaters and skaters into members of a theatrical troupe, CdS turned to world champion figure skaters and ice dancers, Kurt Browning and Benjamin Agosto for help. Two other shows were performed on a cruise ship's specially designed 400-seat £18 million theater. Its jointly undertaken design (by CdS and the cruise line company) had to ensure that everything would be as spectacular as possible while allowing for the movement of the sea. The same 16 performers were in both shows, having a major part in one and a minor role in the other, and had to agree to be at sea for six months.

The Role of Partnerships

Like the relationship with the cruise company, CdS has engaged in many partnerships in order to develop and put on its shows. For example, CdS's eight Las Vegas shows are undertaken in partnership with MGM Resorts. Its show *Believe* is a partnership between Criss Angel, regarded as the top magician/illusionist in the world, and CdS. Toruk was inspired by James Cameron's Avatar movie franchise. Cameron himself participated in the project as a creative consultant.

CdS has also staged a few productions built around musical artists, including The Beatles, Michael Jackson, Elvis Presley and Argentine rock band Soda Stereo. In the latter case 50,000 tickets were sold on the first day of sales in Buenos Aires, breaking a record in Argentina. The music was to be heard both in the show and on an album set to be released to coincide with the show's premiere. CdS's Creative Director and others spent months immersing themselves in the band's world, interviewing the band and its fans, and immersing themselves in its Latin American culture. In some of these shows, for example, those based on Michael Jackson's music, new technologies were employed to enhance the artistry through immersive hologram projections and lasers, cutting-edge sound systems and specially designed loudspeakers located in the headrest of each seat.

Strategic Capabilities

The capabilities involved in running the actual shows are not the only ones that CdS has had to develop. At its peak as many as 19 touring shows were running concurrently across the world. This in its own right was an enormous step above anything that a normal circus would do, and CdS has developed innovative capabilities in moving very complex equipment across large distances. Danielle Savoie, Vice-President of Information Technology and Knowledge Management at Cirque du Soleil, describes erecting a big top as in effect building a self-sufficient village (Rivard et al., 2012):

> It's a village of about 150 people, and it needs the very best technology to meet their needs ... And this is a village that moves every six or seven weeks, which means the village has to be constantly torn down and set up again ... Every part, hose, wire, piece of rigging and bolt has its place ... Imagine the logistics when over 55 trailer-loads of equipment have to be hauled from place to place, and at each site, it all has to be in working order within 30 hours.

It took three Boeing 747s and a 777 to get the entire set of Toruk – comprising more than 1,000 individual items – to Sanya, where the production was staged inside a massive temporary arena, capable of seating up to 3,000 spectators. It was built from scratch in just 22 days. Others are so large that they travel the world in 38 shipping containers or three cargo planes.

CdS's personnel come from more than 40 countries and speak more than 25 different languages and dialects. At one point CdS's casting director was on the road for months at a time seeking out new acts. With expansion CdS began to need more than 100 new artists every year. Because performers sometimes came from remote locations such as small villages in Africa, China or South America, CdS would request that at least two friends or family members accompany the performer to help ease the challenges of the different language and cultural environments. Language courses and educational opportunities were provided for both performers and their children.

Knowledge Management

Being able to replicate shows in different places requires a high-quality knowledge management system. Rather than simply automating activities, CdS's IT systems are used to capture and transfer knowledge across projects and processes (Rivard et al., 2012). All CdS's shows are high-tech, nomadic and long-lived, with a typical lifespan of 15 years. CdS Memory is a knowledge repository described as a comprehensive custom-developed "bible" for the organization. It's accessible online in five different languages and is used to store detailed information about each show, from design to delivery. Memory saves the images, videos, sketches and notes that served as sources of creative inspiration for previous shows. Kooza, alone, has 75,000 documents. It contains over 5,000 costume designs and 4,000 alteration notes, ensuring that the quality of each show is consistent despite unforeseen events and replacements (Rivard et al., 2012).

The Kin-Cirque app (another part of Memory) ensures that the over 20,000 categories of equipment used in its shows are tailored to the exact physical measurements and needs of the performers. To achieve this a great deal of technical documentation needed to be developed to record usage as well as compliance with international standards. Linguistic software had to be developed in order to standardize over 150,000 terms used to describe the equipment and to integrate with other technical information in their database. The Kin app allows physical fitness specialists to optimize each artist's muscular development and along with the Medi-Cirque app – also part of CdS Memory – keeps detailed information on artist injuries and incidents. It generates medical statistics on all artists and analyses typical injuries for different acts. It even establishes recovery times and relapse rates, and it provides CdS with an overview it can use to manage the risks of injury in its many acts. Medi-Cirque also has the ability to find replacements for injured artists. From its database of over 24,000 files, the application suggests replacement artists whose height and weight match those of the injured artists. In this way, CdS is able to avoid downtime, in addition to eliminating costly costume redesigns.

IT-Based Communications

The other way that CdS uses technology is through its website and social media. It uses this to extend the ways in which consumers can experience CdS shows, through multimedia experiences as well as to promote its work and attract potential performers from across the world. It also uses it to seek ideas for improving its performances. Staying ahead of the latest artistic trends is vital and employees are invited to share their discoveries from the performing or visual arts, design, food, music, technology or architecture under "Open Eyes", a digital platform for sharing new ideas. These Open Eyes postings can be shared and provide inspiration to all CdS colleagues who access the portal.

In its management of social media CdS partnered with a software company, Stackla, to develop AI-powered content curation. It uses Stackla's machine learning algorithms to evaluate published content, analyze how their customers interact with it and receive predictive recommendations for what content will perform the best (Nosto, 2021). Content created by their employees is posted on their website as well as on social media channels, a good way of communicating to potential new recruits exactly what is involved in being a Cirque performer as well as showcasing the firm to potential customers and collaborators. By 2020 its #CdSWay campaign had reached 2.8 billion people, about the same reach as Facebook. On CdS's YouTube channel, one of their performance videos reached 9.4 million views (thecreativeconversation, 2020).

Another way that CdS promotes its work, and gains additional income, is through the digitization of its performances, to be bought on DVD or downloaded. It has often allowed film and TV program makers to film behind the scenes as performers rehearse, or to tell the story of the Cirque "family" as it travels around the world. It has also increasingly generated content on other media. CdS Media, a joint venture between CdS and broadcaster Bell Media, joined with Samsung to produce a virtual reality version of one of its shows, to be viewed on its Galaxy smartphones. In 2015 CdS launched *Luna Petunia*, a new animated series to be shown worldwide exclusively on Netflix, and to include a franchised consumer products line, interactive digital content and a live tour. A number of Virtual Reality Experiences have been produced by CdS Images, the multimedia production division of CdS, jointly with Felix & Paul Studios, specialists in cinematic virtual reality.

CdS in the Future

In 2015 Laliberté sold 90% of his stock in CdS to a group headed by a US private equity firm, TPG, its Chinese partner Fosun International, China's biggest private conglomerate and one of the country's most acquisitive firms and Quebec pension fund Caisse de dépôt et placement du Québec. The head of Fosun is a Chinese billionaire Guo Guangchang known as the Warren Buffett of the East. Fosun had recently acquired Club Med, Thomas Cook and Center Parcs. Laliberté maintained a 10% stake in the company and continued to provide strategic and creative input. The deal was a sensitive one, with the Canadian government concerned that it would lose the creative and artistic development in Montreal, as well as Canadian employment. It permitted the takeover, reassured by the acquirers' commitment to maintain the centrality of its Montreal headquarters and ensure that at least 70% of the senior management in Canada is Canadian. TPG was to also provide annual progress reports to the federal government. In February 2020 Laliberté sold his remaining 10% stake to Caisse de dépôt.

In the last few years CdS's biggest bet has been on China. Daniel Lamarre visited China often in order to better understand its people and customs, and suggested that China might eventually represent 20–25% of the company's sales. In this CdS is in line with companies around the globe that are trying to capitalize on the increasing spending on leisure by China's growing middle class. CdS, which had suffered from falling profits in recent years and had become a bit "flabby and passé" (Austen, 2015), was considered ripe to expand into China. It planned to open a permanent show in Hangzhou, very much like those in Las Vegas. But it would be a story about China, with 50% of the artists and 75% of the crew Chinese.

However, COVID loomed. In March 2020 CdS announced that all 44 active shows worldwide would be suspended and that 95% of its staff would be temporarily laid off, and in June 2020 the company announced it had filed for bankruptcy protection: the company had debts of over $1 billion (Hill, 2022). The intention was to rehire the majority of employees once coronavirus-related shutdowns were lifted and operations could resume. On 17 July 2020, a takeover proposal by the company's creditors was approved by the Quebec Superior Court. The company was to be sold to the former CEO of MGM Resorts International Jim Murren and investment company Catalyst Capital. On 24 November 2020 CdS emerged from bankruptcy.

With the exception of two resident shows which reopened with limited capacities in the summer of 2020, CdS did not reopen its shows for over a year following its suspension. In the summer of 2021, the company began gradually reopening several of its shows, beginning with all its Las Vegas-based resident shows and some of its touring shows in late 2021 and 2022. In November 2021, a resident show Drawn to Life launched, CdS's first new production since the start of the pandemic. And in November 2021, Daniel Lamarre stepped down as president and CEO, moving into the role of Board Executive Vice-chairman. Former chief financial officer and chief operating officer Stéphane Lefebvre would take over as president and CEO (Kelly, 2021).

Case study questions for discussion:

1. Does CdS rely on any complementors? If so, how can it ensure that these are useful to CdS?
2. Who are CdS's major collaborators? What capabilities and knowledge does CdS need in order to benefit from these collaborations?
3. How does CdS manage its innovation risks?
4. Will CdS retain its creativity and innovativeness now that Guy Laliberté is not formally involved in the company? What should its new owners do to maintain its innovative capabilities? Does the appointment of a finance/operations specialist as the new CEO signal a move away from invention to exploitation?
5. How does CdS exploit its innovations?

NOTE

1   Source: personal communication Jonathan Mayes, Clore Foundation.

REFERENCES

Agyeman, K. H. (2019). Top 10 museum trends you should know. Available from: https://medium.com/museum-tech-trends/top-10-museum-trends-in-2019-3c5582ed8253. Accessed August 20, 2021.

Alsop, R. (2021). Intangible, invisible and eternally nascent: Designing sound in Australian performing arts. *Scene*, 9(1–2), 117–132.

Amans, P., Mazars-Chapelon, A. and Villesèque-Dubus, F. (2015). Budgeting in institutional complexity: The case of performing arts organizations. *Management Accounting Research*, 27, 47–66.

Ángel Marín, P. M. (2021). Challenging the listener: How to change trends in classical music programming. Available from: http://resonancias.uc.cl/es/N%C2%BA-42/challenging-the-listener-how-to-change-trends-in-classical-music-programming.html. Accessed March 23, 2022.

APN. (2018). The world's largest theatrical producer Cirque du Soleil to perform in Mumbai in November this year. June 1. Available from: https://www.apnnews.com/the-worlds-largest-theatrical-producer-cirque-du-soleil-to-perform-in-mumbai-in-november-this-year/. Accessed March 9, 2022.

Armstrong, J. E. (2021). Person-environment relationships: Influences beyond acoustics in mical performance. (pages 246–260) In James Williams, Samuel Horlor (Editors) *Musical Spaces: Place, Performance, and Power.* New York: Jenny Stanford Publishing.

ARTnews (2020). What's next? 18 Trends that will move the art world forward. *ARTnews*, June 24, 2020. Available from: https://www.artnews.com/art-news/news/art-trends-that-move-art-world-forward-1202692078/2/. Accessed December 15, 2021.

Asher, T. (2020). Shaping museum stories with neuroscience. *Museum Next*. Available from: https://www.museumnext.com/article/shaping-museum-stories-with-neuroscience/. Accessed January 15, 2022.

Atkinson, S. & Kennedy, H. W. (2018). Extended reality ecosystems: Innovations in creativity and collaboration in the theatrical arts. *Refractory: A Journal of Entertainment Media*, 30, 12.

Austen, I. (2015). Sale of Cirque du Soleil aims to open doors in China. *New York Times*, April 20.

Bakhshi, H. and Throsby, D. (2009). Innovation in Arts and cultural organisations. *NESTA Interim Research Report*, December 1.

Bakhshi, H., Mateos-Garcia, J. and Throsby, D. (2010). Beyond live: Digital innovation in the performing arts. NESTA. Available from: https://media.nesta.org.uk/documents/beyond_live.pdf. Accessed July 14, 2022.

Bidgood, J. (2017). How to get the brain to like art. *New York Times*. March 11, 2017. Section S, Page 5. Available from: https://www.nytimes.com/2017/03/11/arts/how-to-get-the-brain-to-like-art.html. Accessed June 15, 2022.

Bowman, N. D., Cohen, E. and Döveling, K. (2021). Emotion and digital media: Emotion regulation in interactive, on-demand, and networked media. (pages 316–328). In Katrin Döveling, Elly A. Konijn (Editors) *Routledge International Handbook of Emotions and Media*, 2nd Edition, First Published 2021. London: Routledge.

Bulut, M. (2018). *Digital Performance: The Use of New Media Technologies in the Performing Arts. A Thesis.* Aristotle University of Thessaloniki.

Byrnes, W. J. (2019). Getting on the Balcony: Deploying adaptive leadership in the arts. In *The Routledge Companion to Arts Management* (pp. 155–169). Routledge.

Charr, M. (2021). Museum uses artificial intelligence to curate better exhibitions. Available from: https://www.museumnext.com/article/museum-uses-artificial-intelligence-to-curate-better-exhibitions. Accessed August 20, 2021.

Cirque du Soleil (2022). Available from: https://www.cirquedusoleil.com/press/kits/corporate/about-cirque. Accessed March 9, 2022.

Coates, C. (2021). How museums are using augmented reality. *Museum Next*, July 17. Available from: https://www.museumnext.com/article/how-museums-are-using-augmented-reality. Accessed June 6, 2022.

Cuseum (2020). Advised by Dr. Pawan Sinha, Massachusetts Institute of Technology. Researchers: Molly Cornell and Lauren Nathan. Neurological perceptions of art through augmented and virtual reality. July 2019–May 2020. Available from: https://cuseum.com/neuroscience. Accessed March 3, 2022.

Dare, E. (2019). Art fair innovations in Shanghai and London. Available from: https://researchonline.rca.ac.uk/3982. Accessed March 3, 2022.

Davies, A. and Brady, T. (2000). Organisational capabilities and learning in complex product systems: Towards repeatable solutions. *Research Policy*, 29(7–8), 931–953.

DeFillippi, R. (2015). Project based organizations in creative industries. In Jones, C., Lorenzen, M. and Sapsed, J. (eds.), *Handbook of Creative Industries*. Oxford: Oxford University Press.

Donelli, C. C., Fanelli, S. and Zangrandi, A. (2021). Inside and outside the boardroom: Collaborative practices in the performing arts sector. *International Journal of Arts Management*, 24(1): 48–62.

Dooley, R. (2019). The Neuroscience of art museum design with Dr. Tedi Asher. *The Brainfluence Podcast*. April 11, 2019. Available from: https://www.rogerdooley.com/tedi-asher-museum-design/. Accessed February 8, 2021.

Drobnick, J. (editor) (2006). *The Smell Culture Reader*. Berg Publishers. p. 360. ISBN 1-84520-213-9. Available from: http://motioncapturesociety.com/. Accessed February 8, 2022.

Dziurski, P. (2016). Success in creative industries: A discussion about critical success factors. *Journal of Management and Financial Sciences*, 9(24): 87–100.

Eberson, S. (2018). Cirque du Soleil picks up speed with new ice show. Pittsburgh Post-Gazette, January 13, 2018. Available from: https://www.post-gazette.com › 2018/01/15. Accessed March 6, 2022.

Ford, V. and Mandviwalla, M. (2020). Can digital engagement transform the performing arts? In *Proceedings of the 53rd Hawaii International Conference on System Sciences*.

Galiana, M., Linares, C. and Page, Á. (2016). Impact of architectural variables on acoustic perception in concert halls. *Journal of Environmental Psychology*, 48, 108–119.

Gander, J., Haberberg, A., and Rieple, A. (2007). A paradox of alliance management: Resource contamination in the recorded music industry. *Journal of Organisational Behaviour*, 28(5), 607–624.

Gay, M. (2016). Peabody Essex Museum breaks new ground on expansion. *Boston Globe*. December 9, 2016. Available from: https://www.bostonglobe.com/arts/art/2016/12/08/peabody-essex-museum-breaks-ground-expansion. Accessed February 10, 2022.

Greenberger, A. (2018). Let's hang: with space-sharing programs, galleries band together to battle an uncertain market. *ARTnews*. September 27, 2018. Available from: https://www.artnews.com/art-news/news/lets-hang-space-sharing-programs-galleries-band-together-to-battle-uncertain-market-11044/. Accessed December 15, 2021.

Hall, N. (2022). *Concert Lighting and Its Effect on The Concert Experience*. Falconer Electronics. Available from: https://falconerelectronics.com/concert-lighting-affect/. Accessed April 3, 2022.

Haberberg, A. and Rieple, A. (2008). *Strategic Management: Theory and Application*. Oxford: Oxford University Press.

Han, S. Yoon, J.-H. and Kwon, J. (2021). Impact of experiential value of augmented reality: The context of heritage tourism. *Sustainability*, 13, 41–47.

Hausmann, A. and Poellmann, L. (2013). Using social media for arts marketing: Theoretical analysis and empirical insights for performing arts organizations. *International Review on Public and Nonprofit Marketing*, 10(2), 143–161.

He, J. and Huang, X. (2018). Agglomeration, differentiation and creative milieux: A socioeconomic analysis of location behaviour of creative enterprises in Shanghai. *Urban Policy and Research*, 36(1), 79–96.

Hill, A. (2022). Cirque du Soleil's Daniel Lamarre: from $1bn to zero revenues in 48 hours. *Ft.com*, January 9. Available from: https://www.ft.com/content/c29d17f7-368f-457b-acc2-76f9aea7a812. Accessed July 21, 2022.

Innovate (2022). How innovative AV is the force behind Vivid Sydney's spectacular success. Available from: https://integrate-expo.com/digital-signage-engagement/vivid/. Accessed June 27, 2022.

Jaffe, J. C. (2005). Innovative approaches to the design of symphony halls. *Acoustical Science and Technology*, 26(2), 240–243.

Jochum, E. A. (2013). Deus ex Machina. Towards an Aesthetics of Autonomous and Semi-autonomous Machines. Doctoral dissertation, University of Colorado at Boulder.

Kampanngroup.com (2021). When the time ball gets stuck-Six years' delay in construction cannot harm the prestige project that is the 'Elbphilharmonie' Available from: https://www.kampmanngroup.com/Kampmann-Today/Reportages/when-the-time-ball-gets-stuck. Accessed June 29, 2022.

Kelly, B. (2021). Cirque du Soleil picks finance veteran as president and CEO. *Montreal Gazette*, December 1. Available from: (https://montrealgazette.com/business/local-business/cirque-du-soleil-names-stephane-lefebvre-as-president-and-ceo. Accessed May 5, 2022.

Kennisland (2010). (UK National Portrait Gallery vs. Wikimedia) vs. the Public Domain. Available from: https://www.kl.nl/en/opinion/uk-national-portrait-gallery-vs-wikimedia-vs-the-public-domain/. Accessed July 21, 2021.

Khanna, T., Gulati, R. and Nohria, N. (1994). Alliances as learning races. *Academy of Management Proceedings*, 1, 42–46. Briarcliff Manor, NY, Academy of Management.

Khlystova, O., Kalyuzhnova, Y., and Belitski, M. (2022). The impact of the COVID-19 pandemic on the creative industries: A literature review and future research agenda. *Journal of Business Research*, 139, 1192–1210.

Kim, W. C. and Mauborgne, R (2015). *Blue Ocean Strategy*. Cambridge: Harvard Business Review Press.

Knardal, P. S. (2020). Orchestrating institutional complexity and performance management in the performing arts. *Financial Accountability and Management*, 36(3), 300–318.

Kohn, B. (2020). Sundance 2021 reveals how the virtual festival will work for 70-plus films in 7 days. *IndieWire*. December 2, 2020. Available from: https://www.indiewire.com/2020/12/sundance-2021-how-virtual-festival-will-work-1234601903/. Accessed May 12, 2022.

Labaronne, L., and Tröndle, M. (2021). Managing and evaluating the performing arts: Value creation through resource transformation. *The Journal of Arts Management, Law, and Society*, 51(1), 3–18.

Marinkovic, P. (2022). Hologram artists: The future of live performance. *Medium*. Available from: https://medium.com/predict/hologram-artists-the-future-of-live-performance-9851d2e02ae1. Accessed June 24, 2022.

Marketing Interactive (2021). The future of events in a post-COVID era. Available from: https://www.marketing-interactive.com/the-future-of-events-in-a-post-covid-era. Accessed April 12, 2022.

Mistek, R. (2021). Why we need hybrid film festivals. *Hyperallergic*, September 9. Available from: https://hyperallergic.com/675747/why-we-need-hybrid-film-festivals/. Accessed March 9, 2022.

NEA Research Report #58 (January 2015). *When Going Gets Tough: Barriers and Motivations Affecting Arts Attendance*. National Endowment for the Arts. Available from: https://www.arts.gov/sites/default/files/when-going-gets-tough-revised2.pdf. Accessed June 13, 2022.

Nogare, C. D. and Murzyn-Kupisz, M. (2021). Do museums foster innovation through engagement with the cultural and creative industries? *Journal of Cultural Economics*, Springer;The Association for Cultural Economics International, 45(4), 671–704, December.

Nosto (2021). Cirque du Soleil creates immersive digital experiences with user-generated visuals. Available from: https://www.nosto.com/case-studies/cirque-du-soleil/. Accessed May 20, 2022.

Ohnishi, T., Matsuda, H., Asada, T., Aruga, M., Hirakata, M., Nishikawa, M., Katoh, A., Imabayashi, E. (2001). Functional anatomy of musical perception in musicians. *Cerebral Cortex*, 11(8), 754–760. doi: 10.1093/cercor/11.8.754. PMID: 11459765.

PACA (2019). Performing spaces. Available from: https://paca.org.au/wp-content/uploads /2019/10/Performing-Spaces-2019-Final-Singles-1.pdf. Accessed July 14, 2022.

Pastukhov, D. (2019). The mechanics of touring: How the live music industry works. *Soundcharts* blog, April 28. Available from: https://soundcharts.com/blog/mechanics -of-touring. Accessed July 3, 2022.

PEM (2021). Peabody Essex museum neuroscience initiative. Available from: https://www .pem.org/neuroscience-initiative. Accessed August 20, 2021.

Pine II J. and Gilmore, J. H. (1999). *The Experience Economy*. Boston: Harvard Business School Press.

Pisano, D. (2010). IMAX–Not the first but close. *National Air and Space Museum*. May 3. Available from: https://airandspace.si.edu/stories/editorial/imax%E2%80%94not-first -close. Accessed July 14, 2022.

Porter, M., Bernard, M., Chaturvedi, R. S., Hill, A., Maddox, C. and Schrimpf, M. (2012). Tennessee music cluster. *Microeconomics of Competitiveness*, May 4, 2012. Harvard Business School Student Project.

Rivard, S., Pinsonneault, A. and Croteau, A-M. (2012). Information technology at Cirque du Soleil: Looking back, moving forward. *International Journal of Case Studies in Management*, 10(4), December. Available from: link.gale.com/apps/doc/A330027 167/AONE?u=jrycal5&sid=googleScholar&xid=2b08902e. Accessed September 6, 2022.

Sassi, M., Jyrämä, A., and Pihlak, Ü. (2019). Using the strategy tripod to understand strategic management in the "evaluation-friendly" organizations of cultural and creative industries. *The Journal of Arts Management, Law, and Society*, 49(5), 324–346.

Sharp, J. (21 June 2012). 4DX: Here come the feelies. *Sight and Sound Magazine. British Film Institute.* Available from: https://www2.bfi.org.uk/news/sightsound/4dx-here -come-feelies. Accessed May 9, 2022.

Sundance Institute (2021). 2021 Sundance film festival announces audience attendance. Available from: https://www.sundance.org/blogs/news/2021-sundance-film-festival -announces-audience-attendance/#:~:text=48%25%20of%20the%20participants %20were,and%20the%20U.S.%20Virgin%20Islands. Accessed May 5, 2022.

Thecreativeconversation (2020).Cirque du Soleil takes you on a hypnotic journey from your living room. Available from: https://thecreativeconversation.wordpress.com /2020/05/12/cirque-du-soleil-takes-you-on-a-hypnotic-journey-from-your-living -room/. Accessed October 10, 2021.

Towse, R. (2013). *A Handbook of Cultural Economics*. Edward Elgar.

Trunfio, M., Lucia, M. D., Campana, S. and Magnelli, A. (2022). Innovating the cultural heritage museum service model through virtual reality and augmented reality: The effects on the overall visitor experience and satisfaction. *Journal of Heritage Tourism*, 17(1), 1–19.

Tschmuck, P. (2016). From record selling to cultural entrepreneurship: The music economy in the digital paradigm shift. In Wikstrom, P. and DeFillippi, R. (eds.), *Business Innovation and Disruption in the Music Industry* (pp.13–32). Northampton, MA. USA: Edward Elgar.

Tschmuck, P. (2020).The music industry in the covid-19 pandemic-live nation. December 16, 2020. Available from: https://musicbusinessresearch.wordpress.com/2020/12/16/the-live -music-industry-in-the-covid-19-pandemic-live-nation/. Accessed July 13, 2022.

UNESCO (2020). *Museums around the World in the Face of COVID-19*. Available from: https://unesdoc.unesco.org/ark:/48223/pf0000373530/PDF/373530eng.pdf.mult. Accessed December 20, 2021.

Venables, M. 2013. The technology behind the Las Vegas magic of Cirque Du Soleil. *Forbes*, August 30, 2013.

Vietoris, A. (2018). *Rock and Roll Never Dies-Will Holograms Dominate Live Performances in Rock Music in the Future?* [Utrech University, Master's thesis]. Available from: https://studenttheses.uu.nl/bitstream/handle/20.500.12932/31246/Will%20Hologram %20Technology%20Dominate%20Live%20Performances%20in%20Rock%20in%20the %20Future_Final%20MasterThesis%20Alina%20Vietoris.pdf?sequence=2. Accessed June 25, 2022.

Walmsley, B. (2019). Engaging audiences through digital technologies. In Walmsley, B. (ed.), *Audience Engagement in the Performing Arts: A Critical Analysis* (pp. 199–224). Cham: Palgrave McMillan (Springer Nature).

Webster, A. (2021). The pandemic was inescapable at the 2021 Sundance film festival. *The Verge*. February 3, 2021. Available from: https://www.theverge.com/2021/2/3/22262520/sundance-film-festival-2021-pandemic-these-days-pink-cloud. Accessed May 12, 2022.

Wikstrom, P. (2022). *The Music Industry in an Age of Digital Distribution*. Available from: https://www.bbvaopenmind.com/en/articles/the-music-industry-in-an-age-of-digital-distribution/. Accessed July 26, 2022.

Innovation in a Post-COVID World

Implications for the CCIs

Alison Rieple, Robert DeFillippi and David Schreiber

Chapter 6

Introduction

Many of our discussions around innovations in this text
have centered on developments that can be categorized
as transformational products/services, processes and
business models. Product innovation through digitization
was most transformational in digitizable media industries,
with the greatest impact occurring in recorded and live
music, filmmaking, publishing and photography. Process
innovations appeared to be most transformational in the
physical products industries, with the emergence of digital
technologies for tracking, communicating and collaborating
among manufacturing value chain participants. Business model
innovations were particularly notable in digitizable media
industries, with streaming technologies and their associated
innovative payment systems revolutionizing the procurement
and payment of media.

As we conclude our discussion about innovation in the CCIs,
much of which has been a historical journey into the most

DOI: 10.4324/9781003207542-6

impactful of innovations, we turn our attention to what is to come. We have yet to know whether some of these innovations in the CCIs are indeed transformational, but as we observe the impacts they have had or are currently having, it helps us to consider where they may be taking us into the future. Some show true potential in transforming the creative landscape while continuing to improve upon previous products and experiences, even though they currently seem novel in the infancy of their development and application.

AI (ARTIFICIAL INTELLIGENCE)

Innovations in the exploitation of abundant digital data by so-called machine learning and the associated practices of Artificial Intelligence are starting to impact the CCIs. We've included AI as a future driver due to the potentially profound influence it may have in the CCIs beyond what we are already seeing. These trends are an extension of the digital revolution but really represent a transformation in data analytics and prediction. AI has either supplemented or replaced human agents in many sectors of the creative industries, including analysis of consumer trends in choice and preferences for goods and services, predictions of patterns of demand for CCI services, and security of live performances by audience scanning, identification and detection of risks. Also, the ability to plan and coordinate large, complex, CCI projects is now being transformed by the deployment of AI's findings and recommendations. In some instances, AI-based recommendations for product and service offerings, as well as scheduling of service provision, are shaped by algorithms.

AI has also entered the world of the CCIs insofar as specific AI learning models have created original poetry, print copy for news and entertainment media, advertising copy and imagery, realistic video stream imagery, interactive stories, including movie screenplays, and multiple forms of original music in a variety of genres (Economist, 2022b). Chapter 3 recognized digitization as a general-purpose technology that can affect an entire economy and have the potential to transform preexisting economic and social structures (Lipsey et al., 2005). These criteria seem increasingly applicable to AI technologies; investment in these technologies in North America alone amounted to 114 billion dollars in 2021 (Economist, 2022b).

A challenge of AI deployment is the tradeoff between the efficiency of AI solutions and the value of human experience in making judgments on practice and process options. In a number of both CCI and non-CCI industries, it has been established that AI algorithmic analyses and predictions can be more accurate than those made by human agents (Pecherskiy, 2017). And in one controversial recent case, even artists appear to have the potential to be replaced by AI (Roose, 2022) as an AI-generated picture won an art prize at the Colorado State Fair (Figure 6.1).

As a result, the displacement of business analytic practitioners by computer-based agencies will be transformational throughout both the CCI industries and elsewhere. Similarly, the ability of AI to mimic and in some cases surpass the creative output of artists raises difficult questions about the evolving relationship between AI technologists and creative artists in an expanding number of CCI sectors. Discussions about ownership and Intellectual Property rights will continue and will no doubt be a challenge to overcome as government policy, human creativity and copyright intersect with these new technologies. This is nothing new of course, governments are often late to respond to Intellectual Property issues as technologies push markets

Figure 6.1   AI art – Théâtre D'opéra Spatial © 2022 Jason M Allen – https://www.jason allen.com/

forward, but when the question of "who" or "what" created the algorithm that created the copyright begins to blur, the answers to these questions aren't so clear.

ENHANCEMENT OF SENSORY EXPERIENCES AND WEARABLE TECHNOLOGIES

In addition to the potential innovations brought upon by the emergence of AI, developments within the enhanced sensory and wearable technologies sector are showing potential to transform audience experience. Historically, exposure to these technologies in ephemeral experiences was provided within the physical site of a live performance, for example, in the form of enhanced audio quality and digital imagery, special effects based on computer imagery graphics (CIG) and even experiments with enhanced aromas and fragrances to match visual and auditory stimuli. Although attempts at visual and audio stimuli were met with mixed reviews in its infancy in prior decades, new developments in technology and consumer interest are providing a renewed interest in sensory-enhancing experiences for audiences. Innovation includes the development and more widespread use of 60-channel immersive audio like Dolby Atmos or DTS:X that allow for a spatial sound experience that is interpreted as three-dimensional (Morrison, 2022). 4DX theaters are also increasingly adopted around the world. A modern take on "smellovision", where odor is released during the projection of a film, 4DX theaters immerse the viewer in 3D technology with seats that move, environmental effects like snow, rain, wind, "ticklers" at your feet and even odor to enhance the special effects. There are currently 141 4DX cinemas across 21 countries in Europe (Malouchou, 2019), and in the coming years, 85 theaters in the USA alone will be transformed to provide this experience to audience goers (Scripps Media, 2019). These innovations will cater to an audience seeking a more experimental experience.

Wearable technology is also likely to be increasingly employed to replace both the human experience and even the physical performance space itself, with self-guided and portable digital assistants that provide enhanced user experiences and insights. These wearable technology applications may be in the form of downloads to your preferred device (e.g., phone, watch or wearable clothing) and thus can accommodate a wide array of user preferences. Watches may be preferred by users who do not want to be encumbered by phones, and wearable tech may be experienced as more fashionable and more convenient than alternative devices. Some ideas currently in concept development are clothes that can hear, which will be able to detect heart rates, applause or other activities, and sweat-powered smart watches (Hughes, 2022). Such wearable technologies are fostering complementary innovations between industries: fashion, health services and the technology developers themselves.

THE BLOCKCHAIN AND NFTS (NON-FUNGIBLE TOKENS)

Recently, new types of payment and ownership systems have emerged. Blockchains, non-fungible tokens (NFTs) and cryptocurrencies are transforming the ways that intangible products are being sold and monetized. The NFT is a digital asset that provides value through verifiable "proof" on the blockchain that a digital creation is original. The blockchain, better known for securing cryptocurrencies such as Bitcoin and Ethereum (Conway and Mansa, 2021), is a "system of recording information in a way that makes it difficult or impossible to change, hack, or cheat the system" (Euromoney .com, 2022). It is a digital ledger that records transactions and exists on a system of computers across a computer network. Because of this level of security, NFTs allow for the ability to add "smart contracts" to transactions. A smart contract is a program that allows for a certain outcome when specific conditions are met. They act in a way that enables security and efficiency in workflow when transactions take place on the blockchain. Simply, they are "if/when" statements that are written in the code and offer a safe, secure and efficient way to register products or release funds to other users when needed. The contracts are automated, buyer "A" pays seller "B" by directing pay-outs for resale or secondary market activities. In the first half of 2021 $2.5 billion in NFT transactions were recorded (Crawley, 2021).

Although the role and impacts of the blockchain and NFTs in the creative industries remain unclear (Economist, 2022a), a few forward-thinking artists, musicians and other authors have experimented with monetizing the inherent scarcity and authenticity that is created when an NFT is sold. In essence, artists are maximizing "fandom" by creating exclusivity of their products and creating that scarcity in a market that didn't previously exist. This technology has the potential to monetize digital content in new ways.

Through creating an NFT any musician, artist or copyright holder is able to create a one-of-a-kind digital version of their product. Some of the most expensive NFTs sold as of 2021 include the first "Tweet" by the founder of Twitter Jack Dorsey. He turned a static image of a five-word tweet into a digital file stored on a blockchain. It was sold for $2.9 million. Others include a *New York Times*' article discussing the NFT, which sold for over $500,000, and the ever-popular YouTube hit Charlie Bit Me which sold for $761,000. In addition, promoters such as Live Nation have sold NFTs of concerts while professional sports leagues like the NBA have sold videos of well-known "dunk shots" for thousands of dollars, modern-day version of baseball or Pokémon cards. Even artists are designing digital versions of their works while musicians are selling VIP ticket experiences, merchandise and full-length DJ concerts, one example being Destination Hexagonia sold by Don Diablo for $1.2 million.

Allowing them to participate in this additional source of revenue will have positive long-term implications for the creative class. Artists will be able to offer merchandise bundles and a myriad of additional fan experiences. NFT and blockchain-backed ticketing for live events has the potential to eliminate "scalping" or the illegitimate secondary market by verifying the legitimacy of tickets. Any revenue generated above "retail" on the secondary markets can then be shared through the smart contract back to the original promoter, artist team or event organizer.

The challenge with the NFT market is that artists or their rights' holders still retain the copyright in their works. Although a digital artist may sell an NFT of their drawing for $25,000, they still own the rights that are inherent in the original work. What, then, is the long-term viability of this model? Especially considering many creative industries are based on copyright exploitation; entire revenue streams like the recording industry, music publishing and film/TV production exist due to the ownership and exploitation of these rights.

As of this writing, the NFT market continues to be volatile and expensive: in an auction in April 2022 no one bid more than $280 for Jack Dorsey's NFT of his first Tweet (Kauflin, 2022), indicating that the necessary resale market may be unavailable to NFT owners. It also isn't suited to the "Do-It-Yourself" (DIY) or small market copyright holders since the monetary exploitation works better for well-known artists or video clips of highly sought-after events. While the technology may have the potential to make these transactions efficient, they don't yet allow for the subtle nuances needed for the licensing of creative works. Additionally, the legal validity of these contracts could and will likely be put into question at some point. Their resolution, and under what circumstances or jurisdiction, is not yet known.

REALISTIC HOLOGRAMS

Holograms are certainly not a new concept. They have been discussed in science fiction and pop culture for decades. But like many of the innovations discussed in this chapter, it will take a significant amount of power, bandwidth and data transfer capabilities to allow holographic innovations to be accessible on a wide scale. As we illustrated in Chapter 3, we are already seeing the use of holograms in live entertainment with the "guest appearances" of legacy artists who have died or are even still alive. However, until the hologram can achieve realistic portrayals, it will be a novel concept that sits on the fringe of user experience. Its potential for market transformation is still questionable.

Realistic holograms are still a challenge to engineer on a grand and realistic scale. However, researchers from Cambridge University and The Walt Disney Company are getting closer to achieving them, with newly developed "Holobricks". Holobricks tile holograms together to form a large seamless 3D image (Li et al., 2022; University of Cambridge, 2022). This enables the potential to have practical implications of large realistic 3D images. In order for this to be achieved, however, the amount of data transfer is substantial. For example, our familiar 2D HD television displays need an information rate of about three gigabits per second, but a 3D display of the same resolution would require a rate of three terabits per second, something which is not yet available (Li et al., 2022). It appears that the proof of concept has been achieved, but it is still the practical and market application of such an innovation that will need continued development.

VIRTUAL, AUGMENTED MIXED AND EXTENDED REALITY

The current application of augmented and virtual reality has been repeatedly mentioned throughout this book, with its influence permeating all three clusters. And although we are only seeing glimpses of their transformative potential played out in the current marketplace, the possibilities for their use in the future are only limited by our imaginations. As the technology, bandwidth capabilities and users' willingness to continue integrating technology into their lives evolves, the greater the impact they will have on CCI products and experiences that are offered.

One such example that we have not yet touched on in this text are the developments surrounding extended reality (XR) or virtual reality universes like the metaverse. The "Metaverse" is an embodied Internet mostly accessed through virtual and augmented reality, that all of us can simultaneously interact within. Those close to its development claim it will dwarf the World Wide Web as it provides a visual and immersive experience the Internet is unable to provide. With the potential interconnectivity, flexibility and exchange of data, it will also provide an optimal opportunity to integrate AI, providing a place for it to learn and develop (Hughes, 2022).

When Facebook changed its name to Meta in 2021, its ambition to become synonymous with the technology and experiences of virtual worlds became apparent, but they are certainly not exclusive to it. Each metaverse is owned by different companies or individuals, and they can be used in a number of ways. Game developers like Epic Games are interested in the development of digital avatars within their virtual gaming platforms (Dolan, 2022). The Metaverse's influence on the live entertainment sector is already being seen with the launching of virtual concerts. COVID-19 massively accelerated the move of fashion companies into the metaverse. The use of social media to discover and shop for clothes increased over the course of the pandemic as customers who were unable to visit stores spent more time at home scrolling through their feeds to socialize as well as shop.

We know the development of NFTs on the blockchain by artists and musicians is encouraging the development of the virtual market, but how will the creative world leverage this exclusivity in the future? With metaverse parties and exclusive "meet and greets"? How will this digital interaction be best monetized into new business models and further product development? Branding and marketing and the use of gamification can surround all our activities while audio engineers leverage the latest developments in immersive sound experiences.

The investment in XR technologies continues to increase with 2021 (Metinko, 2022) seeing the second best year ever for VR/AR investment with nearly $3.9 billion going to venture start-ups, a 229% increase from 2020 (Sprigg, 2022). Currently in the city of Seoul, they are investing €3 billion to create the infrastructure for a virtual space that reflects the Seoul cityscape that will enable cultural interaction, tourism and more (Hughes, 2022). With existing creative industry firms and venture capitalists investing in the future of this technology, the market innovations that will begin to emerge will impact CCIs in new and profound ways.

CONCLUDING THOUGHTS

As authors of this text, we can't begin to proclaim what new innovations will transform the CCIs, but we can certainly predict that the changes already stimulated by the CCIs' response to the COVID pandemic will continue to transform the means of production and distribution and will change the way that we all experience and interact with culture and creativity.

REFERENCES

Conway, L. and Mansa, J., (2021). *The 10 Most Important Cryptocurrencies Other Than Bitcoin*. Available from: https://www.investopedia.com/tech/most-important -cryptocurrencies-other-than-bitcoin/. Accessed May 12, 2022.

Crawley, J., (2021). *NFT Sales Climbe to $2.47B in First-Half of 2021: Report*. Available from: https://www.coindesk.com/nft-sales-climb-to-2-47b-in-first-half-2021-report. Accessed July 14, 2022.

Dolan, J., (2022). The Metaverse: A new world of creativity. *Wavve.com*. Available from: https://wavve.co/the-metaverse-a-new-world-of-creativity/. Accessed July 22, 2022.

Economist, (2022a). *The Market for Non-fungible Tokens Is Evolving*. Available from: https://www.economist.com/finance-and-economics/the-market-for-non-fungible -tokens-is-evolving/21805856. Accessed March 5, 2022.

Economist, (2022b). AI'S new frontier. Briefing artificial intelligence. *The Economist*. June 11, 2022, pp. 21–24.

Euromoney.com, (2022). *Blockchain Explained: What is Blockchain?* | Euromoney Learning. Available from: https://www.euromoney.com/learning/blockchain -explained/what-is-blockchain. Accessed March 5, 2022.

Hughes, A., (2022). *The Metaverse Could Become a Wild West if We're not Careful* | *BBC Science Focus Magazine*. Sciencefocus.com. Available from: https://www .sciencefocus.com/future-technology/addiction-crime-and-data-breaches-the -metaverse-could-become-a-wild-west-if-were-not-careful/. Accessed June 27, 2022.

Kauflin, J., (2022).Why Jack Dorsey's first-tweet NFT plummeted 99% in value in a year. *Forbes*. April 14.

Li, J., Smithwick, Q. and Chu, D., (2022). Holobricks: Modular coarse integral holographic displays. *Light: Science & Applications*, 11(1), 1–15.

Lipsey, R., Carlaw, K. I. and Bekhar, C. T., (2005). *Economic Transformations: General Purpose Technologies and Long-Term Economic Growth*. Oxford: Oxford University Press. pp. 131–218.

Malouchou, V., (2019). Rocking the Old Continent: Immersive Seating in Europe Faces Unique Challenges . *Boxoffice*. Available from: https://www.boxofficepro.com/ immersive-seating-in-europe-4dx-dbox-mx4d-flexound/. Accessed February 20, 2023.

Metinko, C., (2022). VR/AR investments increase just as metaverse talk heats up—But that may not be the only reason. *Crunchbase News*. Available from: <https://news .crunchbase.com/startups/metaverse-augmented-reality-virtual-reality-investment/. Accessed June 27, 2022.

Morrison, G., (2022). Dolby Atmos: Everything you need to know about the spatial audio format. *Cnet*. Available from: https://www.cnet.com/tech/home-entertainment/dolby -atmos-what-you-need-to-know-about-the-spatial-audio-format/. Accessed July 22, 2022.

Pecherskiy, V., (2017). Council post: Will AI replace creative jobs?. *Forbes*. Available from: https://www.forbes.com/sites/forbescommunicationscouncil/2017/10/11/will-ai -replace-creative-jobs/?sh=1ec3ad5896a2. Accessed August 28, 2022.

Roose, K., (2022). An A.I.-generated picture won an art prize. Artists aren't happy. *New York Times*, September 2. Available from: https://www.nytimes.com/2022/09/02/ technology/ai-artificial-intelligence-artists.html. Accessed September 7, 2022.

Scripps Media, (2019). Regal at Opry Mills is now showing movies in 4DX; putting movie goers in the movie, with weather effects and moving seats. Available from: https:// www.newschannel5.com/news/regal-at-opry-mills-is-now-showing-movies-in-4dx -putting-movie-goers-in-the-movie-with-weather-effects-and-moving-seats. Accessed July 22, 2022.

Sprigg, S., (2022). XR trends 2022 (12/12): Investment in XR and the metaverse. *Awexr .com*. Available from: https://www.awexr.com/blog/Investment-in-XR-and-the -Metaverse. Accessed June 27, 2022.

University of Cambridge, (2022). Stackable 'holobricks' can make giant 3D images. Available from: https://www.cam.ac.uk/research/news/stackable-holobricks-can -make-giant-3d-images. Accessed June 27, 2022.

Index

Busson, A. 17

CAD-CAM *see* computer-aided
design and manufacturing
Cameron, J. 188
Capitalism, Socialisms and
Democracy (Schumpeter,
1942 treatise) 1
Cardin, P. 98
Caves, R.E. 25, 31
Christensen, C. 4, 15
Cirque du Soleil (CdS) (French for
Circus of the Sun) 40; #CdSWay
campaign 191; degree of brand
predictability 186; in future 192–
193; IT-based communications
191–192; knowledge management
190; mission statement 185;
partnerships 186, 188–189;
in permanent locations 186;
principal business 184; product
coherence 186; product
innovation 186–188; strategic
capabilities 189; technological
innovation *185*
cloud-based CAD software 100
clusters *see* digitizable media
industries; ephemeral experience
providers (EEPs); physical
products
collaborative capabilities,
ephemeral experience providers
(EEPs) 174–178
collaborative innovation 11
colored zirconia (Swarovski) 3
color filmmaking 13
commercial failures 24
community-crowd
transformation 73–75
compact disc (CD) 64, 65
complementary assets 25, 29–30
complementors, power of 34
computer-aided design and
manufacturing (CAD-CAM)
99–100
computer games developers 33
computer generated imagery
(CGI) 68–69
computer imagery graphics
(CIG) 202
concert hall design 161–164,
162, 163
Condo and art gallery
collaborations 176–178

coordinate measurement 112
copycat products 29
copyright infringements 29
copyright laws 26, 28–30
counterfeiting 30, 123
COVID impact: digitizable media
industries 80–82; ephemeral
experience providers (EEPs) 183–
184; physical products 120–125
Crash the Super Bowl contest 72
Creative and Digital Industries 16
creative collaborations 179
creative crowdsourcing 70–75; idea
contests 70; simple contests 71;
stage-based contests 71; talent
and skill identification 71
creative economy 16, 18
Creative Economy Coalition (US)
(arts.gov) 17, 32
creative milieux 31, 179
creativity, definition 3
critical success factors: cultural
products 25; economic
peculiarities 24–25; innovation
ecosystem 30–32; intellectual
property (IP) 26–30; product/
service creativity 23–24; role of
prescription 25
crossover phenomena 58
crowdsourcing-type open
innovation 11
cryptocurrencies 63, 125
cultural intermediaries (roles of
prescription) 24, 25
cultural tourism 153
curious bind 24
customer-to-manufacturer (C2M)
(Kutesmart) 111, 112
cyber risks 123, 124

DAW *see* Digital Audio
Workstation (DAW)
DeFillippi, R. 27, 31, 75, 176, 179
derivative products 24, 29
design process innovation 99–100
design rights 26–28
diffusion of innovations
theory 66–69
Digital Audio Workstation (DAW)
60, 60–61
Digital, Culture, Media and Sport
(DCMS) 17, 32
digital currencies 8
digital innovations 30, 122, 157

digital manufacturing 110
digital prints 47
digital "product passports" 123
digital revolution 46, 62
digital technology
convergence 47–48
digitizable media industries 2;
adoption of innovation 66–69;
artistic innovation and discovery
46, 57; audience 44; bottlenecks
in distribution 62; conglomerates
45; content distribution 62–66;
content transmission 33; COVID
impact 80–82; creative content
45; creative crowdsourcing
70–75; critical challenges 33–34;
diffusion of innovations theory
66–69; Digital Audio Workstation
(DAW) music editor 60, 60–61;
digital technology convergence
47–48; Disney 45; ecosystems
of 43, 45, 46, 76–80; filmmaking
35, 47; franchise content 44;
general purpose technologies
(GPTs) 46–56; monetization
62–66; new content 44; popular
literature 44; popular television
series 44; pre-digital barriers
62; process innovations 45;
product categories 35; product
innovations 45; social and
cultural changes in audience
tastes 56–61; subscription
models 45; Tencent 82–89
digitization 6, 35, 45–56, 62, 76, 96,
170, 179, 191, 199, 200
digitized entertainment, piracy 30
direct customer monetization
models 50
disinterest in economic reward 23
Disney 11, 45
disruptive innovation
(Christensen) 4
dominant design 2
donation (philanthropic)
economy 38

economic contribution 18, 19
economic peculiarities 24–25
ecosystem theory 31–32
Elbphilharmonie 161–164
electronic data interchange (EDI) 9,
62, 96, 101, 103, 114

electronic point of sale (EPOS)
technologies 107, 129
ephemeral experience providers
(EEPs) 3, 152; artistic
organizations 38, 179; audience
and visitor engagement 155–
168; augmented reality (AR)
154; BigData 40; collaborative
capabilities 174–178;
coordination challenges 178;
COVID'S impact 183–184; critical
challenges 38–39; donation
(philanthropic) economy 38;
first-of-a-kind challenges 180;
governmental actors 178; human
resource challenge 179; micro
enterprises 38; museums and
art galleries 153; online media
tools 180; project-based ventures
179; reputation 180; resources
obtaining and managing
178–183; technical capabilities
of equipment 39; theater/opera
productions 153; touring of
standardized offerings 40;
tourism destinations 154; virtual
and hybrid experiences 168–174;
virtual production ecosystems
179; virtual reality (VR) 154
eSports 53–56; sponsorships 54, 55
Evrard, Y. 17
extended reality (XR) 206, 207

fair dealing (fair use) 28
familiarity 24
Fanning, S. 64
fashion manufacturing 9, 30, 106,
110, 124
fast fashion–supply chain business
model innovation: acrylic 128–
129; components of 127–128;
cost minimization 127; design
process, innovation 128; future
of 130–132; H&M 125–132;
logistics technologies 127, 129;
manufacturing 129; new clothing
collections 126; nylon 128–129;
polyester 128–129; profit margins
126; store design 130; supply
systems 129; throw-away ethos
125; Zara 125–132
filmmaking 13, 35, 47, 62
"Fintech" business 88

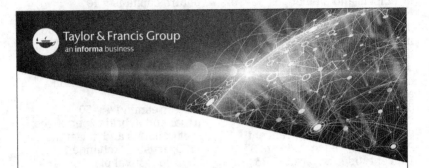

Printed in the United States
by Baker & Taylor Publisher Services